5/08

ALSO BY LISE FUNDERBURG

Black, White, Other

PIG CANDY

Taking My Father South,
Taking My Father Home—A Memoir

LISE FUNDERBURG

FREE PRESS

New York   London   Toronto   Sydney

*f*P
Free Press
A Division of Simon & Schuster, Inc.
1230 Avenue of the Americas
New York, NY 10020

First Free Press hardcover edition May 2008

FREE PRESS and colophon are trademarks of Simon & Schuster, Inc.

For information about special discounts for bulk purchases,
please contact Simon & Schuster Special Sales at 1-800-456-6798
or business@simonandschuster.com

Designed by Suet Y. Chong

Manufactured in the United States of America

10 9 8 7 6 5 4 3 2 1

Library of Congress Cataloging-in-Publication Data

Funderburg, Lise.
Pig candy: a history of my father, race, and place / by Lise Funderburg.
p. cm.
1. Funderburg, George Newton. 2. African Americans—
Georgia—Jasper County—Biography. 3. Cancer patients—Georgia—
Jasper County—Biography. 4. Fathers and daughters—Georgia—
Jasper—Biography. 5. Jasper County (Ga.)—Biography. 6. Jasper
County (Ga.)—Race relations. I. Title.
F292.J2F86 2008
975.8'583004960730092—dc22
[B]
2007035990

ISBN-13: 978-1-4165-4766-2
ISBN-10:   1-4165-4766-5

CONTENTS

PIG CANDY

ELEVATION 690 FT.

IN MARCH OF 2004, just when the urge to rake out garden beds and plant summer bulbs is too strong to resist, despite the possibility—the near certainty—that snow will come again to Philadelphia, I pick up my father and his wife and head south.

We drive from their suburban retirement community to Philadelphia International Airport, then fly to Georgia, them in business class, me in coach. In Atlanta, we rent a car and aim for Monticello, a small town surrounded by small towns: Zebulon and Sparta, Musella and Smarr. This is Monti-*sello*, not *chello*, seat of Jasper County, home to the fighting Hurricanes, one-time buckle on the

Georgia peach-growing belt, birthplace of my father, and the town he shunned for decades, until twenty years ago when he gave in to a childhood dream and bought a farm a few miles from Monticello's town square.

Across the seat of our full-size sedan, I see my father, George Newton Funderburg, grow more energetic with each mile. He looks out the passenger-side window as big-box malls trickle away, replaced by pine forest and signs for barbecue. My father is a handsome man. I tend to look at him through a lens in which surface and shape hardly register, except as conveyers of emotion, but I can see that at seventy-seven, he has barely a crease in his skin, much less a wrinkle. He is still in the vicinity of his peak height, five feet eleven inches, and his close-cropped hair, never grown long enough to complete a kink, is slightly more salt than pepper. His face and body are well-proportioned, except for the large-belly/no-posterior dilemma that plagues many men after a certain age, and his gray-blue eyes and meticulously flossed, brushed, and later-life-orthodonticized teeth sparkle with charm and good humor when the spirit moves him. Down here, most people look at his skin, the color of faded parchment, and call it "high yellow." Up north, most people assume he's white.

Dad interrupts his own reverie with projections: how we'll occupy ourselves on this trip, what changes we'll encounter, what will have stayed the same. He anticipates, accurately, that we will find his 126-acre farm-cum-vacation home in pristine condition, thanks to the attentions of Troy Johnson, a friend and fellow retiree who watches out for the house and three ponds, the ancient grove of pecan trees that yield seemingly on whim, and several well-manicured pastures Dad rents out to the cattle-farming Howard brothers, forty-eight-year-old identical twins named Albert and Elbert.

* * *

DOWN SOUTH, spring has advanced. Pear trees are in full bloom, naturalized daffodils stripe the just-greening pastures with yellow, and deep red camellias dot walkways and yards, sentries at every door. Sweaters need to be kept nearby but not on, windows are cranked open to ensure a cross breeze. We make good time from the airport to the farm, just over an hour, and Dad and I don't bother to unpack before we turn our attention to the two items on our agenda: roasting a pig and getting him some chemo.

First, the pig. In January, my father read a newspaper article that chronicled the author's experiment with cooking a seventy-pound pig in a Cuban-American–designed roasting box called *La Caja China* ['kä-hä 'chē-nä]: a simple plywood cart lined with metal and designed to suspend coals above rather than below the meat. The outcome, sweet and savory, succulent and crisp, earned the paradoxical moniker "pig candy."

Pig candy?

Dad ordered the largest model *Caja* from its Miami manufacturer and had it sent to the farm.

Clever inventions and well-prepared food both make my father's list of favorite things. Together they were irresistible. My father has always displayed a fascination for crafty mechanics, for improved ways to clean and fix and open and close. Over the years he has plied Diane, Margaret, and me, his three daughters, with laundry tables, vises, fingernail buffing systems, magnetic polishing kits, and Evelyn Wood Speed Reading Dynamics. Efficiency is his aesthetic, and in any given room of his various abodes, you are assured of finding flossing materials—waxed thread, plastic, and mint-impregnated wood—in the drawers of ubiquitous side tables that support the ubiquitous lamps (*You can't read in the dark*), coasters (*Put something under that glass*), and Kleenex (*Who's sniffing? Blow your nose!*).

Dabbling is my father's über-hobby. He'll become possessed with something new (thank-you notes, golf, people's middle names), and, like polar bear club swimmers on a winter beach, he'll plunge in completely, then retreat from the depths, shaking off water and done with it all. If there's an instructional video, all the better. Sometimes watching that is enough and he won't expend energy on the actual doing of the thing. This was the case with net fishing and square-foot gardening, horse whispering and harmonica playing.

Dad uses word of mouth to support his passing fancies. In Monticello, population 2,500, with its intertwined bloodlines and relationships, word gets around. Dad tells everyone we run into about La Caja China, or "pig box," as we have come to call it. He informs anyone he can corner that he's looking to find a whole pig: that he needs it dressed and delivered and preferably one hundred pounds, which is the box's stated maximum capacity. He mentions this to Connie, the cashier at the Tillman House Restaurant. He inserts this into small talk when he's charging wigglers and deer feeder pellets at Monticello Farm & Garden. He broadcasts it at Eddie Ray Tyler's barbershop, where one or two men sit in the defunct shoeshine stand that serves as a waiting area whether someone's in Eddie Ray's cutting chair or not.

At Eddie Ray's, the men sit for hours, reading the paper and talking about politics and the land's yield, which, these days, is suburban sprawl. Every few months, another local farm is subsumed into Atlanta-orbiting subdivisions. The prefabricated houses are vinyl-sided and asphalt-shingled, central-air impervious to barometric shifts and connecting to the state capital by way of long, arduous commutes. Developers swallow up fields and pastures, enticing title holders to abandon the land that ate up their parents' lives, maybe broke their parents' hearts. In the year of my dad's birth, 1926, Georgia had more than 250,000 farms. Now there are fewer than 50,000, with no signs of that number going anywhere but down. Since 1959, when I was born, Georgia land dedicated to farming has been cut by half.

As with seemingly everything else in Monticello, the demise of farming is intertwined with race. My grandfather used to say that once land went from black hands to white, it never went back. My father has found that to be true in Jasper County, except for this farm of his and a parcel of property bought by the city manager. *Those are exceptions*, Dad says when I raise them. *But they don't take away from the truth of your granddaddy's point.* When I investigate the claim, I find that Georgia farming is an overwhelmingly white enterprise. The state's black population is almost 30 percent, according to the 2000 U.S. Census, but nonwhites own only 3 percent of its farmland.

MY FATHER'S LIFELONG LOVE of farming has never wavered, even as the romance of living off the land seduces fewer and fewer people. And it truly is a romance, marked by all the irrational fervor that accompanies infatuation. Obstacles for the individual farmer are vast and varied, from agribusiness competition to the disdain of the local labor force—what dwindling labor pool remains.

Still, Georgia is a farming state. It ranks first in the nation in peanuts, pecans, and rye. It is also the number one producer of broiler chickens and thus, not coincidentally, eggs. Jasper County, covering 374 square miles, grows mostly corn and wheat. And despite the seemingly irrevocable tumble toward suburbanization, a direct link to nature endures among its people. Concern for weather is deeply embedded, locked into their consciousness along with the taste of summer's first ripe fruits and the smell of a coming storm. Everyone talks about how it's been raining too much or too little, been too hot or too cold. Crops are growing too fast or not fast enough. Pecans and peaches are coming in good this year or they're not.

Dad discusses these topics with endless enthusiasm, but his interest is largely theoretical. Beyond fertilizing the pecan grove and ponds, weed-whacking the fence line, and mowing the pastures, most of which falls to Elbert and Albert, Dad's property is as much nature preserve as it is agricultural enterprise.

Alfred Johnson, Troy's older brother and a Monticello fixture five years my dad's senior, remembers my father calling when he purchased the property in 1985. Dad had bought it over the phone, sight unseen, knowing only that it sat next to farmland his own father had once rented. *Bubba,* my father said, using Alfred's nickname. *Bubba, I bought a pig in a sack.*

Before Troy, Dad formed a partnership with Bubba. My father had the funds and the spirit of adventure, but Bubba had the skills. He had been the town's first black plumber-electrician, spent years as the local demolitions expert in a terrain where holes couldn't be dug in the red clay soil as easily as they could be blasted, and worked at Georgia-Pacific's lumber mill for more than twenty years. Bubba's grandfather owned more land than any other black man around, a nine-hundred-acre farm in nearby Gladesville, where Bubba spent much of his childhood. Bubba knew how to work the land.

From the start, and aside from the occasional trash pickup or brush removal, my father farmed primarily by phone. His hands are big but soft, not like Bubba's. Dad pored over agricultural how-to articles and wore out phone books looking for experts to call. He built his cattle chute based on a pamphlet he saw on the county agent's bulletin board, and its efficiency in holding cows for worming and tagging still prompts visits from the curious and the admiring. He frequently prevailed on the University of Georgia's Extension Service for information: on beaver control and management, whether topical surfactant treatments would kill the persimmon seedlings that grow out of cow dung, and what price per inch he should pay for fish to stock his ponds with.

In the 1980s, with Bubba riding shotgun, Dad attended viniculture seminars and cattle auctions. He and Bubba bought a bull and thirty head of beef cattle, Herefords and Angus mixed, and enough grapevines to plant fifteen rows, six vines per row. He joined the American Chestnut Foundation, which counted fellow Georgian and former President Jimmy Carter among its members, and Bubba planted the ten whips that came by mail. In only the slightest nod to his and Bubba's advanced years, Dad had a roll bar and seat belt installed on the riding mower. When Dad had a sign painted for the entrance to the farm, he asked Bubba what he'd prefer to be called: manager or overseer? Overseer, Bubba said, without a moment's hesitation, choosing a title that, in their youth, black men never held and that Dad immediately had printed in black block letters across the bottom of the sign. *Alfred Johnson, Overseer.*

Every farm-related transaction was calculated for its impact on both individual and community. *People are more likely to make themselves available to you,* he explained, *and no one feels taken advantage of.* When Dad hired people to do anything, he paid more than the going rate, which he based on whatever various laborers told him they earned, or, in the absence of such information, on what bag packers earned at Ingles, the recently opened "American-owned" supermarket just around the bend. Next to the Georgia-Pacific plant, a little ways down Highway 83, Ingles was the county's biggest private employer.

My father made Bubba a signatory on a local checking account so Bubba could be the one to write checks when supplies had to be bought or work was done. *I never paid anybody,* my father says. *They had to go to Alfred to get a check. And, boy, there's nothing that improves relations better than having that kind of buying power. People would come to Alfred and say, "Mr. George want to buy any more land? I got forty acres out here." "No, Mr. George don't want to buy any more land."*

My father's agenda was to draw attention away from the source of funds and to share the power that came with purchasing. Why? By way of explanation, my father tells two stories. The first concerns my paternal grandfather, Frederick Douglas Funderburg, who served as the town's black physician for half a century, starting in 1922. In the aftermath of the Great Depression, my grandfather had just started to earn a decent living. He was walking through town when an old white farmer (*a redneck*, my father says) called out.

Hey, Doc, the man said. *How you doing? I hear you banking a bale of cotton a day.*

A 480-pound bale of cotton was worth about fifty dollars at that time. Somehow the man, although not an employee of the bank, knew the amount of my grandfather's cash deposits. From then on, Grandfather took the month's receipts, wrapped them in newspaper, and carried them off to banks in Atlanta and in Eatonton, the next town due east.

If somebody knew you had money, my father explains, *they'd figure out a way to get it out of you, arrest you, make false accusations.*

The second story takes place in the midst of Prohibition. Because my grandfather had some standing in the white community due to his profession and his light complexion, other blacks would come to him for help negotiating the white-dominated social and legal systems: posting bail, buying property, even arranging private loans, using their houses and livestock as collateral. A neighbor named Charlie Couch earned his living making moonshine and trapping rabbits. My grandmother was a regular customer for the latter, often buying one rabbit for fifteen cents or two for a quarter.

Mr. Couch came to Granddaddy and said, *Doc, I got this two thousand dollars. I want to put it somewhere where it's safe.*

Don't put it in the bank in Jasper County, Granddaddy told him.

Well, could you help me out?

Grandfather took Couch to the bank in Eatonton.

Hello, Doc, the banker said as soon as Granddaddy and Couch walked in.

I have Charlie Couch here. He wants to open an account.

What kind of account you want to open, Charlie? How much money you got?

Two thousand dollars, my grandfather said.
Come right in, Mr. Couch.

THANKS TO MY FATHER'S PENCHANT for order and Bubba's ability to implement it, often by himself, the pig in a sack turned out to be a prize. The farm became a beautiful sprawl of cleared pastures, well-fertilized pecan trees, manicured ponds, and freshly painted gates.

As purchased, the farm came with a house, a single-story wood-frame building topped with a corrugated tin roof. A small sitting porch faced away from the entrance road, partially shaded by the largest, oldest pecan tree on the property. The farmhouse, as purchased, came with tenants: Paul Marks and his family. Marks worked a long career at a sawmill but had been forced into early retirement by emphysema, the lung disease that would make him weak, chain him to an oxygen tank a few years down the road, then take his life.

Beyond any reluctance he might have felt about dislodging the Markses, my father never considered living in that building, which he refers to by its address, 294 Fellowship Road. Instead, he and Lois, his second wife, stayed at his boyhood home. By then, the street he'd grown up on had been renamed Funderburg Drive, in honor of my grandfather. Funderburg Drive had also been paved since Dad's childhood, and the smaller, surrounding houses wired and plumbed.

Two years after Dad acquired the farm, Granddaddy passed away, and the house in town was willed to his children. My father promptly bought out his siblings' shares. But that house presented problems that made it, too, an unlikely base of operations. Nothing was modern about it, despite past claims to cutting-edge technology. It was, after all, the first house on Colored Folks Hill to have indoor plumbing and electricity, although the latter consisted of bare bulbs hanging from the ceiling by a cord. No similar innovations followed those early glory days, and from the day Granddaddy moved out in the late 1970s until my father took up part-time residence, the house had been tenanted by an eccentric local dentist who considered himself a health-care protégé of my grandfather, who grew juice-bound wheatgrass in wooden crates that seemed to take up every available kitchen surface, every counter and tabletop.

It wasn't the house's dog-eared kitchen or wood-paneled den that troubled my father once the dentist moved out and he and Lois moved in. It wasn't the enduring decrepitude of the neighboring shotgun shacks, wood-frame boxes packing in one generation after another of the same families. The problem with the house, to my father's mind, was its location. It sat squarely inside one of the town's remaining all-black sections, the other sections bearing names like Frogtown and Blue Ruin, as in the popular brand of bluing, the laundry-whitening additive so many black women had used to do white folks' washing. My father was sure most white people would feel uncomfortable coming to a house on Colored Folks Hill, even if they were too young to know that name for it or too polite to use it. He was bound and determined that he would never host a segregated event in Monticello. So he turned his gaze to the farm, outside of town and free of racial associations, at least as much as a place owned by a black man could be.

My father decided to build his own house. He and Bubba discussed its siting: Dad leaned toward breaking ground along the farm's northernmost edge, parallel to Route 16. Bubba disagreed. There was the noise factor, first of all, between general traffic and the constant rumbling of lumber trucks: forty-foot trunks of freshly sawed wood jostling against one another, straining against their chain-link lashings with every bump in the road. More important, Bubba thought, there was the hill.

Along the property's southern boundary, five yards or so from the cattle fence that signals the beginning of a neighbor's pasture, was the farm's highest point. Bubba had noticed its panoramic view during a foray on the riding mower. You could see thirty miles to the south, he figured, all the way to Forsythe and beyond. The next time my father came to town, Bubba drove him to the apex. Dad looked out over the swells of grazing land and forest and decided, on the spot, that Bubba was right.

It seems only logical that the house you build from scratch is going to embody your dreams. You might think that. You would not be my father.

He had initially handed over to Lois the design aspect of the project, but when her dreaming began to spin out of his control, he took the project back and called up the architects who designed Waverly Heights, his retirement complex ten miles from the center of Philadelphia. Waverly has town houses and apartment buildings and a medical wing fused onto a 1912 manor house built for a railroad executive. Dad flew Waverly's designers to Georgia, told them what he wanted, and wrote a check. They measured the site, noted the direction of the sun, and drew up a plan re-creating the single-level villa in which Dad and Lois currently reside.

Granted, there are slight modifications: more square footage to each room, higher cathedral ceiling, extra bedroom and bath, sun porch, and the designation "354 Fellowship Road" rather than "Villa 13." Still, the overall effect is the same, as are the materials, down to the brick wainscoting outside and slate hearth inside. And because Lois is so constant in her household organization and spare decor, a quirk has resulted: in photographs of family gatherings, it is nearly impossible from backgrounds alone to tell the location.

When the house was built, exactly ten years after Dad's purchase of the property, he changed the "Funderburg Farm" sign. He relocated it from the rental house entrance to the new driveway laid for 354 and had it amended to read "George's Hill." He also had Bubba's name painted over. After eight years of partnership, serious stomach troubles and surgeries gone wrong forced the seventy-five-year-old Bubba to step aside and his brother Troy to step in. Bubba cut back to tending just his own vegetable "patch" of twelve and a half acres, his grapevines, flower beds, dozen cows, and three dogs. In place of Bubba's name, the farm sign read "Elevation 690 ft."

One morning, Dad and I look out over the biggest pond, the one that has a white sand bank surrounding its dock, the sand installed subsequent to my sister Margaret's offhand mention that a beach would be nice. Morning mist hangs over the water, the sun just beginning to burn through, and a majestic heron rises up from the opposite shore. It flies across the pond and into a tree with vast, slow-moving wings that seem to defy gravity. *Look!* I exclaim, the city child ever thrilled by manifestations of the natural world. My father follows my pointing finger in time to see the bird alight onto a branch.

Hunh, he grunts. *He's eating the dollar bass.*

2.

A PRODUCTIVE
MEMBER OF SOCIETY

D AD MENTIONS HIS PIG QUEST to Marshall Tinsley, a handsome man close to sixty with a strong, open face and a brilliant
smile, despite a few missing teeth on the bottom row. Marshall is
a mason twice over: by trade and also as a thirty-third-degree Free
and Accepted Mason of the Most Worshipful Prince Hall Grand
Lodge of Georgia, for which he serves in the office of Worshipful
Junior Grand Steward. Marshall's first visit to Dad's farm was to fix a
screen door. His skill and thoroughness caught my father's attention,

and now Marshall comes to Thanksgiving. He even brought the turkey once, which he'd deep-fried at three minutes per pound.

Marshall is somehow related to Holsey Tinsley (the childhood sweetheart and now second husband of my father's sister, Chase, which makes Holsey, I realize a few years after their marriage, my uncle) and directly related to the owner of Dave's BBQ & Soul Food restaurant, who is Marshall's brother, Dave Tinsley. Marshall has a bad back and a bum knee that collapses under him without warning. It looks like he's doubling over with laughter, except it's weakness and pain. He went through "the cancer," as some people here put it, and when he hears that Dad's prostate cancer has come out of a fifteen-year remission and that he'll have to have chemotherapy, Marshall recommends strawberry-flavored Ensure, which he drank when chemo killed his appetite, which was all the time. Dad is sure to mention the pig quest to Marshall because Marshall is well-connected through the Masons and work and church activities and through taking at least one meal a day at his brother's restaurant on Frobel Street, one block east of the town square. One of Marshall's closest friends is a heavily networked bus driver/prison guard/chicken farmer who goes by the nickname of Tater and is Marshall's partner in a venture concerning a herd of goats.

Before Marshall has a chance to make headway, Dad finds a pig. His pork conduit is Ben Tillman, owner and head cook of Tillman House, a restaurant twenty steps west of the town square, a square through which eighteen-wheelers still pass and people recognize one another's vehicles with honks and waves. In his off-hours, Ben does catering. If clients want help serving and cleaning up, he brings his little sister, Sissy Tillman Hulsey. Sissy may well be older than Ben, but she is a quarter of his size. He is monstrously solid, heavy but not truly obese. He's just big, as is his daddy, Mack, the former sheriff who bought the restaurant in the late 1970s but has since sold it to Ben and now just helps out, pouring sweet tea into to-go cups and putting Styrofoam containers into bags.

Ben's place is open only on weekdays from 6 A.M. to 2 P.M., but it easily does as much business as the nearby Hardee's and Dairy Queen and Big Chick combined, even though their doors stay open longer. Dave's comes closest to Tillman's in its menus and cafeteria line setup. The main difference is that most of Dave's sit-down clients and all of his staff are black. Most of Tillman's clients and all of his staff are white.

The morning after we arrive, Lois is still asleep when Dad and I leave the doppelgänger house to go to Tillman's for breakfast. Inside the restaurant's front door, Dad takes off his taupe Stetson and places it on an empty chair. Cowboy hats are not a popular head covering in central Georgia—I can't recall seeing one on anybody else's head—but my father has never been a slave to fashion. He adheres to a foundation of cleanliness and good repair, but beyond that, function and comfort prevail. And innovation. For some years, he favored a stiff polyester traveler's blazer, the blue one with hidden pockets he had ordered from a stamp-sized ad in *The New Yorker*. He treats clothing as a uniform, a necessary accoutrement of living but nothing more.

Tillman's business is brisk, as it is every morning, yet there are still plenty of open tables. We sit up front, near the entrance and cash register and recently expanded retail product line: shelves of jams, barbecue sauces, and peppered vinegar locally brewed and bottled and canned. My favorite is "The Enhancer: The Sauce that Demands Your Imagination." We order eggs, sausage, and grits from Connie, whose long brown braid swings down the back of her Christian rock concert T-shirt as she pads around the restaurant in high-top cross-trainers. She swallows the ends of words in the local fashion, talking about a husband who keeps her out of *troub-* and wondering at the end of our meal if we want anything *el-*.

The restaurant's cafeteria line and three seating areas are carved out of the first floor of a large, old, wood-framed house, obligatory porch out front. On one wall a horse halter hangs between two fur stoles sagging on metal coat hangers. Atop an upright piano, Little League team portraits alternate with historic shots of the area collected by Benny, the UPS delivery man who is also an amateur historian. In a picture from the 1930s, a white man sits on a horse-drawn cart, legs primly crossed and hands in lap, presiding over dozens of black men in prison stripes and shackles.

There was a time, before the Tillmans bought the business, when we could not have passed through these doors and sat at a table. As Coloreds (or Nigras or Mulattoes or Blacks or whatever term was in fashion), we would have been relegated to the back door of the restaurant to buy our food and take it away. To my father, this past is direct, personal, and constant, etching itself into his instincts. My father is as fair-skinned as I am, so the restrictions he grew up under, so largely tied to skin color, were, in his case, not actually because of the color of his skin, but because of the idea of skin color. To me, this past is historical, his story abstract. As a white-looking mixed-race girl, growing up in the urban, integrated North in the 1960s, I have only heard of such customs.

WE ARRIVE ON A TUESDAY. The pig fest is set for Saturday. In the interim, Lois will ensconce herself in the sunroom's BackSaver lounger, set at full recline. Lois and my father have established fairly separate activity orbits in the thirty years they've been together (twice the length of his marriage to my mother). Dad finds projects, obsessions, intrigues to pursue, either telephonically or in person. His modus operandi is all operandi, all the time. Lois watches English mystery series and reads whodunits. While we're at the farm, the sunroom is her headquarters, and she has a mystery novel in hand, telephone and remote control within reach. She gets up only to use the bathroom and for meals, in both cases relying on a walker to keep her upright. Her mind is sharp but her balance is gone. It's brain chemistry rather than inner ear, the doctors tell her, and her only protection from dizziness and imminent collapse is to remain horizontal.

Lois seems relieved whenever my sisters and I are around. For better and worse we absorb our father's attention, and more than once, his tendency toward irascibility has prompted a reactionary alliance. I credit Lois for establishing the noncompete policy under which she and I operate: I was twelve when she became a part of my family, too young to do much more than feel resentful. Toward me and my sisters, and her own four children, as far as I can tell, she displays a curious blend of being unsentimental but generous, uninterested but accommodating. As physically inhibited as she is, she seems fairly content, and so I do little for her while we're in Georgia other than to bring her a glass of water, no ice, when she descends into one of her chronic coughing spells, or to ask her if she needs anything when I'm going to the store. Only rarely will she ask for something, and only when I'm already headed out on an errand.

In Georgia, my father lives from errand to errand, repair to repair, enterprise to enterprise. He keeps lists in a small spiral notebook or on index cards or the backs of envelopes, and he scratches off items as each is accomplished. Ever since August of 1985, when my sisters and I flew down with him so that all of us, including him, could see the farm for the first time, one of his to-do items is to bestow allowances at the start of every visit.

The Chamber of Commerce welcomes you to Monticello, he says, then proffers a handshake, a crisp fifty-dollar bill (and after a few years and in a nod to inflation, a hundred) folded into his palm. He singles out each of us to do this, delivering his welcome in a low voice, as if the transaction is a secret to be kept. This largesse, this whimsy, from a man whose cash gifts for most of my life consisted of birthday checks for five dollars, half of which had to be given to charity and the other half deposited into a savings account. My sisters and I come to call his presentation the Golden Handshake, and the joke of it is that, beyond purchasing nail polish from the drugstore or The Enhancer from Tillman House, there is nowhere to spend the money.

Tuesday's to-do list is shorter, less ambitious than usual. My father seems to have misplaced his up-and-at-'em. He has trouble climbing in and out of his high-riding ten-year-old Isuzu Trooper, a small truck manufactured before consumer comfort was incorporated into SUV design. He alley-oops one leg into the truck using progressive swings, then shifts his body weight into the center of the passenger seat in labored increments before picking up the other leg with both hands and pulling it up after him. Sometimes during this process he lets out a little laugh, a chortle I take to mean: This is how it is. We'll just carry on. Do not pity me.

Old age is hell, is the most he'll say out loud. Or, tacking on the nickname coined for me by his one grandchild, *My legs don't work so good, Leesee.* For my father, this is as bare as he's willing to get. It's more than I am used to.

WE TURN OUR ATTENTION to chemotherapy on Wednesday, after breakfast at Tillman's. Dad's errand list is tucked into his breast pocket, and we climb into the Isuzu, which doubles as a mobile toolshed. In the rear cargo area, paper towel rolls commingle with green plastic five-gallon buckets that once held pond fertilizer and now await either the day's catch, pecans (when it's a good year), or roadside trash. Clever devices are always close by, most designed to save the operator from bending over. This includes two three-foot poles attached to wire cages that are rolled over the ground to snag fallen pecans. For efficiency's sake, Dad likes to operate both at once. Also, a long-reach, two-clawed trash grabber sits near a bag of used supermarket bags that are wedged between rectangular plastic tubs, one filled with fish kibble, the other with fish trap bait that resembles dried horse manure. Pliers and deerskin work gloves tend to remain up front, stuck between driver and passenger seats. A condition of using the vehicle is that one must keep the glove compartment locked at all times. It holds a loaded pistol. Inevitably, Kleenex boxes are within reach and miscellaneous tools are strewn around. You never know when you'll need to tie a hammer to a rope, heave it up and over the nut-laden branch of a pecan tree, and tug at the two rope ends until nuts shake off and fall to the ground, after which you can roll over them with the picker-upper cages.

Today, I drive. Dad began to criticize my shifting technique a year or so ago, wincing and groaning whenever the clutch-gas-shift interaction fell below his standards. Which was every time. But this day, he looks out his window and says, apropos of nothing, *My vision seems to be getting fuzzier,* and for the rest of my visit, the job of driving will fall to me by unspoken agreement. We must travel thirty miles to meet an oncologist whose offices are in the town of Covington. Dad no longer radiates disapproval when first gear hiccups into second or second stutters into third, but while I drive, he steadies the manila envelope filled with test results in his lap and dispenses orders.

Turn left, he instructs as I approach an intersection, *after you stop at the stop sign.*

Otherwise, we are mostly silent. I drink in the landscape as we drive north on Highway 83. Everything I see demands translation. I don't know the seasons, only that the azaleas here will be long gone before the ones back in Philadelphia come close to blooming. Wisteria, with its grape-bunch flower clusters, climbs up into the trees the way I know ivy to do, and kudzu druids loom at the highway's edge. Roll after roll of baled hay line recently shorn fields, and unpaved red clay roads splinter off to the left and right, marked by various signs promising religious fellowship, fresh eggs, or, come election time, the best bet for sheriff.

Pastures and pine forests dominate, interrupted by long, low poultry barns and pecan groves. The land in Jasper County yields up its bounty unevenly, and farmers are increasingly drawn to whatever requires the least amount of labor. One man can grow a hundred-acre stand of pine trees by himself. One family can run a poultry operation of a hundred thousand broilers, the Chicken McNuggets and shrink-wrapped family packs of tomorrow, bred and plumped in six-week cycles. Crops take more hands than most farmers can find, none more labor intensive than peaches and cotton, the two that at one time made certain Jasper landowners rich.

I don't know many of the trees we are speeding past, why they grow the way they do, what it means when a stand of pines has burned down to charcoal, if that's a good or bad thing. Topography, too, confounds me. I understand the anonymity of urban grids, the consensual distance that exists between apartment buildings and front doors squeezed up against one another. But these one-lane highways are necklaces stringing together small-town pearls, each one a community in which relationships link across generations. The string itself puzzles me: I can't bring it into focus, but I suspect that an adage pointing up the regionally distinct ways in which discrimination is articulated socially and socioeconomically might be of help: In the North, supposedly, blacks can get high but not close; in the South, close but not high. In the South, the possibility of having some shared history if not ancestry is great, unlike the autonomy I grew up with in the North, in the nation's fourth-largest city.

I don't know this world at all.

IN CAHOOTS WITH OUR FATHER, my sisters and I have devised a plan that should allow him to continue spending spring and fall here without disrupting the chemotherapy that he is supposed to start and that, according to his oncologist at home, he'll stay on until it stops working. One of the mildest forms of chemo there is. Once a week, three weeks on and one week off. Not meant to cure—it's too late for that—but to slow the rampant climb of Dad's prostate-specific antigen (PSA) level, a number that indicates prostate gland activity and that has been doubling every month since the first spike was noted last year.

I presume cessation of treatments will be concurrent with death or in close proximity to it, since the cancer has already metastasized and can only be slowed now, not stopped. But chemo is chemo, my sisters and I reason: regionless. Surely the treatment will work better for him if administered in "Big Foot Country," as he has started to call Jasper County. So far, Dad's plan is to drive himself to and from these treatments. *I'll pull over if I'm sleepy,* he says. This reasoning, along with his diminishing vision, does not reassure.

The man we're going to see this morning, Dr. Carter, has provisionally agreed, pending the examination he'll conduct today, to administer chemotherapy to Dad in Georgia. Consistent with small-town interconnectedness, Dr. Carter was recommended by Bubba's son Troy, an emergency room physician in the nearby town of Milledgeville who was named after the uncle now watching over Dad's farm.

At the start of the appointment, we find out that Dr. Carter has taught at Emory University in addition to running a private practice, and that he is a natural instructor of the best sort. In the tiny examination room, he delivers an exuberant, extemporaneous lecture on prostate cancer: its origins, method of progression, and available treatment modalities, along with their pluses and minuses. He is in constant motion as he talks, pushing his glasses back up onto the bridge of his nose, gesturing and hopping about the room, practically acting out the disease and the steps we can take to combat it. He touches my father's arm from time to time, as if to seal a mutual understanding.

On the paper sheet that covers the examination table, Dr. Carter spells out *estramustine* and *antigen-resistant* with a thick black marker. He also makes cartoon renderings of the spine, the cancerous lesions that weaken it, and the weight-bearing bones of the body that are likely points for "spot-welding" radiation down the road. *A fractured skull won't kill you*, he explains, *but a broken hip is usually the beginning of the end.*

He pulls more paper from the roll above the table's headrest, joking that his nurses give him heck for wasting their supplies. He says "heck," not "hell," which may be related to the Pentecostal literature that fills the waiting room magazine rack and side tables. I brace myself in case he brings up God, not one of my father's favorite topics. When Dr. Carter leaves the room briefly, I walk over to the examination table drawings.

I'd love to take these home, I say.

Ask him, my father commands. *When he comes back in.*

A lab technician samples and processes Dad's blood while we're with Dr. Carter, and the minute the doctor has confirmation that Dad's PSA level is in the mid-300s, he advises us to schedule chemo with the front desk as soon as possible.

My husband, John, and our friend Claudia are coming from Philadelphia for the weekend, and we have reservations to return together on Sunday afternoon. When Dr. Carter says treatment can start on Monday, I decide to let them go back without me.

On Thursday, my father's day, and therefore mine, is organized around waiting for a fish broker to come restock the ponds. The man didn't show on Wednesday, claiming truck problems, and my father is anxious to cross the task off his list. When the fish man finally does arrive, in a heavy red truck with oxygenated water tanks on its bed, his rail-thin wife is riding shotgun. She has no duties that I can see, other than to watch what happens, smile when greeted, and smoke cigarettes.

Dad and I follow the red truck in the Isuzu, and we are still establishing our photo-taking position when the fish release begins. It takes less than ten seconds for three hundred pounds of catfish to cascade into the biggest of the farm's ponds from a long metal chute swung out from the side of the truck. The fish are about eight inches long, which Dad hopes is big enough to stand a chance against the pond's extant bass and bream and grass carp.

Catfish dispensed, the truck turns back through the woods and up to the paved driveway, across a pasture, and down through a sloping stand of pines to the smallest pond, where Dad is introducing carp to keep down the vegetation. This pond is not named, nor is the midsized one on the other side of the pecan grove. Curious, since my father is obsessed with signs. It's not clear if he's just amusing himself or trying to share the "ego massage" he says he got from having a University of Pennsylvania building (actually an information kiosk inside a building) named after him upon donating several properties to the school when he retired from his real estate career. To whatever end, there are signs bolted to trees and railings all over the farm property: Carolyn Funderburg Fish Pond Road (named after his niece); Diane Funderburg Fish Pond (his oldest daughter); Margaret Funderburg Beach (his middle daughter); Phoebe Funderburg Moore's Woods (his cherished granddaughter); Lise Funderburg Motor Boat; and, in a less expansive nod to his sons-in-law (one of whom has been painted over a previous name, due to divorce and subsequent remarriage), the shared Greg Moore & John Howard Ladder.

For his carp delivery, the fish man stops the truck halfway down the hill and walks close to the small pond, tamping the earth with his feet to check its solidity. There's been steady rain in the last few weeks. Satisfied with the firmness of the terrain, he returns to the truck, eases it close to the bank, and keeps the motor running.

The man brought three sterile carp rather than the requested four, but these are so big, he promises my father, they'll clean up the pond in a minute. And even though they're bigger, he says, he won't charge my dad extra. My father, not a fan of having transaction terms changed without his consent, says nothing, just waits and watches. The fish man wrestles the fish out of their tank one at a time, using a heavy-gauge net with a thick metal pole for a handle. The carp he's brought certainly are big, fifteen to twenty pounds each, and can grow to sixty pounds, apparently, with nothing to stop them. They have no natural enemies, the fish man tells me, and that's why it's illegal to possess the fertile variety. Even with the nonreproducing fish, the authorities keep careful track. *These three here?* he says. *The state of Georgia knows each one of 'em by name.*

The carp don't cooperate. They recoil from the net and once trapped, thrash about, requiring the fish man to hold on to the pole with both hands. I see one carp attempt to leap out of the tank, seemingly standing on its back fins while assessing its future. I sense panic.

No one panics outright after the fish man has finished and tries to leave and his truck spins its wheels in the red clay of the pond's edge, sliding a few inches toward the water with each gunning of the engine. My father has been standing to the side of the goings-on, leaning on a cane and observing from under the brim of his black Stetson, the camera he calls his "shoot and run" holstered to his belt. Once the truck is clearly stuck, he switches into action mode.

Take me to the shed, he commands. We drive up and out of the woods, through the pasture gate, and to a tilting equipment shed that came with the property. I park facing its wood double doors, and Dad stays in the Isuzu, directing me through the piles and cobwebs in search of a towing chain. I find only a twisted wire cable, stiff with age and disuse. Clearly dissatisfied but without other options, he orders me back to the truck, back around the cow gate, back through the pasture, and down to the embedded truck.

At this point, my father decides to drive. He pulls himself up into the driver's seat by the steering wheel, his arms doing the bulk of the work, his legs trailing behind. He thrusts the Trooper into four-wheel drive and backs it close to the embedded truck's front bumper. The fish man finds enough give in the old cable to fasten the two vehicles together, and his wife stands a few yards away, puffing on a cigarette with new vigor. *Rev, rev, rev.* Nothing. Not even a budge. *Revvvvvv.* A burning smell seeps out from the Isuzu's hood. Dad gets the fish man to unhook the vehicles and orders me back behind the wheel. Back we go to the shed, where Dad unfolds himself, picking up each leg with his hands in order to set it on the ground. He approaches the John Deere, a thirty-year-old tractor he bought after reading a farm bulletin that promoted diesel-motored equipment as a prophylactic against an anticipated fuel shortage. Dad bought it from the man across the road, whose extensive collection of used farm equipment borders on the pathological.

Dad tries to climb onto the John Deere's driving platform but can't reach its seat, mounted a good four feet above the ground. He tries to swing his legs, to lift them, hands gripping the seat and steering wheel, knuckles blanching as he tries to hoist himself up.

Shit, he says.

I have been trained over a lifetime and by this man not to interfere at such tense moments, but to stand completely still, to cause no distractions, to breathe quietly, and to say nothing. I have also been taught to be helpful. I step in.

Here, I say. *I can get you up there.*

I crouch underneath him, the lower half of my back wedged under his rear end. I start to count aloud, making *one* and *two* into two-syllable warm-up words. *Wuh-un . . . Too-oo . . .* He joins in, and at the one-syllable burst of *three,* I push upward. On this first try, thank goodness, he makes it. For a moment, the tension is broken. We are effervescent with success.

The engine turns over after several false starts, and Dad drives back to the pond. I run ahead to the pasture gate so I can close it after him. I watch his face as he passes. As he thins and ages and ails, Dad looks more like Granddaddy, when he was close to the end of his own life. Dad's upper lip is a half circle facing down, his bottom lip a horizontal, unbending line.

Once hitched, the tractor merely rocks the fish man's truck in the muddy furrows its wheels have formed, and on the biggest heave-ho sets it sliding sideways, several feet closer to the water's edge.

Dad, usually dogged beyond reason, has had enough. We call the local towing company from my cell phone and request a wrecker. We drive the tractor back to the shed and leave the fish man and his fumy companion to wait by the pond while we return to the house. An hour passes, and as I drive out to pick up the midday meal from Tillman's (Thursday is fried pork chops, thin as a dime, and if I'm lucky, sweet and earthy boiled rutabaga on the side), I can see through the pine trees that the wrecker, an impossibly big truck in a land of big trucks, is working away at its task. When I return ten minutes later, the wrecker and the fish man are gone.

But not forgotten. Storytelling is a Funderburg pastime, the way other families once might have gathered around a radio or sung hymns. Key elements include self-deprecation, suspense, and endless marveling at natural or mechanical wonders. How big those carp were! How quickly the catfish slid down that chute and into the water! We depict each other and ourselves as characters who frequently straddle the line between haplessness and ingenuity, both of which are substantially embellished. As long as no one has come to bodily harm, mishaps and embroilments constitute the farm's canon. Stories are replayed and further embellished for newcomers, visitors, whoever comes within hearing range. By the end of a trip, any of us can tell any story, our actual participation immaterial.

FRIDAY IS AN EASY DAY. We're waiting for the pig to be delivered and then for John and Claudia—whose deep cultural identification with being Jewish in no way precludes a love for pork—to come prepare it. I'm a good cook, but my interests lean more toward outcome than art. My husband and our friend, on the other hand, are fierce, inventive, and impassioned at the stove. Also bossy. The combined force of their talent and opinions is too much for me, and when they get together in a kitchen, I find reasons to go elsewhere. Until plates hit the table.

To quell my father's back-seat hosting and finger-wagging aphorisms, which include, *Leave nothing to chance* and *The challenge is in the moment; the time is always now*, I have stopped by Tillman's to confirm the three-thirty pig delivery time, tabulated charcoal needs, inventoried paper napkin reserves, and searched the Web for recipes that will approximate the citrus, garlic, and cumin *mojo* marinade one traditionally injects into a *Caja China* pig. For the task, my father has somehow procured not one but two veterinary injection needles. I raise practical and logistical questions. *How many bags of ice will we need to keep the pig cool overnight? What's the forecast?*

Call Troy, Dad says in answer to each query, then barks out only the last four digits of Troy's telephone number, since all of Monticello shares the same area code and three-digit exchange.

Troy is the fifth of eight children (Bubba, the second). After fifty years of working in a Connecticut textile factory, ending up as a foreman and union leader, Troy retired, and he and his wife, Dorothy, born and raised in Monticello, came back home to live next door to her retired schoolteacher sister and mother. Actually, the sister and mother live two doors away, but Troy and Dorothy own the house in between and keep it empty. They don't want to be bothered with tenants.

We call it our closet, Dorothy says.

Troy took over caretaking my father's property after Bubba got sick. The terms of the arrangement have shifted slightly in that Dad pays Troy for his labor and Troy, more outgoing than his brother, takes a more active role in the care of the house, in the directing of the twins, in the planning of projects and anticipating maintenance needs, from water pumps to lawn mower blades. In the wake of Dad's disintegrating health, Troy keeps the farm going.

For an hourly wage that is left to Troy to track, he does some mowing, some minor repairs, a lot of checking up on things, and various pond-related tasks, from filling Dad's motorized wildlife feeders to testing the pond's algae levels. As soon as Dad comes into town, sometimes before going to the farm, he'll head for the Johnsons' house to resolve outstanding debts.

Got to keep the money straight, he'll say to Troy.

If Dad orders something while in Pennsylvania, he has it sent to Troy's. Exhibit A: *La Caja China.* Troy has been curious about it ever since the two fifty-pound shipping boxes containing its unassembled parts arrived. He wants to see the thing in action, and he says he's going to be there on Saturday from start to finish. Any kind of pig roasting requires that one be in attendance through the entire enterprise, Troy says, primarily to stand around, *drinking beer and talking trash.*

Friday afternoon and thirty minutes ahead of schedule, Ben Tillman pulls up to the garage of 354 Fellowship Road in a glossy black Chevy 1500, his truck bed lined in corrugated plastic and filled with a plastic cooler and a plastic-swaddled pig, forty-eight inches of pale pink flesh stamped by government inspectors and curved into a semifetal position.

Ben is close to forty, although I'm not sure on which side of it, balding and close-cropped. His well-fed stomach stretches the fabric of his blue T-shirt, and his skin is as pink as, maybe pinker than, the pig's. Troy happens to be at the house. He's come to pick up two largemouth bass I've caught but don't want to skin or gut, and he edges around the periphery of this delivery, watching as Ben hoists the package under one arm like a sack of flour and heads into the garage.

That's one hundred pounds? I ask.

It was before they took the head off, Ben says. *Now it's about eighty-five.*

* * *

ONCE BEN RELEASES the headless, hoofless pig from its shroud, Troy steps in. He pulls a paper-towel roll from the garage's cluttered workbench and begins wiping down the carcass, cleaning off blood that has pooled in the neck area, a wound only a few hours old.

With eleven bags of ice from Ingles, we turn the *Caja China* into a temporary cooler. The plan, after long-distance consultations with Claudia and John, is to cool but not freeze the meat. John, whose credo is that flesh should come to room temperature before it is put on a fire, would probably let the pig sit uniced overnight, but too many others in the pig roast inner circle have expressed concerns about trichinosis, hog cholera, foot-and-mouth, and other festering scenarios.

Talkative, easygoing Troy has gone silent in the presence of Ben. Not unpleasant, but decidedly uncharacteristically reserved. I take his picture with Ben as they stand over the pig. Surely this is the first time they have ever shared a photographic frame.

As I look through the viewfinder, I wonder if Troy is thinking about when Bubba was a sheriff's deputy, the first black law officer in Jasper County. Bubba agreed to take on the task, my father has told me, but at the end of his five-year term, he was more than glad to leave. This was in the late 1960s, and Bubba wasn't authorized to arrest whites, wasn't even supposed to answer calls from white homes. He was, however, charged with monitoring the crowds during a Klan rally that came through town. As the story goes, he stood along the sidelines as the leader of the parade walked by, a Grand Titan or possibly Grand Giant in the Klan's hierarchy. Cloaked in a sheet and white hood, the leader's identity was meant to be protected. But Bubba looked at the head of the parade and apparently recognized the boots of Mack Tillman, Ben's father, poking out from under the hem of the white robe.

In one version of the tale, the elder Tillman hadn't yet run for sheriff, and over the years I've heard that as an explanation for why Bubba never would vote for him. In other versions, Mack already held office. Today, I wonder how many times Troy has heard the story and if it's replaying in his head as he and Ben look into my camera.

After a few more minutes of standing around, conjecturing about how long the pig will take to cook, Ben gets ready to take off, telling us he'll be coming early tomorrow.

I got to see this, he says.

To do so, Ben will have to come by twice. First to observe, then to serve. In recognition of Ben's finding the pig, Dad immediately hired him to bring the side dishes and dessert, and Sissy to set up, mind, and clean up the buffet. My father is constantly calculating cost and benefit, debt and repayment.

THE RENTAL CAR RUMBLES over the farmhouse cattle grate well after dark. John and Claudia spill through the door with bumper-to-bumper traffic tales and hearty appetites. Dad has been waiting in his favorite chair, a swiveling, wheeled number, upholstered and armed, in which he anchors himself at the head of the long oak kitchen table. He can helm from here. He doesn't have to get up to reach the garage door or the counter behind him, the one that separates the eating and cooking sections of the room, and he can see who's coming from three directions: driveway, sunroom, and entryway. I call everyone for dinner, or supper, as the day's third meal is called around here, and Lois walkers her way in halting, shaky intervals to the chair on Dad's right.

What is this, Claudia asks when I pull a sheet of takeout ribs from the oven. *A pork warm-up?*

We plow through the rack purchased from Supreme Wings, a side concern of the pasture-renting Albert and Elbert in collaboration with their sister and nephew, and after supper, we head out to the garage to address the pig. John presses down on each side of the rib cage, putting all his weight into flattening the carcass so it can be sandwiched between two metal grids that will suspend it inside the *Caja*. When his efforts fail, he takes a hatchet to the pig's spine, then steps on it when no one's looking, cracking the ribs free with the weight of his body. Claudia sits on the riding mower parked nearby, pretending to steer it over bumpy fields and shouting *Yee-ha*.

Eventually, Claudia and John sit on either side of the pig, injecting marinade in bilateral, synchronized spurts. The fluid inflates pockets of skin like balloons, causing Claudia to roar with laughter. My father watches from a utility stool he can wheel around for a better view. He likes Claudia. In matters of business or finance, her messy ebullience would offend him, but he's drawn to her enthusiasm for the farm, for the pig, for the prospect of so much succulent pork. Before the weekend ends, he will name the driveway after her and place an order for its sign.

When the pig will hold no more marinade, we leave it and collapse into our respective beds, delivered to sleep by the night's sounds, cicadas vibrating and lumber trucks heading to the Georgia-Pacific plant a few miles down Highway 83.

3.

LA CAJA CHINA

Troy offered to come start the coals at eight-thirty Saturday morning. He arrives at seven-thirty. What is it with these rural people and prepunctuality? The sun has barely hoisted itself up into the sky. The household is still on its first pot of coffee. Troy parks his dented brown pickup in one of the parking spaces laid into 354's paved cul-de-sac entry, then walks around to the back door. Where you set your emergency brake, which entryway you believe is yours implies comfort, respect, subservience, tradition, and, occasionally, simple happenstance. More than once, I have looked to my father to translate the race and class koans that surround us. His inclination is to answer by way of illustration.

> *One of the twins came up to the house one day. He came to the back door and knocked, sort of hat in hand. I said, "Why didn't you come to the front door?" I said, "Don't come to my back door anymore." He let it pass. When he left he said, "Thank you, Mr. Funderburg. And I ain't coming to your back door no more."*

Troy's early arrival is no surprise to John, whose cherished North Carolina childhood is stirred up by time spent at the farm. John has already wheeled the *Caja* to a corner of the garage driveway and emptied it of ice. He and Troy lift the trussed pig and heave it into the roasting box. The sandwiching metal grid has legs at each corner, which set the pig several inches above the box's floor, allowing hot air to circulate around the meat. The morning is cool, and my father, observing from a slight remove, wears deerskin work gloves and a quilted vest over his button-down shirt. He leans on the cane he now takes everywhere. Under his watchful eye, the younger men lay the sheet metal lid in place and pour two mounds of charcoal onto it, per instructions printed on the box's plywood exterior. Rationalizing that fumes cannot contaminate the pig as they would in a conventional roasting setup, John pyromaniacally douses, drenches, and soaks the briquettes with lighter fluid, then steps back to let Troy do the honors. Using a box of safety kitchen matches, Troy lights each pyre. Twin peaks of orange inferno climb two feet into the air: Troy, John, and my father stand mesmerized.

Already, the pig roast work is mostly done. Nothing to do but stand around, talk trash, and, at this point in the day, drink coffee. I give Claudia a full tour of the house. *This place looks like a Marriott,* she says. *A nice Marriott,* she adds, but a generic, tidy Marriott nonetheless. It's true. Only a few stamps of individuality exist. Along one kitchen wall, a series of framed photographs taken more than seventy years ago depict Monticello life: a gas station, the west side of the square, cotton bales passing through town atop mule-driven carts, and a whites-only hotel that has long since burned down and which, according to Uncle Holsey, had a mean owner and a parrot on its porch, trained to swear at any black people who walked by. A photograph of my niece surrounded by blueberry bushes is in one room, and an enormous, larger-than-life portrait of Lois, taken by one of her sons, is in another. There is a watercolor of a black cowboy, a poster from a Martha's Vineyard fair, and a poster of Schloss Burg an der Wupper, a castle that supposedly links our line of Funderburgs to its white, European ancestry. At least eighteen Kleenex boxes dot the seven-room, three-bath house, each offering up white tissue (*Who's sniffing? Blow your nose!*). Some are sheathed in brass covers, out of the same dignifying impulse, perhaps, that drove Lois to insist until recent years that condiments be decanted into serving containers. The desk in the living room, the bookcase between kitchen and sunroom, the workbench in the garage, and the cabinet portion of the bedroom wardrobe are pure Dad, clutters of useful and useless items, tape and stamps and fastening doohickeys of every stripe. Recently abandoned interests linger, in the form of instructional booklets and videos. Drawers and desktops and bookshelves hold reference books and magnifying glasses and always, always, emery boards and diamond-cut metal files with cuticle pushers and pointed cleaning ends.

At a yard sale several years ago, Dad paid a dollar for a junk-filled cutlery tray. Boredom might have propelled him, as my sisters and I went through piles of linens, pillowcase by pillowcase, and marveled at the sociological import of advertisements in a dog-eared *Life* magazine from 1963. The junk Dad purchased ranged from rubber bands to bolts and paper clips. When we tried to make fun of him, he argued that if he were to find one nail or screw in that tray when he needed it, saving him a trip to the hardware store, he would feel it was money well spent. Thus far, from what I can tell, he's still out a buck.

Once my house tour ends, Claudia and I set off in the rental car to seek adventure. We hit the local attractions: the fruit stand where you can ask for a "five-dollar lemon" and get a jar of moonshine in return; the Ingles shelves filled with syrups and cornmeals and pork products on a scale unknown outside of Dixie; and, finally, the flea market in Flovilla that seems from its roadside clutter that it might offer up some treasure, then doesn't. Claudia's heart flutters slightly when she sees a stack of *Playboy* magazines that she could sell in Philadelphia to Hefnerian connoisseurs. But on inspection they're not old enough, not classic or collectible enough, and so, she says, not worth the schlep.

We return to Monticello. Claudia should see the town square, stately and pristine. Often, each corner swarms with fund-raisers hawking Krispy Kremes: for the deer festival, for band uniforms, for a school field trip. But today, no doughnut ambush awaits us, and I take her by the Funderburg homeplace, the two houses my grandfather bought in 1925 and joined together, a few doors below the crest of Colored Folks Hill.

The house, always painted white, has a pitched roof and a screened-in porch where my father and his siblings would lay out the Sunday paper's comics, practically piling on top of one another in order to read them. On the porch swing that still hangs off to one side, my father read his favorite boyhood book, *The Autobiography of Benjamin Franklin*, which he dug out of a box his oldest brother, Fred, had shipped home from college the summer he went to work on a Civilian Conservation Corps project in Alabama. Out back, behind a massive pecan tree, stands the barn, where cows and hogs and chickens and horses once were milked and butchered and shod. And just outside the kitchen door, one thick-stemmed stubble of an ancient rosebush hangs on, planted by a rose-loving grandmother I never knew, since only a few months passed between her death and my birth.

Less than a hundred yards down Funderburg Drive, I turn into the civic project my father has instigated and whose completion he anxiously awaits. It is called Funderburg Park, which he sometimes finds flattering, sometimes doesn't, and it is composed primarily of fifteen acres he inherited or bought from his siblings and then donated to the city. Inside city limits, few undeveloped parcels of this size remain. This one has escaped transformation in part because of location. Despite its fairly flat grade and easy walk from the center of town, it is surrounded by shotgun shacks and a barrackslike low-income housing project. And it is surrounded, almost completely, by black people.

Perhaps my grandfather held on to the land long enough to leave it to his children because it was such an accomplishment to have purchased it in the first place. When my father and the Johnson boys attended the Jasper County Training School for Coloreds, sections of the property served as a muddy playing field. My grandfather used most of it for farming, a joint venture he undertook with the school principal, G. J. Van Buren, who was  the only black person in town my grandfather found to be his cosmopolitan and educational equal.

Perhaps holding on to the land was Grandfather's way of memorializing Van Buren, who moved to an even more rural Georgia community after several years in Monticello. One night, Van Buren heard a noise and went onto his porch to investigate. A shotgun fired, from close range, and my grandfather's friend died instantly, blown in half by the blast. The crime was never solved, the murderer never found.

I drive Claudia past the only completed portion of the park project: a community center set close to the entrance. This building is a welcoming, one-story bungalow, surprisingly handsome for low-budget municipal architecture and similar to many houses in the better sections of town. It has been named the Get-Ahead House, and for now hosts delinquency deterrence programs run by the police department.

The playing fields and outdoor pavilion have yet to be constructed, and Dad has grown antsier than ever. The clock ticks. He donated the land more than five years ago, and promises from city officials remain unfulfilled. Now and then he goes through a spate of letter-writing and e-mailing and phone calls, checking for status reports about this or that aspect of construction or grant making or permit seeking. Depending on the results of his badgering, he is either temporarily appeased or too frustrated to further aggravate himself and he backs off for a while. Maybe as his health diminishes he will back off for good, not by choice but from lack of energy.

As Claudia and I circle back toward the farm, curious to see how the pig is faring, we have a stroke of luck—a yard sale. At a quick glance, not that promising: plastic time-saving gadgets and ingenious devices that can only be bought on TV. But at the center of the yard, a boy has spread out his collection of pocketknives across a card table. Claudia zeroes in, her attention lands. Over the six years I've known her, I've come to see that she has a keen eye for . . . for what? For curiosities, for quality, for stuff that other people will want, for things she can sell on eBay. These knives are alternately squat and thin, sleek and rounded, bulky and small. Their casings are horn and wood, metal and bone. Some are shiny from wear, some are simply worn. Some she discards, the ones whose blades have been snapped off, having been employed in tasks beyond their capacities. But others, especially where the brand name is stamped into an end or the inlay is detailed, she gathers into a pile.

How much for all of these? she asks the boy.

Sixteen dollars?

Great, Claudia says, opening her wallet.

* * *

SHORTLY AFTER NOON, Mack Tillman comes to see the pig. The former sheriff drives up in a gleaming white truck, winding along Claudia Raab Driveway at a crawl, giving everyone in the house time to speculate on who we're peering at through the sunroom windows. This is a testimonial to the degree of curiosity the pig box has inspired in town, that Daddy Mack would come by, uninvited. No question whether he'll stay for the party—he won't—but he wants to see. For the rest of the day and into the next, the black party guests mention this to one another in low voices. *Know who came by? Guess who stopped to see the pig . . .*

According to John's calculations, the coals, already twice replenished, should be lifted off in another twenty minutes so that the pig can be turned and the skin browned. The *Caja China* instructions stress the importance of keeping the box closed for the first several hours, then opening it only once. For Mack Tillman's bene-fit, though, John opens the box. Everyone crowds around to see.

Claudia squeals. Others inhale deeply. The pig is well on its way, shades of umber and brown, even blackened at points.

John retrieves a knife from the kitchen and carves off tastes. Mack accepts a piece, puts it in his mouth, and contemplates it, saying nothing. Behind his big square plastic eyeglass frames, his look is impenetrable. There is a general silence after each person tries the pork. It is salty. Horribly, wretchedly salty. Apparently, this is a case of overenthusiastic overinoculation with overly briny brine.

It is a little salty, Mack Tillman concedes, once someone else has said so.

Claudia cocks her head to one side while she concentrates on a contemplative chew. *Maybe it's the spot we took it from,* she suggests. John seems less optimistic but carves from a different section of the pig's belly. The second sample is marginally less saline. We hold on to the hope that this sliding scale might continue to slide in other parts of the pig. John and Troy turn over the grid-encased carcass, make crisscross cuts in its skin, and close up the box for another few hours until the guests are likely to arrive. At least the contamination-sensitive among us will be assured of a fully cooked pig. John worries it will be overcooked.

Troy leaves to change for the party, from red flannel shirt to blue flannel, one bill cap to another. He comes back an hour later with Dorothy and her brother, Howard Smith, the A.M.E. church organist and retired schoolteacher, in tow.

My father believes that for a meal to reflect southern hospitality, it should include hot plates, hot food, and hot bread. And so, while I knew Ben Tillman would bring a pan of corn bread, I wanted to be sure that we'd have some fresh from the oven. I called Dorothy on and off all day, trying to get her corn bread recipe, leaving messages of increasing urgency.

Miss Dottie, I have a question . . . Miss Dottie, I'm in a pickle . . . Miss Dottie, only you can help me . . .

When I finally got through, she suggested I make crackling bread instead and dictated a shopping list that included which brand of pork cracklings to buy (Lord's) and which self-rising cornmeal mix to get (White Lily). Now, when she comes through the door of the farmhouse and into the kitchen, to my great relief, she takes charge. She cooks in the local method, with no measuring device other than the cupped palm of her hand. She fluffs the flour with a fork in lieu of sifting, and inspects each egg she uses for irregularity. A speck of blood, she explains, and she will throw out the whole thing. She is similarly squeamish about the dead, and while she will attend viewings of loved ones, she will not, she admits, approach the casket and look at remains.

I admire her cooking technique, but she tut-tuts the praise. She can't really bake, she says, not anymore. *When I say I'm going to make cookies, Lise,* she confides in a whisper, *neighborhood children run in the opposite direction. Really, they are so bad, no one will eat them. I used to be able to bake, but no more. Lise, I don't know what happened.*

A MONTH AGO, before I escorted Dad and Lois down for their annual spring visit, I proposed we break in *La Caja China* while I was with them. Dad seized on the idea immediately, but that led to the question of whom to invite. Legwork would fall to me, I knew, so I argued for a limited list, only the people most like family. With the exception of Jerry Goldin, a wisecracking, storytelling, animal-loving, Jewish former state trooper who had befriended my father a few years earlier, everyone on my list was black. But my father diversified and added, partly on principle, and partly because he had social courtesies to repay. The Pig Party head count grew to fifteen, all of us knowing that Dad would add names at the last minute, depending on who he ran into the day before or morning of.

Guests arrive throughout the afternoon. No one knew when the food would be ready: Some guests were told to come between five and six, and some were told simply to "Come early and stay late," a phrase as worn in our family as "There's plenty more in the kitchen." Sissy was told to start serving at five or five-thirty, but she and her brother show up hours ahead of schedule. Sissy busies herself with setting up. Ben carries aluminum trays of collards, sweet potatoes, corn bread, and cobbler into the house, then heads back outside to watch the pig.

People gather chairs onto the driveway next to the *Caja China*. We have carried and dragged them from the garage, the toolshed, and the patio in order to surround an inert plywood container. Troy and Dorothy and Howard, my cousin Carolyn from Atlanta, Ben, John, and Claudia. All of us worshipping a box that is completely inert. Even the ashen coals appear dormant, sending their heat downward into the mystery of the interior.

Dad and Lois stay inside, sitting in the sunroom with Mary Jim and Mackie, the couple who live on the next hobby farm over and whose other-than-us all-white Super Bowl party Dad and I attended months earlier: five televisions scattered around a great room the length of a bowling alley, Chex Party Mix and taco salad on offer, and a betting pool that cost ten dollars a square and was won by Mary Jim's daughter-in-law.

Jerry Goldin wanders between the sunroom and pig box contingents, bridging each trip with a refrigerator beer stop. Outside, Ben tells us tales of pig roasts he has known, enterprises that took all night, trash talking usurped by boredom halfway through, inevitably ending with participants swearing they'd never do it again.

By four-thirty or so, the smell is irresistible, and, manufacturer's calculations be damned, the guests are uniformly restless. Only those who tasted the salt-lick slices earlier in the day hesitate about the imminent deboxing. John and Troy take the coal tray by its handles, lift it off, and rest it sideways across the roasting box's long metal arms.

The crowd gathers in for a look. There it is, skin ranging from golden to charred, savory perfume pouring forth. In light of its immensity, various observers decamp to find platters and a surface on which it can be carved. There is some discussion about putting the whole thing onto the kitchen table, where Sissy has already laid out the side dishes, plates, and desserts. Those could certainly be moved, it is decided, but there are spillable juices to be considered, and moreover, molten grease that could easily drip onto the floor.

I ask Troy if there might be plywood scraps in the small utility shed behind the house. He says yes, and I head off to investigate.

Ben follows me, Troy follows Ben. Plywood is found, power tools are enlisted to saw off protuberances, and a box of aluminum foil is fully exhausted in covering the board. The shimmery litter is laid across two plastic lawn chairs positioned next to the pig box.

John unleashes the pig from its grid, which requires wire cutters. The pig was too thick to secure with the metal S-hooks provided with the box—this pig would have required more of an **S** than an S— so John jury-rigged a porcine orthodontia, having dug through my father's workbench mess to find a sufficiently pliable gauge of wire.

John carves with an intuitive logic, aware that there is a right way to do this even if he is not privy to it. The sheriff's deputy Dad hired for "parking and security" sidles over to watch. He doesn't have much else to do, since all the cars have been parked and no segregationist agitators have appeared. The deputy is in his twenties, pink and fleshy, and, as he lets on, the son of a butcher. John immediately solicits advice: how to find the joints, what to do once they've been found.

Claudia, a tactile cook, assists by ripping hunks of meat apart by hand and chucking them onto the platter. Jerry Goldin, clearly hungry and perhaps more accustomed to eating among his houseful of dogs, peels off a ten-inch, loinlike strip with his fingers, then steps aside to devour it immediately, raising it above his tilted-back head. The less aggressive or more recently fed guests stand in close, watching every move, identifying which pieces they hope to get onto their plates.

The actual consumption of the pig is less theatrical. As it turns out, the salt problem has either cooked away, dripping down into the catch pan that now holds inches of liquid lard, or was overconcentrated only in parts. The cooks agree that, in fact, there could be more seasoning next time, especially garlic and cumin and orange juice. Still, the repugnant carcass has emerged from its sarcophagus, transformed into crisped, caramelized skin and tender, succulent meat. Pig candy has been achieved.

Outside, guests fill their plates and take them into the dining room, while the sunroom crowd stays in the sunroom, propping plates on coffee tables and footstools and knees. Jerry Goldin still wanders between the two.

At the dining room table, a mahogany behemoth that came from my grandfather's house, the hush of consumption subsides after only five or ten chewing-filled minutes. Claudia produces her penknives for show-and-tell. Troy and Howard are enthralled. Troy asks several times where *exactly* this sale was, despite Claudia's repeated assurances that it was a onetime event and that she exhausted the stock. Seeing how fascinated both men are, Claudia invites each one to take his pick. They say no, too polite to accept a gift from such a new acquaintance. But Claudia repeats her offer, repeats it again, and they capitulate. Troy chooses a bigger knife with antler casing, and Howard picks one with painted enamel, a Canadian Mountie depicted on the side.

Ben sits with us in the dining room. He doesn't have his father's reserve. He doesn't hesitate to answer Claudia's questions about whether southern people worry about their diets (*No*) and if not, whether they worry about how they look (*No*). When she asks about life in Monticello, Ben talks about going to Tuesday night city council meetings just for something to do, that he'd go even if the meetings were held on a Friday night since there's nothing else going on—no movie theaters, no bars, no Starbucks. In the face of Claudia's curiosity and Ben's guilelessness, Troy warms up, and the tale-telling begins to bounce around the table, a ball kept in constant play, stories about beloved pen knives, pig roasts gone by, bootlegging school bus drivers, and creative ways to use crackling.

Dad insists on giving away the leftovers, and he calls out for me to fill another Ziploc whenever someone stands up or buttons a jacket. His appetite has left him, and the food will rot if it's left behind. He orders me to make up more packages than there are guests: one for Marshall Tinsley, who is out of town, and another for

George Davie Mohorne, the neighbor who cleans the farm's property line along Fellowship Road and Route 16, a task that involves collecting jettisoned beer cans, Dairy Queen Blizzard cups, and the occasional deer carcass. Dad once cracked Troy right up by telling him that the clean fence line made black folks proud and white folks envious.

Late into the evening, after most of the guests have gone home, saddled with gallon-size bags of meat and side dishes, Troy's brothers Lorenzo and Bubba arrive. They are in their eighties and live together at Bubba's house. Like several of Troy and Dorothy's siblings, Lorenzo spent half a century in Connecticut, but after Bubba's wife, Bertha Kate, passed away, and Lorenzo and Bubba were both alone, the family convinced Lorenzo to come home.

They didn't want me to die up there by myself, Lorenzo tells me. *They didn't want me to die like a dog.*

Whenever Lorenzo and Bubba visit, talk turns to the old days. The Funderburg and Johnson children grew up together, along with Dorothy and her brother Howard, who lived next door to my father. They all attended the Jasper County Training School, a simple wood-frame building made out of salvaged lumber from the demolished white high school. In class, boys were taught to build outhouses, girls to sew, and what book learning could be fit in beyond that was based on outdated textbooks cast off from the white school.

The Funderburg, Johnson, and Smith families belonged to the same church, Saint James African Methodist Episcopal, on Funderburg Drive, then called Warren Street. And when the boys weren't in class or doing chores or in Sunday school, which my grandfather taught, they played. They shot marbles and spun tops, sharpening the spinners' points and hoping to knock one another's off balance with a carefully aimed launch. Troy remembers that my father would stand on the curb with a pocketful of nickels, promising one to any boy who would go and hit his own head against a light pole.

45

Did you ever earn a nickel? I ask Troy.

No, uh-uh, he says. *No way. But it was funny. It was just George being George.*

Boys of my father's generation learned how to shoot by the age of ten, and while my father didn't have his own gun, he always had access to one. Sometimes he would take the household's utilitarian .22, used for chores such as putting a bullet directly between a pig's eyes at hog-killing time. Other times, he would use his brother Fred's double-barreled shotgun when he went hunting for quail or rabbits. It was a .410, lightweight and with minimal kick after firing, but my father wasn't much of a shot and he rarely conquered his prey.

My father and the Johnson boys dug worms for fishing and threw lines into creeks, catching crawfish and minnows, never enough to bring home. Lorenzo, who was my father's main running buddy, excelled at turtle gigging, which entailed spearing the backs of snapping turtles with a barbed hook fixed to a long pole.

In the fall, the children gathered buckets of pecans that fell into yards and along roadsides, as well as in carefully tended orchards. They went sledding on barrel staves down hill paths lined with pine straw; in early summer they ate peaches, and in August, they picked scuppernongs, giant orbs of grapes with a sugar content so high their perfume fermented in the heat of the sun.

Of the three Johnson men I know, Lorenzo is smallest in stature but has a deep, honey-coated voice, and whether he's talking about the science of horse racing or fixing TVs, the authoritative, velvety timbre draws you in close.

The professor, Bubba calls him, though Lorenzo didn't go past high school.

Bubba is harder to understand, his country accent never thinned by living up north like so many of his siblings did. But his face, barely lined, is a rich, vibrant brown, his handsome features more arresting than I'm used to seeing on an eighty-two-year-old.

The two brothers have eaten, they say, but they accept not only the small plates I make up for them but also a mountain of take-home packages. And they'll come back on Sunday for the pan of grease, when it's had a chance to congeal. My father's Monticello peers do not waste: scraps of any kind are used until they disintegrate. The grease will go to Bubba's dogs.

Leftovers are so aggressively distributed, my father riding herd whenever anyone starts to make a good-bye, that by the end of Saturday night, the refrigerator holds only enough meat to make a handful of sandwiches.

LATELY, MY FATHER'S BEEN ON A TEAR about religion, particularly Christianity as exploited by white capitalists to justify the economically beneficial practice of slavery. He is offended by the worship of a God whose subjects subscribe to subjugation and segregation, whose church congregations reflect those practices, whose reading of the scriptures suggests that either position is spiritually defensible. Among blacks, he sees religion as a crutch, a palliative, a concession to injustice, a prison in which the incarcerated hold the key. At Tillman's or Eddie Ray's, Dad looks for opportunities, often makes them, to mention Dr. Martin Luther King Jr.'s comment that eleven A.M. Sunday mornings was, and still is, the most segregated hour in America. As often as I've heard that notion over the years, the shock of it can still grab me. The friction between secular reality and Christian ideals—the aspiring to a better self and conduct, liberation from the petty jealousies and insults of daily life—is eternally stunning.

At eleven A.M. on this Sunday, the day after the Pig Party, Jerry Goldin drives up to the house with a man he introduces as the one other Jew in Jasper County, an electrician named Resnick. Jerry's arrival is odd, a recent awkwardness. Jerry used to come over regularly to talk politics and local gossip with Dad, a practice that started after my father made an impression on Bryant Larmon, one of the early risers who ate breakfast at Tillman's when it opened, as my dad did. Bryant is a few years older than my father and has been dairy farming full time since the age of five. Dad and Bryant talked cows, toured Bryant's dairy occasionally, and had small adventures together: to a county fair where they had their feet massaged, to Bryant's family place in the north Georgia mountains. One day, Bryant showed my father his pride and joy, a plaque he carried in his truck citing the second-lowest bacteria count in Jasper County. My father went home, wrapped an unopened bottle of brandy in aluminum foil, and topped it with a Post-it note: "Congratulations on the second-lowest bacteria count in Jasper County." He delivered it the next morning at breakfast.

Shortly after that, Jerry introduced himself to my father in a telephone call.

You don't know me, Jerry said into Dad's message machine. *But I'm Jerry Goldin and I thought you should know that ever since you gave Bryant Larmon that bottle of booze, he's stopped showing people his plaque and now he shows them the booze.*

That message sparked a friendship that went strong for a number of years, then frosted over. On doctor's orders, my father cut out booze and cigars, both of which had fueled Dad and Jerry's sessions, but Jerry's absence is more directly connected to the time my father banned one of Jerry's dogs, Happy, subsequent to an incident that involved a plate of hors d'oeuvres, the low-slung coffee table in 354's great room, and insufficient subsequent remorse, human or canine. Jerry is a love-me-love-my-dog kind of guy, actively involved in the local animal shelter and the owner of a small menagerie. After the Happy Ban was levied, Dad's invitations and Jerry's visits ceased altogether.

But with the passage of time and perhaps the change in my father's health, the winds have shifted. Jerry came solo to the pig roast, and as Dad's decline grows increasingly obvious, Jerry seems eager to help out. Today, he has brought Resnick to look at a problem Dad mentioned during the party.

Shalom, y'all, Jerry says, prompting the northern-born-and-raised Claudia to guffaw.

Jerry heads for the refrigerator to get a beer and offers to get one for Resnick. Resnick declines. *Alcohol and electricity don't mix [mee-yucks],* he says as he climbs a ladder to examine a failing fluorescent light in the garage.

Claudia and John leave for the airport at noon, hours earlier than the trip demands, spooked by the traffic on their way down. I wave at the retreating car, wishing it would turn around. For the rest of the night, Dad and Lois roost in the sunroom, the old console TV from my grandfather's house flickering satellite stations into the room. At the dining table, I set up a digital photo printer my dad recently asked me to order for him. I churn out four-by-six pictures taken over the last few days, archiving the event of which we are still in the midst, cataloging it for safekeeping, for proof.

I see in the pictures that life is leaking from my father. I have seen it, watched it seep out of him in the last few months and now, in close quarters, from one day to the next. My sisters and I go to most doctors' appointments with him, inserting ourselves to his combined relief and annoyance. We do it for him—so much information to keep straight, so many medications to keep an eye on—but also for ourselves. I go because I need to understand what is happening, and because even the smallest actions feel like fortification against what is yet to come.

I conspire now to give him pleasure. He has grown easier to be around: his bullying and snappishness less stinging, his moments of charm and humor and irrepressible curiosity more magnetic. I spend most of Sunday night with the pictures, editing down to the best shots, ordering them into a chronology, and then sliding them into the miniature album I picked up at the drugstore across from the Uncle Remus Regional Library and a block from Dave's.

I want my father to have a record of the Pig Party. I want him to be able to look back on it whenever he wants, to show it off to fellow Waverly residents, to his doctors, to the odd visitor to his apartment. I want to construct a memento of the trip that could be his last.

MY FATHER HAD KNOWN for two months that his prostate cancer was back before my sisters and I—or Lois, for that matter—found out. In those two months, John and I got married, and in the informal style of second marriages, we celebrated with a midsummer barbecue in our Philadelphia backyard. The event was potluck, except for the main dish, ribs. In the earliest stages of planning, there was a fleeting notion that John, such a good cook and lover of fire and meat, would produce the main course. But he would either be exhausted by or endlessly occupied with the effort, and so we decided to job out the task. Local purveyors proved problematic: the most talented one didn't answer her phone, the reliable one produced tough, dry meat, and the one who was a former Black Panther apparently likened our request to university speaking gigs and demanded ten thousand dollars, more than triple the entire event budget.

Dad called to see how preparations were going, and I mentioned my rib quandary. He said nothing, but a half hour later, he called back and began a campaign of suggesting that he order the ribs from Dave's. If I stall, I thought, perhaps he'll give up.

Dave's does make good ribs, I said, *but how would we get them here?*

Dad launched into an investigation of shipping options and thawing times, calling me every few days to detail his progress. World peace could be achieved, I thought more than once, were his energies to be redirected. When it turned out that FedExing the meat would prove cumbersome, logistically and financially, he made delivery arrangements with Marshall Tinsley. My father did not ask if this was okay, did not ask if we'd decided on Dave's, did not pay for the ribs. This was simply the best and therefore only solution, and I was expected to proceed accordingly. And so the day before the party, Marshall picked up forty racks of ribs, iced down and accompanied by jugs of sauce. He filled the trunk and backseat of his Lincoln Town Car with coolers, plucked a nephew out of the local pool hall for company, and drove straight north. On the morning of the event, John still ended up spending two hours prepping. He cleaved apart the frozen slabs into easy-reheat individual portions, cramping his cutting hand into a four-Advil state. But the meat was the hit of the reception. *After the ribs came out*, Marshall recalls, *all you could hear was a hundred and fifty people chewing.*

Two days later, we found out about Dad's cancer. John and I were having dinner with Claudia on her front porch. My oldest sister, Diane, walked up the driveway, having heard voices from our yard, two houses away. Normally, she would call out "Hola," and launch into some line of questioning about what we were eating or where we'd been all day or what flowers Claudia had planted in her yard. But she saw me and said nothing.

What's wrong? I asked.

She started to cry. She had visited my father that day. As often happens, he asked if she wanted to see his recent correspondence. We find out news of relatives, travel plans, and his current causes and campaigns from these letters and e-mails, sent and received, all printed out and double-hole-punched at the top of each page so they can be slid onto a two-prong fastener made by the ACCO office supply company. Thumbing through, Diane happened across a letter from the urologist, confirming that after fifteen years of Dad's prostate cancer being in remission, its activity levels were increasing and a course of treatment would have to be determined.

That's how we came to know.

DIANE AND I JOINED DAD on his first treatment-related appointment a few weeks later, and after he had his physical, she and I were

ushered into the examination room to wait with him for the oncologist to return and give us her assessment. We chatted about nothing
in particular as we waited, cracking jokes and debating lunch plans
to fill the space. But then we lapsed into silence for a few minutes,
and Diane and I both looked over at our father and saw something
we'd never seen before. He was crying. It didn't last long. Before I
could get up and put my arm around him, he had rubbed the tears
dry and pulled himself back from whatever sadness or fear or grief he
had momentarily succumbed to.

After the appointment, he treated us to one of his favorite foods,
Peking Duck. Diane was quiet. Dad and I chatted as we devoured
the envelopes of thin pancake stuffed with scallions and plum sauce,
duck meat and strips of crisp, fatty, flavored skin that deserves, truth
be told, to be called duck candy. At one point he said, *If I become a
basket case, I want you to pull the plug.*

Dad, Diane said, half wail, half reproach.

I'll do it, I said between bites. *Unless I'd get in trouble.*

I don't want you to get in trouble, he said.

Well, I'll figure out a way. I've got your back.

Thanks, Leesee.

4.

IF IT IS HUMAN, IT WILL ERR

THE MONDAY AFTER the pig roast, Dad and I head out for his first Taxol treatment. First we stop for breakfast at Tillman's, because Dad hopes to capture any postparty buzz that might be floating about. Alternatively, he's prepared to stir up his own, and to that end he instructs me to bring along the little photo album. It is already in my bag.

Even though he did no heavy lifting for the party, other than his wallet, my father seems exhausted. He shuffles from the car to the restaurant, leaning deeply into his cane, occasionally pausing to straighten up and catch his breath and just hold on for a minute.

He has recently developed an inventory of comments for those who await him. If he's in a good mood, he'll say, *I'm comin', I'm comin', I'm comin'*. To the daughters and friends and strangers who routinely ask if he needs help, often crowding in too close, he'll say, *I just need time*, which can come across as jovial or reproachful, depending on his level of intimacy with the other party or, perhaps, his level of discomfort.

Give me a minute, he'll say. *I'll get there.*

Tillman's back room is where Dad says the "good old boys" tend to cluster, many of them the same people who patronize Eddie Ray's barbershop. Dad's use of the moniker isn't completely clear to me, except that "good old boys" never refers, obviously, to women or young people. It also doesn't refer to Latinos or Asians because Monticello, despite the expanding tortilla section at Ingles, is still a mostly black and white town. Most specifically, the term never refers to blacks.

Dad lowers himself into a chair at one of three available tables, as far as possible from the other diners, which in such close quarters is not far at all. Today's crowd is indeed all white and, with the exception of Ben Tillman's wife, all men. Lots of talk about the weather here, but also the goings-on in the city, which Dad sops up like biscuits in redeye gravy.

Whatsa matter with you, Mr. George? one of the older good old boys asks when he sees the cane and the shuffling. The tone is teasing. These men complain about the aches and pains of aging almost as much as they complain about politics and taxes.

I have to get some chemotherapy, my father answers, which silences the other man.

At breakfast, you get table service, and so there's no reason to head back to the room that houses the cafeteria-style food line, over which Ben is no doubt presiding. But Dad wants to keep the money straight, and he hands me a check to give to Ben for the catering and a tip to give Sissy. I deliver both; then, seeing Ben's not too busy, I hand him the photo album across the top of the plastic hygiene barrier. Ben flips through the book.

I ordered my own Caja China *the day after seeing yours in action,* he tells me. *I got my stepdaughter to go on the computer for me.* While he turns pages, he calculates the number of days it will take for the check he sent to arrive and then clear and for the pig box to travel from Florida. *I'm going to start with a mess of Boston butts, not a whole pig, and I sure could use that marinade recipe if you have a chance.*

Sure thing, I say.

I know your daddy keeps you busy.

My father and I eat our spicy fresh sausage, scrambled eggs, and heavily peppered, margarine-topped grits in silence and with dispatch. Dad is not a social eater, a food lingerer. Socializing can come after the fact, should the mood strike, but eating is a task to be completed. If the food's exceptionally good or he knows someone's gone to great lengths to prepare it, he might let out a lip smack here and there, but he is single-minded about the purpose at hand.

When he finishes his last bite of breakfast, he turns to the album I've laid by his plate. He picks it up and passes it to two strangers at the next table, his opening gambit: *Ever hear of a* Caja China?

I have heard this pitch before. In 1994, when my first book was published, my father became its staunchest promoter. He was in Martha's Vineyard at the time, the Massachusetts island where he spent summers for several of his early retirement years. He approached the island's three bookstore owners with a proposition. If they would each order ten copies, he would guarantee sales. At the end of the summer, he would buy up any remainders at full retail. No one turned him down.

What an ingenious plan, I said when he told me of the scheme.

I did sell books for a living, he explained. In his youth, my father had been a prize-winning door-to-door salesman: first cookbooks, then encyclopedias, then storm windows. On my book's behalf, he made his quota by approaching strangers on public plazas, in buffet lines, and waiting to pay at the supermarket. At the beginning of the summer, he started soft. *Nice day*, he might say, just to launch the conversation. By August, with his departure date approaching, he ratcheted up his technique.

You'll have to excuse me, he'd say, cutting to the chase, *But I'm a proud father and I want to tell you about my daughter's book.*

His technique with the Pig Party album also reminds me of the year after the book was published, the winter of 1995. During a heavy snowstorm that struck the Northeast, my father started to feel sluggish and achy. The weather was so bad that he ignored the discomfort for two days. The Waverly maintenance department finally cleared the roads, and he drove the quarter mile from his villa to the health center. He collapsed across its threshold.

I got the call late at night, as is always the case with these calls, and caught the next train from Brooklyn, where I was living, to Philadelphia. I knew he had a pulmonary embolism, was in intensive care, but no one had thought to explain one detail that showed itself the moment I stepped into his hospital room.

I bet you're wondering why your dad looks this way, the nurse by his bed said before I could gasp or weep. She explained in a bright but pointed voice, a tone meant to keep me calm and focused: the blood thinners administered to save his life had also made the bruises he sustained from the fall—on his arms and legs and on his face, where he'd landed on his eyeglasses—turn a brilliant purple, as if grape juice had been spilled over him and never cleaned up. Once the nurse finished, my father began to speak, with oxygen tubes in his nose, IV lines in his arms, and monitors chirping above his head. His voice was raspy, raw from the many tubes that had scraped their way in and out of his throat over the last day. He introduced us by first names, then turned to the nurse.

You'll have to excuse me, he croaked, *but I'm a proud father . . .*

* * *

AT TILLMAN'S, the album makes its rounds among the three seating clusters. Some men linger over the pictures, others dutifully turn from page to page, their eyes falling on but not registering the images. Some men tell their own pig roasting stories. The waitress, Ben's teenage stepdaughter, has been explaining to a large man in bib overalls the plot of a popular television show in which a team of tasteful gay men make over the life and person of a tasteless straight one. She takes a look at the book and lets out an *Ewww*.

We had to do that in school, she tells me.

Roast a pig?

A chicken. We were studying medieval history and we all had to do projects. My teacher wanted me and my friend to roast a chicken in the yard. Then we found out she meant for us to kill the chicken, too. The teacher asked us how we planned to kill the chicken, and my friend said she'd swing it around a few times by the neck and then step on it. Then the teacher said could we please buy a dead chicken at the supermarket.

MY FATHER, KING OF THE EARLY, doesn't like how close we cut the time getting up to Dr. Carter's Covington clinic. His irritation fills the car. His silence seethes. Someone is always at fault. Even if, after repeated self-interrogation, I've found myself blameless, I feel guilty. *If it is human, it will err,* he says. *If it is mechanical, it will malfunction.*

When we get to the reception desk, it turns out he'd gotten the appointment time wrong. We're thirty minutes ahead of schedule, most of the staff has yet to show up, and office hours haven't started. I blame him—silently, lavishly.

I sit reading a Pentecostal tract until we are escorted through the maze of interior corridors, to a treatment room lined with leather-look recliners. All six are unoccupied. My father sits in the nearest one. The chairs face inward toward the nursing station, but behind them, plate-glass windows look out onto spring-budded trees and a gloriously sunny day.

The nurse hooks Dad up to an IV of Benadryl, then a blended infusion of Taxol, the actual cancer-fighting drug, and Zometa, a bone strengthener. The Benadryl knocks my father out, and he sleeps through much of the five-hour infusion. A couple of times, he wakes up with an urgent need to urinate. On top of the diuretics he takes to manage another condition, congestive heart failure, he has the beginnings of a bladder infection that will go undetected for a month, falling to the wayside when other, more critical symptoms crowd the days and the doctors' charts and middle-of-the-night calls to 911.

Once Dad is infusing, I leave to explore the area, which means I go to the mall. At one point, while I am dilly-dallying at the local Wal-Mart, buying matching T-shirts for myself and my father in an acidic green, thinking he's probably no longer an extra large but a large, Dad rouses himself to relieve his bladder. He shuffles over to the bathroom, hanging on to his IV pole for balance, but the bathroom is occupied. In the face of limited options and severe torpor, he steps into an adjacent storage room, picks up a plastic-lined wastebasket, and pees into it. Then he returns to his chair and falls back asleep.

Dad sleeps for most of the drive home, then sleeps through the evening. He misses several doses of the nineteen medications he takes each day, a complicated pharmaceutical maze divided across various intervals and to be taken with or without food, with or without water, with or without milk. When I leave for the airport on Tuesday, he barely wakes long enough to grunt a good-bye. I kiss his cheek, tell him I love him, and drive away, sobbing briefly once I am alone in the car, on the short stretch of Fellowship Road that dead-ends at Highway 16.

* * *

MY FATHER HAS NO additional chemotherapy in Georgia. The first attempt was "disastrous," according to Dr. Carter—my sisters and I welcome his plain speaking—and before the week was out, Lois called us
in Philadelphia to say something was wrong, that my father seemed to
be losing control. He'd fallen down, he'd begun to soil himself, and
she needed at least one of us to come back. Margaret flew down the
next day, so anxious she could have screamed when her plane idled
on the runway, when her car hit a red light. When she finally walked
through the door of 354, Dad seemed to have been waiting for her.

I think we need to go to the hospital, he said.

Indeed he did, and the chemo reaction combined with a fever-
prompting bladder infection and diaper-inducing diarrhea gets my
father transferred in short order from the small Monticello hospital
to one in Covington with which Dr. Carter has an affiliation.

Margaret attends alternately to Lois, who's distraught, and to
Dad, who's either sleeping or irritable. She returns after five days,
bringing Lois with her. Diane and I fly down together to take Margaret's place. We arrive at the hospital to find Dad still weak and still
irritable—hostile, even. We stand too close when he's trying to get
out of bed. We ask too many questions of Gladys, the nurse. Diane's
laugh is wrong. I haven't correctly framed a question. We visit too
long when we could be attending to the tasks he has assigned us.

Be an unfriendly neighbor, my father instructs us as we sit by his
bed on our second day. Diane and I are alone at the farm. *If anyone
comes up the driveway and you don't know who it is, call nine-one-one,*
he says. *Tell them that someone is trespassing on your property and you
need assistance.* As is Dad's way, he is giving us not only a general
instruction, but also the script we are to follow.

His warning comes too late. Just this morning, a man pulled up
to the garage, got out of his car, and walked into the kitchen, no
knocking, no hesitation. He was a big man, older but I don't know

how old, and he was shouting. Not angry shouting, hard-of-hearing shouting. *How's George?* he yelled at us. He shouted that he'd seen Dad's truck around town and honked, but no one waved back. He'd seen the truck in the square and at the supermarket and some other place, and each time, a honk and no response. I listened to this big, yelling man, wondering who he was and wanting to feel safe, thinking as he rambled on that this was okay and he didn't seem like a threat, even though I had no clue who he was and Diane didn't seem to, either. The man finished shouting and turned to leave. *Tell your dad Vince Johnson came by.*

Aha. I recognized the name. One of Dad's childhood friends, a schoolmate at the Jasper County Training School, a teammate on the skimpy football team.

I start to tell Dad this story after his 911 instruction. I succumb to my penchant for dramatization and hold back on the punch line of revealing who the man is. Diane interrupts and says his name. Fair enough. Now is not the time to go for theatrical effect, our dad lying there prone and incontinent and weak, facing only uncertainty.

When he is awake for any length of time, he presses us to get his estate in order. We list the farm for sale with a local real estate agent. We give Jerry Goldin the 1970s poster of a highway patrolman that has been hanging in 354's big guest room and that we're pretty sure is Jerry himself. We disconnect the computer and gather it up with the Bose radio and the binoculars and send them all north, because otherwise they will be sold with the house. My father is having us list the house with a Realtor as is, including all of its contents. *All personalty,* he orders me to write as I fill out the seller's disclosure form.

He has shown the same sentiment-free judgment before: without wincing or expressing one iota of regret, he sold his vacation house on Martha's Vineyard when Lois could no longer manage the stairs and he'd long exhausted his interest in socializing with the blackerati whose families had summered there forever or who, like him, had bought their way in recently. He sold that house with the dishes in the cupboards, the towels, the custom-made dining set, and bicycle tire pump and deck furniture and spare lightbulbs and half-used bottle of dish detergent.

Last summer, when the cancer came out of remission, he instantly set about moving out of Waverly's villa and into its apartment complex, a significant step in the march-to-death configuration of such continuing care facilities. In the new third-floor apartment, he'd have no choice but to cross paths with fellow residents, in the halls and elevators and parking garages, robbed of the town house autonomy that so suited him, with its cigar-friendly garage and private entrance. But Lois, who no longer drove or went anywhere unaccompanied, needed to be closer to the doctor and hairdresser and coffee shop. Dad couldn't be relied on, he knew, to be her main source of transportation.

ONE MORNING, BETWEEN TASKS and while Diane is with Dad at the Covington hospital, I fish for a few hours. I catch nonstop, keeping five big bream and three bass. I gladly give all of them to Troy, who gladly takes them when he stops by the pond to check up on me.

Don't leave your car door open, he warns me. *Snakes will get up in there.* In Monticello, you close the doors so snakes won't get in but leave keys in the car so you know where to find them.

One task Dad has charged me with is to fully document the makes and serial numbers of his rifles and pistols. I am to contact the local auctioneer so that I'll be ready to dispose of them when the time comes. I am not to dispose of them yet. At this juncture, it is enough that I have the information on how to do so.

What I don't have is information on how to deal with Jackie. While Dad's in the hospital, I do not call his closest friends because none, to my knowledge, exist. I do not call the scattering of in-laws and nieces and nephews that remain now that all four of his siblings are gone. The Tuskegee Airman, shot down at the end of World War II. The bank president, the air force colonel, the education specialist, all gone in the last six years. Dad probably wouldn't call any relatives, dead or alive. *None of them are doctors*, he'd say. Sharing a bloodline doesn't mean you have to like the other person, he has maintained, especially relatives who have borrowed from him and not repaid the loan, who don't hold jobs or finish schools, who have interests that don't register as worthwhile: music, Christ, Amway.

But this woman named Jackie comes to visit every day. For several years, Dad has been on a campaign to push us, his daughters, into accepting his belief that Jackie is a heretofore secret half cousin. She would be the child of his youngest brother, Charles, the product of a teenage liaison well before Charles went into the Air Force, settled down with Aunt Ruthie, raised their three children, lived a full life, and then left them bereft when he died a few years ago, never having spoken directly to Jackie about the subject. In my father's presumptive way, he promotes his point of view, advocates its adoption.

Your cousin called this morning, he'll say. Or, *I've invited your cousin over for supper tonight.*

This is tricky business. The facts are murky, no one's rushing to take a DNA test, and my sisters and I discuss, in private, how self-serving Dad's motives might be in embracing Jackie as a relation. The connection the rest of us have maintained with aunts and uncles and cousins on his side of the family is largely the work of my mother, even after my parents divorced. But he and Jackie seem to have formed a symbiotic relationship, and the purported family ties may be an embellishment rather than a foundation. He may be taking a moral stand against the stigma of illegitimacy, but his direct benefit from their association is a constant stream of updates about city politics and the Funderburg Park project, thanks to Jackie's position as a member of the city council. She promises him that she'll see the glacially moving park project through to its completion. He is a high-profile supporter of her who shares his status in the community, bestows appliances on her when hers break, and who sold her the family house on Funderburg Drive on favorable financing terms. Last but perhaps not least, she can claim a patrilineage.

One night while Dad is in the hospital, Diane and I have supper with Uncle Charles's verifiable daughter, Carolyn, halfway between the hospital and the Atlanta bank branch she manages, at a mall restaurant that serves whimsically named salads flecked with such accoutrements as dried cranberries and fried Chinese noodles, and that hires only perky young people who'll bring basket after basket of the warm, spongy bread for which their restaurant is known. We see Carolyn more than any other Funderburg relative because she lives closest to the farm and she's easy and fun to have around. Both Diane and I briefly lived with her family: Diane while Uncle Charles, an Air Force colonel, was stationed in Tucson and she started at the university there; I while on a self-fashioned high school semester abroad when he was stationed in Hawaii. Diane also spent a year at Spelman, the black women's college so many of our relatives attended, and Carolyn was her roommate.

We often rendezvous with Carolyn when we come to the farm, but my purpose tonight is to tell her about Jackie while my father is still alive, in case there's anything Carolyn wants to ask him. Not that he seems to know anything with certainty, only with conviction, but I want to offer her that chance, that choice.

Diane doesn't order a cocktail, but Carolyn and I both get parasol-worthy drinks, and each sip stokes my courage. I preface heavily. *I have something important to tell you,* I say. *I hope I'm doing the right thing, and I just feel like you should have a say in what to do with this information.* I tell her everything I know, everything I've heard. She gives no response and makes unrelated small talk through the rest of the meal: what family members are up to, how her new town house is working out, her cats. I want her to talk about the revelation, to divulge how she's feeling, but somewhere in the cloud of my own anxiety, I see that she needs to absorb, to spend a while in shock. For now, I leave it alone.

FOR FIVE MORE LIP-BITING, fast-food–filled days, Diane and I make the thirty-mile commute from farm to hospital, mostly in separate shifts as we watch for Dad to regain the ability to stand on his own. This, Dr. Carter says to Diane and me as he makes rounds one morning when both of us happen to be present, is what he'll need to see before he can release our father. And, he says, now addressing our father directly, it is imperative that Dad try to walk.

You're at a point now, Dr. Carter says, *where you either use it or lose it.*

Back in Monticello, my uncle Holsey is losing it. He's been fighting prostate cancer for years longer than my father, gotten to the point where they do give him spot welding: painful, targeted radiation treatments that don't seem to provide much relief. One night, while Diane is in Covington, I visit Holsey in the eight-bed Jasper Memorial Hospital, just north of downtown Monticello, north and west of the old Blue Ruin neighborhood in which Holsey grew up and in which there is a Tinsley Street. My grandfather helped establish the hospital, the first and still the only one in Jasper County. He spoke in churches to raise money for the building, to match the government funding available under the 1946 Hill-Burton Act, which had been drafted to address a shortage of medical facilities and a particularly devastating shortage of care available to the poor. On the day its doors opened in 1952, he served on the hospital's medical staff, the only African-American among its doctors.

Holsey's room is dark but for the light over his bed, a fluorescent halo above his nearly bald, well-rounded skull. The other patient bed is empty, and a banged-up metal tank, at least four feet tall, stands sentry at the side of Holsey's bed, dispensing oxygen. Holsey moans whenever he shifts the position of his lank, bony frame, his face twisting in a scowl, but he does not complain. I tell the Pig Party and Fish Man stories, and he nods in appreciation of the finer moments, his otherwise fixed grimace softening slightly.

He asks how Dad is doing. I exaggerate the progress but allow that we don't know how long it will take for him to be released.

I can't be doing this much longer, Holsey says. He is nine years older than my father.

I know, I say, *but boy, you did it great for a long time.*

I guess that's true, he says. *I guess you're right about that.*

DAD PRACTICES STANDING and walking several times a day with the help of Gladys, a nurse whose spunk and good humor rival my father's prickly combination of pain and implacability. When Gladys, joking about a wager she's made with our father, exclaims, *He tried to Jew me down!* Diane and I exchange glances but say nothing. She is our ticket out.

After nine days, the doctor's requirement is met: Dad can barely stand or take a step, but enough of each to win release. We seize the chance to bring him back to Pennsylvania on a commercial airline rather than the scenario we've been entertaining: hiring an ambulance or ambulance plane to make the eight-hundred-mile trip.

Merely watching him make the journey home is excruciating. Every transfer, from wheelchair to van to wheelchair to plane seat, takes forever. Flight attendants and captains and gate agents and wheelchair drivers hover and hesitate, trying to help and getting in the way, rushing him when all he needs is just to regroup, to go on his own clock.

Give me a minute, he asks of us all. *I'll get there.*

Finally, we make it back. We are in my car, driving from the airport to Waverly. I am behind the wheel, cautiously shifting from gear to gear. Diane calls Margaret to check in, to let her know we've landed. Margaret says that Julie Oshana, a woman our parents' age who raised her three girls next door to us for twenty years and has been ill for some time, died this morning. Diane hangs up and tells me the news.

Julie always claimed that when I was a baby, I spoke my first word to her. *Birdie* [Buh-dee], she'd imitate. *Birdie*. I feel compelled to honor this woman who helped raise me, whom I loved dearly, whose middle daughter was my best friend, by saying something. Anything.

That's sad, I start to say, more declaration than lament.

Celebrate! my father flashes from the other side of the car before I can finish. *She had a good life, she had three nice daughters, there's nothing to be sad about. Everybody has to go sometime.*

Neither Diane nor I have the energy to spar or argue or even concur. My father's belligerent optimism hangs in the car, icy and silencing, until even he sees its overwrought positivism.

Don't worry, he says. *I'm not calling the Hemlock Society yet.*

BACK STORY

POWELTON

I N THE FIRST TWELVE years of my life, my father was a distant figure, even though we lived under the same roof. In fact, I knew only one version of the man, the one who'd put the greatest possible distance between himself and his past. What could I imagine of his roots: rural and hot and southern small-town conspicuous, on the black side of the tracks and barely one lifetime removed from slavery?

The man I knew worked long hours and every weekend as the

founder, owner, and lead salesman of a residential real estate company in our section of West Philadelphia. He identified houses and people not by architectural detail or personality, but by address: *That's near 313 North Thirty-seventh. They bought 4615 Osage.* Tracking and tagging house keys was a prime occupation for us, his daughters, when we were enlisted to work the office's reception desk on the occasional Saturday or for the summers we hadn't tried hard enough to find our own jobs.

In the earliest days, when providing for a wife and three small children was a hand-to-mouth enterprise, he participated in family life on a cost-benefit basis. One week, and it must have been a good one saleswise, the whole family went to a roller-skating rink. My father fell down during the outing and hurt his knee. It hurt like hell, he would recall even decades later, and he instantly realized how grave the consequences would be if the sole breadwinner were put out of commission.

From then on, with one or two brief, awkward exceptions, he participated in no recreation, took no vacations. Each summer  throughout my childhood, my mother drove my sisters and me, by herself, to the beach in New Jersey and to her family's cabins in Minnesota. She taught us the alphabet game and the license plate game, and if we hadn't fully exhausted her when we got to state lines, she'd pull over to let us walk from Ohio to Indiana, or Illinois to Wisconsin. As a baby, I traveled in a wood playpen set up in the back of our station wagon, while my father remained in Philadelphia, driving clients from house to house in a late-model Impala, air-conditioning perpetually set on high.

* * *

MY FATHER MET MY MOTHER, a white woman from the Midwest named Marjorie Jeane Lievense, in 1954. They were fellow resi-  dents of an integrated Quaker housing coopera- tive in a neighborhood called Powelton Village. She landed at the Friendship Co-op after two years in Germany, repatriating World War II re- fugees for the American Friends Service Com- mittee. He had completed a tour of duty in Korea

 and finished gallivanting with his friends, other young black men, mostly from the South and many of whom went on to be judges and scholars and accom- plished professionals, firsts in their fields, but not quite on that path then.

Dad was ready to buckle down and make something of himself, ready to give up his enviable income as a door-to-door salesman, and had enrolled as an undergraduate at the University of Pennsylvania's Wharton School. To remove himself from his boisterous surroundings, he was about to secure a room at the local YMCA when he saw

an ad in the university newspaper offering "room and board, 12 dollars a week, self-help coopera- tive." He could pay rent and still have spending money left over from his monthly GI stipend of seventy-five dollars. For my mother, the co-op embodied ideas about community and democ- racy. For my father, the rent was low and he'd have a quiet place to study.

Powelton was bordered by a river, a slum, and a university cam- pus. Once it became known for its physical and social diversity, it drew like-minded people in droves. These progressives were of their time. In the '60s and '70s I knew children named Zeus and

God; saw unconventional household configurations (step, single-parented, gay, interracial, international, and interfaith); and, thanks to a neighborhood commune that was suspected of stealing classified government files, learned to spot an FBI agent by his high-water pant hems, New Jersey plates, and tendency to read the *Trenton Times* in an era when, as the local paper's humble marketing slogan modestly proclaimed: *"Nearly everybody reads* The Bulletin."

If my father came to Powelton for the rent, he had come to Philadelphia for the baseball. In the late 1940s, when a floor-sanding enterprise with a cousin-in-law fell through, Dad sold encyclopedias door-to-door in Columbus, Ohio, the company's only black employee. He was great at his job, even though he was selling in all-white neighborhoods. A new manager came in, a man my father described as "tough-looking Polish stock from somewhere in Pennsylvania." The manager decided to accompany my father on his canvassing one morning, to observe his technique. As my father told it, the manager, in an effort to make conversation, asked how my father liked the job.

"I said, 'Well, it's okay.' And that infuriated him. He said, 'What do you mean, it's okay? If you didn't have this job, you'd be changing tires for thirty-five dollars a week.'"

The comment offended my father, and when the two men got back to the office, my father confided to a salesman he liked that he was finished.

"'I'm leaving,' he said. 'I'm not going to work for him.'"

The other salesman, a disbarred lawyer from New York State and my father's beer-drinking buddy, advised Dad not to be so hasty. Dad's pal knew sales managers in Cleveland and Philadelphia, both of whom would be happy to have my father and his commissions in their offices. In response, my father performed a simple algebraic athletic equation that he reconstructed for me:

"Larry Doby had signed as a center fielder for the Cleveland Indians and Jackie Robinson was playing for the Brooklyn Dodgers," he explained. "These were big items for people interested in sports and race."

"Were you one of those people?" I asked. Even I—not a sports fan—knew that Robinson was the first black player to break into major league baseball.

"Oh, yeah," he said, as if his inclusion went without saying. "Cleveland only had one major league team, the Cleveland Indians. Philadelphia had an American League team and a National League team. If I went to Philadelphia, I could see both Larry Doby *and* Jackie Robinson."

NOT ONLY WERE DOBY and Robinson African-Americans, they were also close to my father's age and fellow southerners, Doby from South Carolina and Robinson from the Georgia side of the Georgia-Florida border.

Baseball might have been the seed for making a life in Philadelphia, but marriage and children rooted him there. Diane was born in 1955, Margaret in 1956, and I followed two and a half years later, born a month after Doby's final game. The three girls were distinguished by temperament and birth order but unified in absorbing the informal culture of our immediate surroundings, which was often quite distinct from our father's.

We did not have to call our father "sir" or our mother "ma'am"—he had cast off much of the South's formalities as well as its accent, his speech geographically neutralized, without diphthongs and dropped *r*'s—but we did have to respond to all questions promptly, directly, in audible tones, and while looking him in the eye. Although it was the neighborhood custom, we did not call our parents by their first names (and on this point, even my otherwise informal mother heartily agreed), but we were that familiar with everyone else's parents, as were the other kids with ours.

We did not burn incense (which led to smoking pot, which led to heroin). We did not take food out of the kitchen (ants), we did not lean back on the rear legs of kitchen chairs (linoleum scars), and we did not scrape our utensils against our plates at mealtime (unnecessary noise). And because he was so exacting, his standards at times mutable and unfathomable, we learned very early on that saying less was better than saying more. About almost anything.

In order to receive our weekly allowances, we were required to place an invoice on top of the hulking console television every Sunday afternoon. The invoice was reviewed, questionable line items explained, and a determination made as to how much cash was to be dispensed. As soon as we could write and had learned how to answer the telephone politely, we were expected to complete preprinted pink "While You Were Out" message slips he'd brought home from the office. These were to be filled out in their entirety: a missing phone number for return calls was not merely unacceptable, it was unthinkable. There was a right way to sweep the sidewalk, to stand up straight, to blow one's nose, to breathe.

When we heard his key turn in the lock at the end of the day, just before dinner, my sisters and I shut off the stereo and lowered our voices. We scurried to our respective sections of a long laminate countertop along the dining room wall, each with its own fluorescent strip light, cubbyhole, and drawer, where we would open and bend over our schoolbooks. The worst path you could take, according to my father, was to be an unproductive member

of society. He encouraged us to be anything in life we wanted to be: "I will support you," he would tell us, "as long as you're the best at it."

My mother became a schoolteacher once I started school. Our parents worked hard to meet our needs and give us opportunities they'd never had, maybe never knew existed. We were neither deprived nor overly indulged, but if we desired something remotely educational, both parents tried to provide it. Among the three of us, and decades before the current vogue of the overscheduled child, there were extracurricular lessons of varying duration in piano, modern dance, bassoon, recorder, silversmithing, swimming, flute, guitar, typing, science, photography, art, and ice-skating. When one of us faced a year with a bad teacher at the local public school, all three were transferred to a budget-stretching Quaker alternative for the rest of our primary and secondary education.

Once in a while, my father sang "Ol' Man River," warbling it, terrifically off-key. Or he twisted, just like Chubby Checker, grinding his heel into the floor with one outstretched leg. We were allowed to laugh at him in these moments, and laughter was something he usually shared only with other adults, ice clinking in their whiskey glasses as percussion.

Neighborhood children were uniformly intimidated by my father and gave him a wide berth, which was easier to do, certainly, in those days when streets were safer, before quality time was invented, and children were permitted—expected—to roam free on weekend and summer days. But there were occasions when he'd focus on one of them, particularly a child who'd been hurt or in some way left out or left behind, with an attention and gentleness and charm that would have them, at least for the moment, smitten.

This was the father I knew. Whether in close, daily proximity or even a neighborhood removed once he and my mother separated in 1971, I was afraid of him, proud of him, and confused as to how to garner his elusive, approving attention. I didn't know the adventures that had filled his life as a young man, his dreams of farming the land. I knew a scrap or two: about the sold storm windows when he and my mother first married, and that his cousin, the writer Eva Rutland, had written in her 1964 memoir, *The Trouble with Being a Mama*, that as a boy, young Georgie wanted to be a rural specialist of sorts, a pigpen fixer. To me, accustomed to land being divisible by sidewalked blocks rather than acres, his ambition seemed as exotic as that of becoming an astronaut or a deep-sea diver.

WHEN I CAME ALONG, he'd launched his career of brokering residential property sales, a business whose success went far beyond what he could have imagined for himself. He started buying and selling houses during the turbulence of residential integration and white flight, first for a prointegration Powelton group desperate to stabilize our community, and then out on his own, with his own fledgling company. His work absorbed him. I reaped the benefits. His absence loomed.

Some of his success was probably due to his lack of passion for the work. He was an antisalesman, not given to schmoozing or gushing. He would walk prospective buyers through a house in complete silence unless the client had a question. His clientele, mostly professors and administrators from nearby Drexel University and the University of Pennsylvania, endorsed this approach with referrals and return business. As his company expanded into property management, there were inevitably those tenants and clients—some of them neighbors—who had complaints. I filled out message slips with details of repairs not completed expeditiously, ran into people who'd allude to maintenance not kept up. I never knew if these allegations were warranted, but by the time I was a teenager, my sisters and I would cringe when we met people who recognized our family name, unsure of what they would have to say about our father.

DAD WAS UNSURE of what to say about himself when I first asked to interview him. It was August of 1999. I was forty-two, he was seventy-six. I sat across from him on the patio of the Waverly villa, turned on the tape recorder, and he stiffened in his chair.

"I sort of feel like your granddaddy used to look when you'd point a camera at him, and he'd freeze up," he told me. "Like you're gonna take some part of me I don't want seen." I asked if I should stop. "It's okay," he said. "Go ahead."

Most of my questions were about work. His jobs, I said to him, were the twentieth century writ small. They were palpable manifestations of American history, I said, that I might one day write about. What I thought was, they were safe ground, neutral territory. His area of expertise. My wedge.

My father was sixteen years old when he started at Morehouse College. Morehouse was and still is a highly respected college for black men in Atlanta, Georgia. In 1941, Benjamin E. Mays was president, and in his Tuesday morning sermons, he communicated a sense of standard and purpose. A representative Mays quote: "The tragedy in life doesn't lie in not reaching your goal. The tragedy lies in having no goal to reach."

My father's goal at the time was to be financially self-sufficient. Instead of studying, he washed dishes in a Chinese restaurant, ran a dry-cleaning concession, and was a fast-talking carhop at the Varsity Drive-In, a favorite whites-only hangout for the Yellow Jackets fans from Georgia Tech. Morehouse administrators invited my father to leave before freshman year was out. He headed for Anniston, Alabama, where my grandfather had grown up and where his brothers Earl and Ilon still resided. Uncle Earl ran a grocery store and barbecue called Fat's Place. Uncle Ilon ran a dance pavilion/sandwich stand and a hotel. The hotel's most prominent feature was that none of the rooms had windows. Over the next year, my father's job was to do whatever his uncles asked of him. This included helping with a chicken-raising enterprise Earl tried to launch.

"I knew how to feed 'em and water 'em," my father said as he explained why the chicken business didn't take off, despite his uncle's purchase of the most modern, electrified chicken plucking machine available. "But I didn't know how to make 'em grow. And besides, people started stealing them."

One night a loud-talking woman came into Ilon's hotel café. She was a regular, and she was known for sounding off. A man came in after her—perhaps a spurned lover—and shot her square in the face. The force of the bullet shook the white powder off her shoes and left an outline of where she last stood. After her body was carted away, my father mopped up the dried polish and wet blood.

As little as possible of these Anniston adventures was reported back to my grandmother in Monticello. Still, she knew enough to be unhappy with the company her Georgie was keeping. Dad got word that he was needed to come home and paint some rental houses Grandfather owned. My father would be paid for it, he was reassured, but he needed to leave Anniston, preferably right away.

He did go home, but it soon became clear that the houses didn't actually need painting. Within weeks, my father was looking for where to go next. Then and for the next decade, he was driven by three questions. Where was the money? Where was the challenge? Where was the adventure?

My father picked tobacco in Connecticut, sold cookbooks in Columbus, and in the summer of 1944, took the job I most liked to hear about, on a Detroit Night Boat called the *Western States*. On the waters of the Great Lakes, Dad did more than wait tables and bellhop. He participated in the swan song of a maritime tradition, honed his talent for anticipating other people's needs as a way to meet his own, and witnessed black people operating with an open autonomy and citizenship unheard of in the South he knew.

Night Boats were floating hotels, hulking steamships that used a paddlewheel along each flank to propel them through the water, crushing all but the thickest skins of winter ice. Because boat speeds often peaked at twenty miles per hour, most trips had to last at least one night. Ship architects incorporated sleeping and dining accommodations into their designs, and the result was a practical, affordable method of travel until heavy winter weather made passage impossible. Brochures turned this speed deficit into an asset, promoting an early version of today's red-eye flights as they urged business travelers to "save a day tonight."

Originally constructed of wood, some sidewheelers exceeded three city blocks in length and were as tall as eight-story buildings. Since the early 1800s, they had transported people between such major ports as New York and New London, Detroit and Cleveland, and, in the longest run of all (435 miles), San Francisco and Los Angeles. The 1960s would herald the death of the Night Boats, but when my father showed up at the Detroit docks, before American highway systems had been fully established and roads given hard surfaces, before automobiles and fuel were widely affordable or available, before airplane travel spread beyond the lark of the rich, the boats provided a critical form of mass transportation.

The *Western States,* owned by the Detroit & Cleveland (D&C) Navigation Company, slept six hundred passengers, a respectable number, although bigger boats could take on two thousand. The *Western States* traveled several routes but was best known for service between Detroit and Chicago, traveling Lake Huron and Lake Michigan with a midway stop at Mackinac Island. This was its run during my father's summers aboard, first in 1944, then again in 1947.

The sound of the massive boat's launch stuck with my father. "The paddlewheels started to turn," he said, "and there was a big slushing sound. But once we were out on the water, you'd forget about it." One passenger testimonial described a similar boat: "Great as its speed, its motion is smooth and graceful as that of a swan."

The D&C provided passengers with journey logs, timetables that indicated at which point ships would pass particular landmarks. What could not be logged was the majesty of the lakes themselves. Erie, Huron, Michigan, Ontario, and Superior are a spectacular show of natural forces. They span 94,000 square miles and constitute one-fifth of the world's surface freshwater supply. To coastal dwellers used to the unbounded horizons of oceans, a map of the Midwest may prompt claustrophobia. But stand at the wave-lapped shores of Lake Michigan, and the feeling is like being at the edge of a continent.

My father got his job the way many migrants do, through people back home. Francis Davis, a Morehouse classmate of Dad's older brother Owen, owed my father sixteen dollars. Francis promised to pay Dad back through the job he'd held the two summers past, working on the boats. "Why don't you come along?" he said to my father, and along with two other college boys Davis had enthralled with tales of high earnings and high-stakes card games, the four paid colored-rate fares and climbed aboard a train at Atlanta's Terminal station for the seven-hundred-mile journey.

Some waiters and cabin stewards made careers out of working on the boats, but most of the crew were black male college students from the South. The summer tourist season dovetailed conveniently with the academic calendar, and there was a presumption of sophistication that many northern whites assigned to that segment of the black population—a relatively small pool from which to draw, considering that only 10 percent of young African-American men were attending and graduating from college in 1940. If you were studying to be a doctor or a teacher, it seemed, only then were you fit to carry suitcases or serve meals.

Dad's pilgrimage fit tidily into the second wave of the Great Migration, the internal movement of black Americans from South to North that spanned the first half of the twentieth century and relocated an estimated six million people. As a result of that shift, the geographical distribution of blacks in the United States flip-flopped completely, from 90 percent living in the South to 90 percent in the North.

The exodus from the South, like any mass movement, stemmed from the convergence of countless circumstances, events, and matters of chance. Wages were higher in the industrialized North, where World War I cut off the immigrant labor supply and contractors had to turn to the South for new prospects. Farming, once the stronghold of the southern economy, had come under attack from every direction, and each assault took with it jobs. Higher production rates that had supported the extra demands of wartime now became surplus, and by 1929, the onset of the Great Depression, farmers had dropped prices by 40 percent. The smaller-scale landowner simply couldn't weather the downturn, and in 1932 alone, 123,000 farms failed.

For farm laborers, what jobs the cotton-decimating boll weevil didn't eradicate, mechanized picking machines did. Shortsighted planting practices of the South's first white settlers had laid the land open to erosion, and the only ways to reclaim the soil were through reforestation and turning the land over to cattle pasture, neither of which required as much tending. As demand grew scarce for the farm labor that had sustained so many offspring of slaves and ex-slaves, southern blacks grew increasingly willing to leave.

My father's restaurant experience of carhopping and diswashing did not prepare him for the linen-topped tables of the *Western States'* dining room or for exotica such as Kadota figs and Long Island duck. Even mundane menu items baffled him.

"When I first got on the boat," he said, "I had never waited tables. One of the first mornings, this man came in and ordered a three-minute boiled egg for breakfast. I said to a more experienced waiter who was at the next station, 'He wants a boiled egg. Isn't that ridiculous?' And he looked at me and said, 'If he wants a boiled egg, get him one.'

"See, I didn't know people ate boiled eggs for breakfast. I'd never heard of that. The only eggs I knew were fried and scrambled. I thought it was laughable. Shows how dumb I was. The world was a whole lot larger than my limited experience. Of course, I already knew that, but this was just something I could not have imagined. It shows you how a country boy from Monticello, Georgia, is shielded from wide exposure to anything. It didn't happen in your family, you didn't go to neighbors to eat, and you didn't go to public places aside from juke joints, where people would eat beef stew or chicken or whatever they were selling. Other times I ate at home."

The *Western States'* chef was also memorable. He was a black man, a large, athletic fellow, my father said, who inspired respect from both sides of the color line.

"He had a tremendous amount of authority over the kitchen and everybody else," Dad recalled, his voice suffused with admiration. "Nobody ever seemed to bother him, but he got things done and he seemed to be answerable only to the captain. He would explain to the captain and the captain would say okay and then everybody had to do what the chef said."

Wasn't it unusual, I wondered, for my father to see such unabashed authority coming from a black man?

"No," he said, suddenly piqued. "I didn't think it was that impressive. He was still a black man working in the heat and the grease."

5.

LABEL BOY

Jasper County soil is particularly adapted to growing peaches of the highest quality, and peach orchards are being extensively planted and rapidly developed. Some commercial orchards are producing as high as $500 per acre. There are now more than one-half million trees in the county, and approximately fifty per cent of them are bearing. Growing peaches promises to shortly become one of Jasper County's greatest industries.

—Jasper County: The Heart of Agricultural Georgia.
Where the Great Opportunities of the Sunny South are
Calling You, *Kiwanis Club, Monticello, Georgia (circa 1925)*

M Y FATHER SEEMS to have stopped reading. His vision has grown so cloudy that I'll find him holding his address book upside down, staring hard as he tries to bring it into focus. When he could still read, he chose history and current affairs and had no patience for fiction. Occasionally he'd read a popular self-help book, such as *The Millionaire Next Door*. Some years ago, he devoured a history of Thomas Jefferson and then three books about an attempted slave rebellion led by a charismatic former slave named Denmark Vesey. As a consequence of his reading, Dad became absorbed in a line of thinking about race and prejudice that as he saw it, removed from the topic a clouding emotionalism. Instead, he embraced a framing of America's racial history as the outcome of economic forces.

We have this market economy that says you can have a free market, he'd say, launching into an explanation of why he no longer calls himself black, but instead says, "American." *People can make their prices and if they can sell their goods at that price they make a profit. We had an agricultural economy, which is labor intensive, so where did the labor come from? From the beginning, why were the Africans brought here? For cheap labor. And all of this bullshit to discredit the slaves as subhuman and so forth was just to keep the cheap labor. To deny them an education and abuse them was just to keep the cheap labor.*

For years after he latched on to the marketplace framework, Dad's philosophy showed up everywhere and anywhere. We'd drive through the grandest section of Monticello and pass a stately eighteenth-century home complete with pillars and veranda. Someone would remark on its handsome profile, and he'd say, *Built on cheap labor.* We'd notice the small sheds behind the stately house and ask if they had been slave quarters. *You want to have your cheap labor easily available.* Dad would talk about a local white man known for his socially progressive actions, then note that the man had a thousand cows and several thousand acres of land. *The source of that wealth had to be cheap labor,* he'd say. We'd talk about the vocational curriculum at his alma mater, the Jasper County Training School, and he'd explain its limited offerings: *designed to produce cheap labor.*

IN THE MID-1920S, Monticello's Kiwanis Club printed a booklet about Jasper County, and it backed up its boosterism with photographs of recently paved roads, the hundred-thousand-dollar "modern" (and all-white) high school, and a one-room cheese factory.

It also celebrated local crops, especially the burgeoning business of peach growing.

By the time my father was born in 1926, peaches were entrenched in the local economy. They replaced cotton, which had been decimated by the arrival of the seed-capsule-eating boll weevil. Even ten years after Dad's birth, after the Great Depression had swept through and foreclosures swallowed up farms, peach trees still blanketed Jasper County, and crops were large enough to keep five fruit-packing operations in business during the harvest season. The county's peach farmers grew a handful of varieties: clingstone and freestone, white and yellow. Among the white-fleshed peaches were the firm-fleshed Hiley (its texture held up well through the canning process) and the flavorful Georgia Belle (too delicate to ship and eventually relegated to backyard growing). Yellow-fleshed peaches included the Southland and Redstone and the tried-and-true Elberta, a large freestone that came to represent a great Georgia peach the way Xerox stands for photocopies.

Monticellans ate peaches straight from the tree, canned and cobbled them, and put them into pies. Fruit too soft or ripe to ship was sold locally and made into ice cream and jam and, in less religiously fervid households, brandy. The fruit's fragility was both threat and reward: it was hard to protect from pests and only available for a short harvest season. Even after the introduction of refrigerated rail cars made peaches less exotic to out-of-state markets, they continued to command a good price.

Jasper County was the center of Georgia's peach belt when Dad was a child, but not for long. The state of Georgia is still a major peach producer, third in the nation behind California and South Carolina. Georgia farmers grow more than forty varieties, but those crops come from further south, where spring frosts are less likely and the land contains more sand and less clay. The disappearance of peaches from Jasper County was largely due to unpredictable growing conditions. You had to care for your orchards the same every year, whether they were producing or not. And increasingly, it seemed, they were not. No one could survive such losses and mis-spent effort.

One of the original selling points of peaches had been that they demanded less manual labor than cotton. But only relatively less, and the owners of peach orchards came to discover that finding workers was actually a larger problem than paying them. The south-ern labor pool already suffered from the exodus north.

Still, when Jasper County peach farming reached its apex, eight million bushels in 1928, the harvesting and shipping that sur-rounded getting fruit to market made it an essential part of the local economy. Harvest season came along in early summer, and when it did, everyone who was available would work in some segment of the process.

My father knew work early on; all children in Monticello did. To start with, running a household was labor-intensive. Even in town, vegetable gardens were essential rather than ornamental, and most families, if they could afford it, would have at least a pig, maybe a  cow staked out in the yard, and a few chick-ens. Adults typically worked more than one job or had more than one money-earning enterprise going. My grandfather's days and nights were filled with treating the patients who came into his two offices, one in Mon-ticello and the other in Eatonton, the next town over. But he also invested in rental properties and owned a farm and grew various crops, including cotton, with varying degrees of success. Next door, Dorothy and Howard Smith's father was a car mechanic who sold wood and charcoal on the side, while their mother took in white people's ironing for the local dry cleaner.

Most black children in Monticello went to work, either after school or during vacations. The Funderburg children were no excep-tion, although my grandmother drew the line at picking cotton. At ten years old, my father took his first summer job. He was a label boy in J. L. Benton's Minneta Packing Company, two miles south of Monticello in the unincorporated Minneta community, a blink of an eye along Highway 83. Now the packing shed is gone and Lake Lumber Company sits on that spot, but in my father's day, hundreds of workers headed for Benton's from May through whenever the last variety came in, which was most likely sometime in July.

Benton's operation centered around a tin-roofed barn that had open sides and a floor set at loading-dock height. The absence of walls eased production flow: flatbed trucks pulled up to one side so that men could drop off wooden field boxes full of freshly picked fruit. The other side was open to a railroad siding. Every morning, a locomotive would switch off the main track onto Benton's spur and drop empty refrigerated boxcars into place, gigantic blocks of ice already lowered in through hatches at the ends of each car.

There was no picking or packing when it rained or when equipment broke down. But when weather cooperated and machines ran smoothly, peach-packing could go far into the night, and workers went to the shed every day for three weeks straight. The common scenario was to fill anywhere from one to three boxcars a day, but my father remembers a record packing day in which workers filled nine.

Pickers, including my uncle Holsey, walked through rows of trees planted in straight lines or checkerboard patterns, filling three-gallon metal buckets. In some orchards, pickers earned according to the number of buckets they filled. They deposited a chit into each one. Chits were counted once the buckets were turned out into field boxes. Pickers at Benton's got a flat rate. In 1936, it was ten cents an hour.

Picking was a nasty job. The fuzz, single-celled hairs that kept fungus spores from settling onto the skin of the peach, broke at the slightest touch. They left sharp ends that could irritate any skin surface but which were especially irksome on a sweaty neck or in the crook of an elbow. Even in the leaden heat, pickers wore long sleeves and neckerchiefs to keep the insidious, itchy hairs off their skin. Some entrepreneur figured out how to collect and bottle the fuzz, and it ended up in novelty shops, sold to any prankster in search of itching powder.

Pickers' boxes were trucked over to the packing shed and turned onto a conglomeration of ramps and devices that enabled workers to sort and grade the fruit. First, the peaches tumbled across rollers covered with hog hair bristles that removed the fuzz. A next set of rollers were set apart at widths that allowed smaller, inferior peaches to fall through to a lower belt. Human graders stood on either side of the belts, culling out rotten or ripe peaches, throwing away the former and sending the latter to be processed immediately at a local canning factory or sold directly from the loading dock.

Peaches that made it through the brushing, grading, and culling ended up in holding bins. A packer—in Benton's shed, only white males held that job—stood on one side of the bin. As he filled each basket, he made sure that the rosiest peaches would end up on the top row, pink sides facing up. Before the baskets could go out to the refrigerated rail cars, they had to be stamped and labeled by label boys. Enter my father.

Labels were printed on thin paper, typically rectangular or square. They were detailed and florid, featuring robust produce and elegant typography, pride in the fruits they advertised. *Jasper Juicies. Fuz-Less. Dixiana. Cloudkist. Rooster Brand: Something to Crow About.* The Minneta label showed the requisite fruits, along with the face of a pretty young woman.

The labels were like long dollar bills, Dad says. I had a bucket of glue and a brush and I'd brush the basket back and forth. You did it carefully, of course, and then put the label on, brushed that side and then brushed this side. Went to the next one.

Bubba worked at Minneta, too, for twice as many years as Dad did. Some years Bubba worked inside the shed and others out in the orchards, picking. Inside, he tells us during a visit to 354, his job was on the opposite side of the shed from my father. Bubba received boxes of freshly picked peaches as they came in from the fields and he turned them onto conveyor belts to be brushed, graded, culled, and packed.

I know by now every job had a name. *What did they call you?* I ask Bubba.

Nigger, my father interrupts. *That's what they called him. Nigger, nigger, nigger. That's what they called all of us.*

Whenever I ask my father what it was like to work with peaches, he tells the same story. As with any tale of Monticello life, he first establishes what family the protagonist of the story comes from, what business the family owned, or the size or nature of its farm. In this case, Billy Jordan, a white boy, was the grandson of J. L. Benton, who owned the packing shed and was related to the Bentons of Benton's Supply Company, the department store and market that took up most of the south side of the town square.

In the summer of 1936, my father and Billy Jordan both turned ten. Billy had a concession stand in the peach shed where workers could get lunch, buying on credit until the weekly payday. To call it a stand, my father concedes, is a bit of an overstatement. A piece of board balanced on top of a box, and stacked on top of the board were potted ham, soda crackers, pork and beans, sardines, and five-cent bottles of pop: small bottles of Coca-Cola and big bellywashers of NEHI and Royal Crown. Wages spent at Billy's stand were no small matter: When my father saved nine dollars one summer, he considered it a small fortune.

What did you do with all that money? I ask.

Not much. For five cents, I could buy a pig ear sandwich at a juke joint off the square, a business owned and operated by your cousin Jackie's grandmother and grandfather. Those were a treat, he tells me, a delicacy, and he licks his lips at the recollection.

Did they really taste that good?

Put on enough hot sauce and anything tastes good.

At the end of one peach-packing day, my father was helping to clean up. *General factotum work*, he calls it. *I'm sweeping the floor and Billy says, "Anybody want anything?" I say, "Yeah, Billy, I want a Coke." And here comes Mr. Bolton,* [the white man] *who's in charge of the migratory workers that followed the fruit season. And he says to me, "From now on, you call him Mr. Billy." I never bought another Coke.*

This is where the tale ends each time my father tells it, on this pinpointing of the defining, inevitable moment in which someone commanded him to humble himself in front of a white peer, direct defiance possible only at great risk of retribution. When that moment came, my father made what was for him an inevitable choice. Even at that young age, he was strong-willed and independent-minded, and he chose freedom over pleasure.

I wonder how such a young boy could make that decision, especially since the pressure to submit to that way of life was unrelenting.

"Yassuh, yassuh, yassuh," he says, imitating the required verbal kowtows, practically spitting out the words even as he slurs them with subservience. *Smiling, smiling, smiling.*

Dad, a natural negotiator, always tries to see more than his own side. He points out that the opportunity for degradation was everywhere. *The more I think about it,* he says, *the more I think it was just as damaging to the oppressor as the oppressed. Because you created a monster on one side and a fiction on the other. Actually, both were fiction because they weren't real people. The monster said, 'I'm white, I'm superior because of my blood, and you blacks must speak to me in this way.' And the conspiracy was that if we can keep them thinking this, we can exploit them for cheap labor.*

And what was the fiction on the other side? I ask.

The fiction was, 'I have to make this pretension of being submissive to please this man who has this extraordinary power over me.' The power was violence most of the time. Well, all of the time, because without it, I don't think they could have controlled the black population.

I realize that my father, always self-employed or working on commission, has spent his life challenging that labor contractor's directive. I suggest that this is evident in his patterns of employment, during which he refused to join the cheap labor force or be the subjugated wage slave.

That's true, he says. I suppose my approach was that I should be paid in accordance with what I produced. And I guess my first jobs were waiting tables for tips and hopping curbs for tips, selling door-to-door for tips.

When he left Monticello, as aimless as the next decade seemed, he was carving out a path of employment that honored one thing he'd always known about himself, even before the concession stand incident.

I never wanted anybody to tell me what to do, he says.

THE INCIDENT LEFT A BITTER, lasting taste, but peaches themselves were not tainted. A couple of years ago, pre–cancer recurrence, I came across a ponderous half-gallon jar of pickled peaches in the refrigerator at 354 Fellowship Road. Peeled fruit, halved and whole, bright red-orange, hung in a viscous liquid.

What are they? I asked, prurience mixed with disdain. Where did they come from?

I used to love these, my father explained, dipping into a momentary reverie, illustrated by a lip smack. His mother canned them when he was a child. She put them up in mason jars alongside fruits and vegetables and sausage patties suspended in lard.

I was stuck on the basic concept. Like pickle pickles?

Food may be paramount to our family—we coordinate entire days around Dave's hours and Tillman's specials—but "pickling" a peach, which uses a blend of dill and mustard seeds, allspice, cloves, pepper, and mace, seemed like the wrong thing to do to this genetic relative of the rose, such a luscious specimen of nature's bounty and one I believed to be solidly ensconced on the dessert side of the food ledger.

Yes, like pickles, he said, impatience edging his response. Pickled peaches had come to Dad's mind, he explained, after decades of not giving them a thought. When my father gets something in his head, it will not go away until it has been brought to resolution. Sooner is better than later. *The challenge is in the moment*, he'll say, *the time is always now*. Once desire had tripped the switch of pursuit, Dad called Mary Howard, the twins' mother, to ask if she knew where he might be able to find pickled peaches.

I wonder if you could help me out, he said to her after the customary exchange of hellos, health, and weather.

Dad often knows the answers to the questions he asks, or at least has an idea that he is in the vicinity of the response he seeks. Case in point: Mrs. Howard makes them herself. She said she'd be pleased to give my father a jar.

Mrs. Howard wouldn't take money from my father for the fruit, noting that Dad had given the twins permission several years running to hold their family reunion in the farm's pecan grove. *We had a good time*, she said. She began sending more jars along with the twins when they'd come to the farm. Because their cows graze on Dad's land, and because their rental agreement brought them by fairly often to mow, bale, and make minor repairs to keep the place looking good, Dad's stock soon multiplied.

LOOKING GOOD IS NOT EVERYTHING, but appearance counts for something. Even in his late nineties, my grandfather still put on a tie before he would go out the front door. During the visit that introduced me to pickled peaches, my father and I made the forty-four-mile drive down to Musella one afternoon, taking two-lane highways to get to the packing house of Dickey Farms, a family peach farm in operation since 1897. We had set up a tour there, interested to see what had changed since my father's day and what had remained the same.

The landscape we passed was mostly pine forests, a smaller portion of it cultivated fields, and, in between, churches, always churches, their portable marquees wheeled to the roadside, beckoning would-be worshipers. "Soul Food Served Here." "This Church is Prayer-Conditioned." "If You Think It's Hot Out There, Try Hell." Occasionally, clusters of houses sidled up to the road. We drove by one lawn cluttered with sagging machinery and furniture worn down by sun and rain.

Black folks live there, my father said. We passed a tidy lawn, clipped grass, nothing out of place. *White folks live there*, he said.

I counted to four on an inhale, counted to four on an exhale. Four, inhale. Four, exhale. I refrained from mentioning the farm that faces my father's, the white-owned property that overflows with rusting and unidentifiable detritus, where cows graze among sprawls of petrified tractors and calcified truck parts. Instead, I pitched my tone to be measured and calm and asked why he thought this phenomenon existed.

Years of deprivation, he said. *Denial of access to education and financial opportunity. The outcome of being relegated to cheap labor.*

This I could stomach. Just when my father has said something that makes me cringe, something ambiguous or critical that hints at a cosmology in which black equals bad (lazy, shiftless, shortsighted), he turns around and shows himself as the race man that I suspect, at his core, he is. Or that I like to think or am desperate to think or long to think he is. I long for him to believe, at his core, in uplifting the race, not denigrating it.

On rare occasions, when I have felt bold or particularly at ease, I have asked direct questions. I noticed, over the course of a few months, that Dad repeatedly invoked the name of Jackie Robinson. After Tiger Woods won a major golf tournament, my father described Woods as the Jackie Robinson of golf. Then, in reference to Bubba Johnson's having served as the town's first black law enforcement officer, he said Bubba was the Jackie Robinson of the sheriff's department. Finally, in telling me a story of his father's career, Dad called Granddaddy the Jackie Robinson of Monticello.

Dad, do you feel race pride? I asked after one of his Jackie Robinsons.

No. I feel human pride though.

But, okay, do you take a particular pride in black people's accomplishments?

Yeah.

So if you take a particular pride in black people's accomplishments, how is that different from race pride?

Well, race would be a factor if they had to overcome blockades set up by racial prejudices. In a sports contest, I root for the underdog if people are being unfair to them. Down in Monticello, black accomplishments have to negotiate race. So, in that sense, yeah, I would say I feel race pride.

Do you also feel a particular pain when you see black people fail to negotiate?

I don't feel any particular pain. I am not impervious to feeling, but I've seen it so much. And you've got to realize that there are just some things that you can't change. And there are ways to succeed in this hostile environment, mostly if you think it through. I realize we are in a market system, and everybody's trying to make money.

AS FOR THE PICKLED PEACHES, curiosity eventually got the better of me. With a long spoon, I trapped a peach against the side of its jar, then slid it up and out into a bowl. I tried to carve off a piece with the side of a teaspoon but the fruit eluded me, and I had to attack it from the top, the downward pressure keeping it in place. I tasted it, slippery but firm-fleshed, and was instantly filled with regret: the pain of confronting lost opportunity, of coming face to face with unrecoverable time! The pickled peaches were heavenly. Savory brine squared off against thick sugar syrup, but in the midst of that contest, the fruit's essential flavor never gave up.

For the rest of that trip, I worked them into every meal. I ate them by themselves. I put slivers of peach and roast chicken on the same fork. I spooned peach halves onto butter pecan ice cream, allowing the piquant syrup to pool into a moat between the melting scoops of ice cream and the sides of the bowl, saving this elixir for last.

After securing my father's permission, I called Mrs. Howard to ask for her pickled peach recipe so I could understand what I'd tasted. Mrs. Howard has raised three sets of children: at twenty her parents died, leaving her and an older brother to raise ten siblings. Then she raised her own ten, and now two of her grandsons. She'd canned thousands of jars over the years. Dad drove with me out to the Howards' place, deeper into the countryside than his farm is. While I went in to visit, he waited outside, talking to Mrs. Howard's grandsons and navigating the drooping, barky beagles that lingered in the dirt and halfheartedly guarded against strangers.

My canning mentor had gone to the trouble of writing up her recipe for me, even though she contended, *It's simple as can be*. But like most cooks who've been at it for decades, the enterprise was second nature to her, and much of it went without saying. "Peel peaches," the recipe began without specifying quantity, and then "soak overnight in 4 lbs. of sugar." The process seemed straightforward enough, if you could determine appropriate proportions. Mrs. Howard's foundations were peaches, sugar, and a package of pickling spice from the supermarket. Her results, however, were transporting.

What other delicacies, I wondered, had my father hidden from me? I liked the local staples well enough: chopped barbecue, ribs, fried chicken, fried catfish, fried pork chops, collard greens braised with streak o' lean. Those were my inheritance, a source of fellow-ship during my childhood with other southern-rooted black people that bridged the miscues of my physiognomy. But these peaches were something else altogether, equal parts comfort and complexity and sweet, sweet, sweet.

So sweet, my father agreed, *the birds hush their singing.*

6.

KLAN SNEAK

My FATHER WON'T LET MARGARET close all of the sunroom blinds to August's wilting midday heat. *You can close most of them*, he says, *as long as you leave two or three open. I want to be able to see the Klan sneaking up on us.*

He is joking and he is not joking. Otherwise, why would he warn us never to open the door to strangers if we're alone at the farm? Why, at the start of this brief weekend visit, would he make Margaret open the garage safe to retrieve his .38 special? And why would he put the gun in the wire basket of his walker, wheel it into his bedroom, and stable it, loaded, in the nightstand drawer?

The sunroom windows cover three walls and look out past the driveway, past the split-rail fence and cattle grate that keep cows away from the house, past the hill's sole pecan tree and over a pasture in which the Howard twins' Herefords and Baldies and Angus occasionally graze. The full length of the driveway, a third of a mile, is visible from the sunroom, gently serpentining out to Fellowship Road and ending at a mailbox that has more than once been used for batting practice, presumably an expression of local pubescent aggression. Most of the time, only daughters traffic the driveway, my father noting when our speed exceeds his preferred ten miles per hour.

We are here to give Dad his second furlough from the Pennsylvania-based chemotherapy he started once he'd recovered from the failed Covington attempt in March. Lois didn't come this trip, claiming the visit was too short, considering the disruption it would cause her.

Dad's first break was in July, all three daughters and John in attendance. On that visit, again mindful that the trip could be his last, and in between the fishing and eating and hovering over my father's needs and whims, I documented the house with my camera. I photographed the bidet, a device my father discovered on a trip abroad and has since installed in every home he's owned. I recorded the overall decor, the pristine but verveless furnishings. Colonialistic. Arts and Craftsish. Scandinavianesque.

I took several views of the master bedroom's perfectly organized walk-in closet: his half across from Lois's, his old John Wanamaker ties collecting dust, his Birkenstocks neatly filed in pairs, standing on their edges on shelves next to plastic takeout containers filled with ammunition.

In July, Dad had cooled on selling the farm and had pulled the listing off the market, but he was still trying to tie up loose ends when he had the strength or as they crossed his mind. He took us up on our offers to help, and hence my ongoing assignment to prepare for the eventual dispossession of the guns. First it was all of the guns, and then Dad decided to hold on to two, the Colt .38 Detective Special and the Browning 9 mm.

We all had our jobs. Margaret became the expert on the two safe combinations and their attendant quirks. The wardrobe-size safe in the second guest room held most of the guns. The old one in the garage, when I last saw it open, held a pair of Dad's undershorts along with two handguns and a pair of binoculars that Dad claims would allow you to see the whiskers on a turkey at three hundred yards. Diane defaulted into being the keeper of financial matters. She kept the books at Dad's real estate company for a couple of years; she still helps him prepare his tax information for the accountant each spring, and he has already informed her that she will be executor of his estate, along with Lois's youngest son.

In July, the three daughters took turns hovering over Dad's pill regimen—an all-time high of twenty medications. Some were adjusted based on a weekly blood test, some were held back if his pulse rate fell too low. The nursing staff at Waverly had recently started to subdivide his pills into blister packs, gridded and glued onto cardboard sheets, which seemed to make it easier for him to keep track, although he claimed there was always some inaccuracy, some way in which the weekly replenishment of pills had been "yucked up."

If it is human, it will err. If it is mechanical, it will malfunction.

THIS AUGUST TRIP, this spontaneous, planned-three-days-in-advance weekend getaway, includes just Dad, Margaret, and me. We get the first sign that it's going to be a good weekend at the Philadelphia airport on Friday. Margaret and I have both taken the day off, we've collected Dad at Waverly, and we are well ahead of schedule when we reach the gate to find the plane's been delayed an hour. We choose a bank of seats, and Dad reads the *New York Times* I've brought for him. I can't tell if he's actually reading it, but he periodically turns its pages. I mention I've brought the pig roast album in case he wants to show it to anyone.

Good work, Leesee, he says.

The gate area is crowded with people and luggage. Across from us there's a family that appears to consist of African parents and their accentless, Americanized teenage daughter; next to them is a casually dressed but self-important woman with hair straightened and pulled skull-tight into a ponytail, oversize sunglasses screening out the fluorescent lights, and a constantly engaged cell phone; and next to her, a mother and her three daughters, all absorbed in magazines and books. Dad folds the newspaper into his lap and studies this foursome for a while, stares unabashedly, then makes his move.

Hey! he calls out, his voice cutting across the aisle and the ambient noise of the waiting area. *Hey, Spelman!*

The girls and their mother shift in their seats, unsure whether or how to respond. I look over and see one has a backpack with "Spelman College" printed on it.

He's looking at your bag, I explain.

My father doesn't need my intercession. He is in full-on charm mode, and within three minutes he has identified that he knows relatives of the family, that this woman's father belonged to the same men's social club he did. He finds out the family's home (Delaware), the purpose of their trip (taking the oldest to start her freshman year at Spelman), and that the mother, Launice, went to Spelman, too. He instructs Margaret to take a picture of them and indicates that if they give us their address, he'll send them a copy. They don't immediately offer up the information. I wonder if this is because he seems odd or because his pants are unsnapped and his fly down, the belt only loosely buckled on top. This is a mode of dressing he's taken to ever since Covington hospital, since the bulky diapers entered his life, and he will not retreat from it, no matter who asks, who stares, or how many strangers try to help out with looks and gestures and euphemisms. *Barn door's open.*

Where's that photo album? he says to me, his prop master.

He passes the album to the family. Each takes a turn looking and asking questions. The mother turns the album back toward us and points to my cousin standing by the *Caja China.*

Is this Carolyn? she asks. They were classmates at Spelman.

In the midst of Dad's campaign, the girls' father comes over from a nearby seat, where he's been occupied with the *Wall Street Journal.* He orbits, asking one of the girls sotto voce if everything's okay, and when she displays no alarm, goes back to his seat without joining the conversation.

The last child to look at the album starts to hand it back.

May I look at that? asks the ponytailed woman from behind her oversize shades. She goes through each page carefully, finding no acquaintances but nodding approval at several points.

DAD IN MONTICELLO is the picture of pleasure: tortoise-paced but full of pep. He takes himself to Troy's to keep the money straight. He comes into the dollar store rather than wait in the car. He comes inside Fresh Air BBQ when we buy quarts of pulled pork to take back to Philadelphia. He hauls his walker into the drugstore in Jackson so he can look for red gum stimulator replacement tips, and when we've both thoroughly combed and recombed the tooth care section to no avail, he notices I'm lingering over a handheld electric flossing wand the way children hover over a coveted item in the toy aisle, counting on the currency of sheer desire. He takes the wand from me and tosses it into the basket of his walker. He leaves me, wheeling purposefully toward the checkout. Anyone looking at him would think, *Now there's a guy with somewhere to go.*

When it turns out the flosser costs thirty dollars, I offer to take it back. Neither of us had looked at the price, never imagining such

AA-battery-powered frippery could be so expensive. *No*, he says, and pulls out his money clip, unfolding a fifty-dollar bill and handing it to the cashier.

It is as if Dad is on vacation from dying. He still tires easily, doesn't do any of the tasks he used to do for fun—raking pine straw off the driveway or throwing fish kibble into the pond—but there's a psychic verve to him we haven't seen in months. When we're coming and going and I ask if he needs help, he inevitably says no.

I just need time, he says.

His to-do list is crowded with what he will ask or hire others to do: enlist George Davie Mohorne to weed-whack the fence line and pick up trash; see if Troy Eugene Johnson can get the riding mower tuned up at Brad's Small Engine Repair Shop; call Troy's neighbor Claudia Andrews (he'll have her middle name soon, it's only a matter of time), who might be willing, Troy says, to hire on for the fall to keep Lois company at 354 when Dad goes out and to fix some of their meals. This last item shows Dad's desire to come back for at least one more stretch, and it's as close as he's come to admitting that he and Lois can no longer manage without help.

We are a family of weight-conscious gluttons, none worse than my father. Disease and medication side effects turn out to be the most effective diet he's followed, and there have been many. The grapefruit diet, the Pritikin diet, and the clear-broth diet come to mind. Each one achieved some rate of success for some time. We have a picture of Dad from a 1980s vacation in Bermuda in which he's tanned and temporarily trim, wearing swim trunks and stretching his hands up to the sky, à la the Royal Canadian Air Force exercise pamphlet from 1962 that shuffled around the house for years. Otherwise, photos show a tendency toward corpulence, face full and clothes stretched taut across an imposing midsection.

In his present state, he could care less about the whole business.

Should we go get some dinner? one of us will ask.

If you want to, he says.

He wants us to have what we need, and for Lois, if she's among us, to be fed, but the children have taken over the shopping, preparation, and cleanup. He continues to pay for it all, handing us a kitty to work from at the start of every trip, crisp hundred-dollar bills fresh from the bank.

Do I need to settle any outstanding debts? he asks periodically, apropos of nothing. *I want to keep the money straight.*

There are certain food-related marks the rest of us try to hit on our visits. Pork is always involved, along with whatever fruits and vegetables are in season. The result, even after a short weekend, is a fridge full of leftovers. Dad has made an arrangement with Dorothy and Troy to clean out the fridge after we go and for them to take what they want, which makes the rest of us less concerned about how much we buy. Still, Margaret and I curb our purchasing on this August trip, sticking to one flavor of ice cream, a single onion in lieu of a five-pound bag, and one package of bacon. No fatback, no country ham, no streak o' lean.

MARGARET IS CLEARING DISHES from the table and finds a half-melted pill in the bottom of Dad's coffee cup, drowning in a missed swig. She retrieves that eroded remainder, centers it on a piece of paper next to Dad's place at the end of the kitchen table, draws a circle around the pill and then an arrow to one side, where she writes its place of discovery and its name, still legible on its blue coating. She leaves the paper for him to find. Later she sees that the pill has been removed. Dad says nothing about it.

The more we can avoid direct contact with our father about his health, the less likely he is to lash out at us. Even in a weekend that's going so well, the topic makes him cross. Our intrusions are unwelcome, even when we are in the right. But unlike the past, when his scorching retorts prompted aftermaths of weeping and lengthy deconstruction, which we saved for the safe harbor of our mother's house, since divorce had only removed her from his direct targeting, we now register the bile without absorbing so much of it. After all, he's dying. Who wouldn't feel a bit on edge?

The catalog of illness-related insults for a man in his situation is unbearably lengthy. He is regularly injected and strapped down and narcotized, tethered to chemotherapy and a walker and diapers and medications that choreograph his every waking hour. But aside from the misplaced pill or worrisomely long nap, this is a good trip. This trip is a joy as much for what does not happen—no 911 calls, no hospitals, no bad reactions to medicines or treatments—as for what does.

HOW'S YOUR DADDY? PEOPLE ask to be polite, they ask because they care, they ask because they know it's expected. The couple who own Monticello Farm & Garden ask when I stop by to pick up a package of fake worms, plastic "Bass Assassins." The drive-through teller asks when I roll up to her window, cashing another check for my father, whom she clearly knows well enough to ask, *And how does he want this?*

Strangers ask while I wait to pay at Ingles or stand in the food line at Dave's. Sometimes they refer to him as "Doc" or "Doc Funderburg," confusing him with his father. Just as he's never corrected them, neither do I.

"He's okay" sounds disingenuous. "Better" sounds like a lie. That first attempt at chemo floored him. This time around, the chemo hasn't cut him down. In Pennsylvania, a milder dose is administered, three (rather than thirty) miles from home. At Waverly, medical professionals and paraprofessionals are on hand to check his vitals, administer tests, and monitor a bedsore ulcer that formed in the Covington hospital bed—a hole at his elbow so deep you could look in and see the core of the man.

So the truth at this moment, for this weekend, is that he is doing okay. By our second day, he forgets to bring his walker along on a car ride and, surprising himself, manages just fine with a cane. When one of us remarks on the development, he lifts the cane from the ground and twirls it, Charlie Chaplin style. And he is better. The low-dose chemo and blood transfusions and careful monitoring have an effect. His bad blood levels have not only stopped spiking, they've started to head downward.

Comfort is relative. To have your PSA level decrease is a good thing, but going from 319 nanograms per milliliter down to the mid-200s is less dramatic when you consider that 10 nanograms is pretty much the definitive line between cancer and no cancer. So when people ask how he's doing, I want to say something like, *Okay, considering*. Or, *Much better, for now*.

What I manage is, *Pretty well. Thanks for asking*.

On our first full day at the farm, I wake up before Margaret and shuffle past Dad on my way to the coffee machine. He sits at his end of the table, dressings laid out in front of him in Ziploc bags.

When you're ready, he says, *maybe you could help me out*.

A bedsore, aka decubitus ulcer, can develop in as little as three hours. Friction against the bed sheet and immobility cut off blood supply, and the skin reddens, then purples, then breaks down. Any bedsore is slow to mend, but with a chemotherapy-compromised immune system, it is even slower. In my father's case, bacteria found their way in, infection developed, and the sore hasn't healed.

Dad's dressing has to be changed once a day. None of us are shy about wounds. We also don't swoon at needles, and we don't wriggle under the dentist's drill. When we were little, Dad put iodine on anything: cuts, scrapes, random mouth sores whether outside or in. Hole left from tooth pulled by paternally administered pliers? Iodine chaser. Splinter removed by sterilized sewing needle dug deep to clear away all remnants of intruding matter? Iodine chaser. Falls off rope swings, stubbed toes at the beginning of barefoot summers, inexpert ducking under motorized toy planes? Iodine chaser. Iodine stung deeply, far beyond the damaged area. It stung through the flesh, down to the bone, into the soul. We sat perfectly still for the administration of the orange-stained Q-tip. No squirming. No whimpering.

Once I've gotten my coffee and gulped down half the cup, Dad rolls his chair over, bringing the dressings to where I'm sitting.

Here's my little talk, he says, *and then I'll leave it to you.*

He goes through each step the nurse went through with him, but then he does not leave it to me. He barks when I'm not moving fast enough, when I don't peel off the old tape correctly. When the tape comes off, so does the folded cotton gauze underneath it. With tweezers, I pull out the old packing, which has become suffused with yellow ooze. Dad asks to see it. *Good*, he says. *That's a sign it's drawing out infection.*

I'm seized with fear that I will infect him, that I will put contaminated tweezers into the bottle of sterile dressing tape before cutting off the strip I need. I fold the inch-long piece of tape into the wound, accordion-style pleats pushed gingerly into the bloodless, ulcerated hole using a sterile cotton swab at the end of a long wooden stick.

Push it in! Dad commands, even though I know from his flinching that the area is tender to him. *It should act as an irritant*, he says more evenly. *At least I think that's why it goes in there.*

I change his dressings every morning. When I retrieve the bottle of isopropyl alcohol from his bathroom medicine cabinet, and two cotton balls, per his specification, the air of the bathroom is thick, heavy with liniments and the powder that coats latex. Once I return to the kitchen and sit next to him, he sticks out his arm, thrusts it in front of me. The elbow is hard to reach, and the wound, just at the tip of the bend, requires that my father contort his body in order to provide me access. We use no iodine in this procedure, but there are plenty of opportunities to inflict pain.

* * *

AT THE AIRPORT security gate on our way to Georgia, Dad's duffel was pulled aside for inspection after it passed under the X-ray machine. The bag held two sealed dressing kits containing metal instruments, disposable tweezers, and scissors that are unmistakably verboten in a post–box cutter world.

Whose bag is this? the inspector asked as the duffel moved toward the end of the conveyer belt. I pointed to Dad a few feet away, a barely standing scarecrow being scanned for metal with a wheelchair and its attendant in wait.

I can see that he needs them, she said, and handed me the bag with kits intact.

I can see that he needs to have his wound addressed and dispensed with as soon as possible, for his sake and mine, so each morning I change the dressing as soon as I get out of bed, before I've had that full cup of coffee, before I can literally see straight. Dad, never a long or late sleeper, has inevitably been up for hours and at first has little patience with my sleepy plodding. By the third day, however, Dad begins to joke with me during the procedure, calling me Doctor and praising my technique. He makes sure to mention how well I "fix him up" when I'm in earshot of his daily call to Lois. Part of me sees through the oblique attempts to appease and praise; part of me sops up every last bit.

MY FATHER PLAYS BY THE RULES, most of the time and within reason. When he drives the Isuzu over to the convenience store that locals call the Stop and Rob to get the papers on Saturday morning, he is not in the door before a man calls out to him.

You're in trouble [trub], the man says.

What kind of trouble? my father asks.

Your tag's expired, the man says.

My father buys the *Macon Telegraph* and the *Atlanta Journal-Constitution* and comes home. He immediately calls the Automobile Association, the motor vehicle registry, and the local police. All tell him the same thing: he's at risk for a ticket until he gets a new registration, which won't be possible until Monday, the day we leave.

Unwilling to risk a citation, my father limits his driving of the Isuzu to within the confines of the farm, except for one run over to Brad's Small Engine. The illicit trip starts with Dad and George Davie Mohorne out on Fellowship Road, having trouble with Dad's weed whacker. Pop Smith, whose family owns the town's black funeral home, stops to exchange greetings on his way home from an unsuccessful fishing expedition. His attempt to help with the whacker is equally fruitless, and he urges Dad to get to Brad's before it closes. Most shops close early on Saturday, don't open at all on Sunday, and close on Wednesdays at noon, the last, my father tells me, a convention left over from Franklin Roosevelt's New Deal days. Eddie Ray Tyler goes a step further: He closes his barbershop every weekday afternoon so he can drive the school bus, then comes back to cut hair and jaw until suppertime.

Aside from driving to Brad's, Dad pretty much abides by the law for the remainder of the trip, except for when he can't wait for late risers to wake up or exercisers to finish on the adjustable incline treadmill installed in his bedroom. Then he takes the rental-car keys and heads out, despite my being its only registered driver and whatever's going on with his eyesight. On Saturday, he takes the rental into town to get a trim and the latest gossip from Eddie Ray, who, in addition to cutting hair and driving children, served as the town's mayor from 1993 to 1995. Eddie Ray wants my father to have some Brunswick stew he made, but doesn't want to inspire the envy of the customers and hangers-on who fill his shop. When Dad goes to use the urinal after Eddie Ray's finished making the gesture of a haircut on Dad's downy-thin Taxol mane, Eddie Ray follows him into the back room, hands him a quart of the tomato, corn, and ground beef porridge, and sends him out the shop's back door.

Dad tells the story to Margaret and me, then to Marshall Tinsley when Marshall joins us for Saturday supper at the new El Giro restaurant (Mexican food! In Monticello!), then once more to Jackie, who joins us when, with the aim of remaining leftoverless, we return to El Giro the following night. Everyone laughs at the story. No one points out the implications of a black man being asked to use the back door, even in 2004. I can't tell if it's my northern paranoia distorting an innocent case of stew-envy management, or if the irony is so obvious it would be like pointing out the existence of air.

MACK TILLMAN, Ben and Sissy's father, dies while we're in town. Dad sees him in the barbershop on Saturday, where Mack complains of stents, the mesh scaffolds that have been implanted into his diseased arteries or vessels or heart (Dad's not sure which) to keep them open. Sunday, Mack's name comes up at El Giro, when Jackie talks about the Klan still being alive and well in Jasper County. Monday morning, the day we leave, Dad commandeers the rental car to head over to Tillman House in anticipation of its 6 A.M. opening. He sits on the steps and waits, only to find out from a passerby that Mack Tillman is dead, died Sunday, unexpected.

How do you separate the man from the Klan, the truth from the rumor, the history from the lore? Did Mack Tillman's boots really stick out from under the white sheet when Bubba Johnson patroled that parade through the square? If something never happened, but the thought of it guides generations of choices and votes and interactions, how different is it from a scrupulously recorded, verifiable history? What credence should be accorded to likelihood? Under the old regime, black people in Monticello regularly saved their own lives by anticipating likely consequences. A fair presumption at the time, but now?

History aside, what did Mack Henry Tillman mean to me? He was a big man, out of proportion to his role at the end of the restaurant's cafeteria line, silently writing up tabs for Connie to ring at the cash register. I didn't know him those sixteen years he was sheriff of Jasper County or the years he was police chief. I didn't know the Methodist he was, the Jaycee, the city councilor, the husband, father, grandfather. When I started going to Tillman House, Ben's ownership was well established. Mack had long since receded into his quiet role of packaging and pouring. What I do know about him is that when he heard Dad was sick back in March, he baked Lois two chess pies, her favorites, and had them sent out to the farm while they were still warm. I do know that to be true.

We are collecting deaths these days. All of my father's siblings are gone, three of them in the last five years. My hard-living cousin Doug; Dad's cousin Buck; and Uncle Holsey this past April, ten days after Dad walked—just barely—out of the Covington hospital and onto a plane. Now Mack Tillman. The closer you come to losing your own parents, the less you have to say when other people die. You know to say something, not to be afraid of how it sounds or if it's the right thing. After a certain age, you know that the greatest mistake would be to stay silent. But you also know that each person's loss is idiosyncratic and, even among members of the same family, to a certain extent unknowable.

Each new death triggers an anticipatory bracing. I find myself squaring off against the future, trying to take stock of something that cannot possibly be measured in advance. I accept that my father will die, that it's completely natural and appropriate, and I suspect I will never get over it. I will never accept his absence from my life.

I SQUEEZE IN SEVERAL BOUTS of fishing on this trip, even though I can't get Margaret or Dad to keep me company. A year or so ago, John, my skilled angler husband, gave me a few pointers, including the seminally helpful "Keep your line in the water." He taught me about identifying the "strike zone" in which fish are most likely to go after your bait. In Dad's largest pond, John figures, that's usually about ten feet offshore; casting in a diagonal line across that magical area is likely to put the hook closer to more fish. I try to fish near underwater "structures," whether the delineation is made by the dock or the light-dark distinctions of a tree's shadow. And in deference to the wisdom of John, who at age seventeen was the Delaware state bass champion record holder for two months, I move to a new spot after five or ten casts, hoping to leverage the element of surprise.

Soon after his tutelage began, I improved. From catching nothing, I moved onto setting a weekend pond record, poachers aside, of more than twenty fish. John diagnosed the pond as being overstocked with bream. I noticed he was not catching anywhere close to my rate.

Most of the folks we know down in Monticello are fond of fresh-caught fish, and unless John was around to clean them, my catches became gifts. Dorothy says she actually enjoys cleaning fish, and Troy's credo is that no fish is too small to fit in his frying pan. John maintained that the bream I was catching were trash fish, crowding the pond and stealing nutrients from the more expensive bass and the pond-cleaning, bottom-feeding catfish. He advised throwing them up on the banks or into the trees to die, then rerigging one's line to appeal to the cagier largemouth bass. Dad endorsed John's suggestions. *Whatever John Reynolds says*, he'd say, appending John's middle name. And yet, one late morning of the otherwise pleasant August weekend, I come back from the pond, park my fishing rod in its stand, and walk into the kitchen. Margaret putters near the sink and Dad is ensconced in his rolling chair.

Do you understand the economics of the fish pond? Dad asks. His tone suggests inquisition, not conversation.

To ask what he means would only prompt a repetition of the

question, and so I say no. Dad launches into a series of calculations, pointing out a cost per unit of catching fish, based not only on their original price tags but also on the expense of fertilizing the pond, the proportionate taxation on the pond acreage as a segment of the whole property, and other considerations I don't follow at all.

My father's tone is stern. He clearly believes I have done something wrong in my zealous angling. This confuses me, as fishing is something he sponsors, making sure to have bait on hand for any visitor. He bought the rods and the stand that holds them, and he's populated the tackle box with hooks and lead weights and elaborately barbed plastic facsimiles of frogs and minnows, some left over from his father's gear.

Would you like me to stop fishing? I ask, trying to get to the heart of the matter.

I didn't say that. I just want to be sure you understand the economic consequences.

At one point, Dad's attention is diverted and I look over at Margaret, who shrugs in confusion and points her index finger at her temple, moving it in a circular motion. We console each other, my sisters and I. We have always done this.

I try to weather the rest of the lecture from an island of neutrality. I answer his questions as well as I can. I repeat back the comments that appear to be crucial. And when he finally seems satisfied that he's made his point, I say, again, that I really enjoy fishing in the pond, but if it is ever inappropriate, I'd be happy to stop, and he just needs to let me know if that's the case. He never speaks of it again.

I CUT BACK on my fishing, but I don't completely stop, and I never subscribe to John's bream-trashing advice. When Holsey, who especially liked bream, was alive, he was always first on my list. He was such a beanpole of a man, it felt good to contribute to his diet. Even before the cancer got to him, he was thin. His Sunday-go-to-church suit hung on his frame like laundry from a line. His skin was a deep brown, and his head, nearly bald, had a ring of closely shorn white hair that he typically covered by a bill cap, a small-brimmed fedora, or a flapped Elmer Fudd hunter's hat.

Almost a lifelong bachelor, he married my aunt Chase, his high school sweetheart, when he was sixty-eight years old. She'd already married, had children, and been widowed. He had told her he'd wait for her, and he did. Not many years after their marriage, she started to lose track of things, become forgetful, confuse names. He nursed her through Alzheimer's and lost her to it, keeping her at home with him up until the very end. Afterward, he still claimed us as family and we him, and he'd come visit each time we were in town, parking himself in a blue leather wing chair in the corner of the sunroom diagonally across from Lois, asking for little but companionship.

He drove up in his Cadillac one autumn day when I was at the fence that separates the house from the pasture. I was on the pasture side, picking up pecans that had fallen from the big tree near the top of George's Hill. He walked through a gate and around to where I stood, and then bent from the hip to gather pecans with me. Folded in half like that, he kept on long after I was ready to stop, kept on plucking up nuts, examining them for wormholes, throwing the bad ones back onto the ground, and searching for good ones until we had filled a five-gallon bucket. We shelled one or two nuts, just to see the quality of their meats.

Shelled pecans used to be like peeled shrimp, a delicacy that signaled special occasions or was the result of hard work. Dad's purchase of the farm, with its grove of mature trees, changed that. If it's a good year for the trees and they give off nuts, the farm's freezer will be stuffed with bags of juicy, shelled meats. Dad will print up mailing labels and send out packages to friends and relatives, and he'll still have enough left to send twenty-five pounds or more to my mom, his ex-wife, so she can make up spiced pecans from her own mother's recipe.

In order for Dad to structure enterprises at the farm so that he is not required to do any of their associated physical labor, he involves himself in all manner of hire, barter, and trade. The low-rent-for-upkeep arrangement with the Howard twins is his most elaborate. George Davie Mohorne is contracted for two hours a week of cleaning the grass between the fence line and the road. Troy Johnson has more than assumed the role his brother played as overseer, and yet the amount Troy charges always seems too small for the work he does. Now that Dad assigns me to keep the money straight on his behalf, I sometimes double-check on Troy's accounting.

Are you sure you're charging for all your time? I ask as I write out a check.

I'm not going to count when I just go out and check on something or go up there to meet the electrician, Troy says. *I'm just going to charge for slave work, like the mowing. That's slave work.*

Dorothy helps Troy clean out the house after we leave, as well as do the laundry and straighten up in the kitchen. I suspect she is not scrupulous in tracking her hours, either. *Just leave everything,* Troy says whenever we're about to leave. *Just lock the door behind you, and I'll take care of it.*

He often stops by on the mornings that we depart. He is a calming force in the midst of our scurrying. At the end of one visit, even though we're running a little close to the wire, Margaret mentions to Troy that she'd like to trim back one of the bushes near the house before she leaves.

Do you think I have time to prune it? she asks.

Troy twists his face into an exaggerated look of alarm. *You don't have time to spell prune,* he says.

In another of Dad's compacts, he has arranged for the picking and processing of pecans on halves. In the years that the trees do produce, Dad goes halves with a man who has a machine that shakes the nuts out of the trees. Dad's half of the yield then goes to a man with a shelling machine, with whom he goes halves. And even after those divisions and after distribution among family and friends, dozens of pounds remain.

On the day that Holsey helped me pick up pecans, it was preshelled nuts I put onto a cookie sheet, not the ones he and I had just gathered.

Holsey, I called out from the kitchen to the sunroom, *how do you fix pecans?*

From the wing chair, he directed me to turn the oven on low, put nuts, salt, and butter into a pan and put them in the oven.

I cut a few dabs of butter onto a cookie sheet, then brought it over to show him.

This much butter?

A little more, he said.

How do you know when they're done? I asked.

When you can smell 'em, he said.

But how long is that? my father interjected.

No specific time, George, Holsey said. *Just a matter of when they're cooked enough to give off a smell.*

Imprecision makes my father's skin crawl. He asked Holsey twice more for a cooking time, then for a guess—an act of desperation since guessing is anathema to my father and treated with the same contempt as lying. When Holsey still had no number to give, my father set the timer for ten minutes. Ten minutes later, it rang.

Well? my father said. *The dinger dang.*

They're not done, Holsey said.

How do you know?

Holsey was gentle and kind, a much-beloved member of the community who volunteered at the Retreat, the senior care annex of Jasper Memorial Hospital, into his eighties. Beloved not just by the black community, either. Eddie Ray, the white barber, called Holsey every morning to check in, and when the white lawyer Larry Lynch started an integrated Bible study group, Holsey was among the first to join. Holsey was a deacon and Sunday school teacher at the Colored Methodist Episcopal church over in Blue Ruin, and he drove his maroon Cadillac so slowly, given his failing eyesight, that a deer once hit him, crushing his fender. But this richly led life is not why I think of him as superhuman. He was about the only person I've ever known to have sustained interaction with my father and show neither frustration nor hurt nor irritation.

Despite my father's obvious exasperation about the pecans, Holsey remained in the chair, his back sunken in and his lanky limbs stretched out, a paperclip unfolded.

I can't smell 'em.

7.

THE SUN HITS
ITS HIGH MARK

JUST WHEN YOU THINK things are calming down—when you think you're looking at a nice stretch of coasting in which you can pay attention to your own health, to the other parent, to nothing at all—something comes along.

The skin on Dad's bedsore has closed over, but after five months, he still feels the tenderness and pain underneath. An infectious disease specialist and an orthopedist confer: the ulcer is probably burrowing into tendon, or, worse, bone. Dad will have an operation to clean out the wound, followed by ten days of wearing a cast to immobilize the joint. Ever since we got back from our August weekend, he's been lobbying to return to Georgia at the beginning of September, hinting around about my availability to escort him and Lois down there, suggesting that John Reynolds Howard and I might enjoy some fishing on the pond. I consider questioning the economics of his suggestion, then bite my tongue.

Surgery can't be scheduled until September 7. This may get in the way of his plan for two months on the farm. This may get in the way of an autumn pig roast redux. This may kill my father. What will be the straw that breaks him? Taking him off his blood thinner for five days prior to surgery? Now that they're going to cut him, they want his blood to clot. But his faulty heart valve has relied on the blood thinner for years now. Putting him under general anesthesia? Canceling a few chemotherapy sessions so that his immune system can rally?

John says that if I'm really afraid my father's going to die during this upcoming procedure, I should talk to a doctor. My husband wants to offer consolation, to calm me, but this is not what I want. There's nothing a doctor could say that will keep my father from dying, either from this setback or some other. I have to say, out loud, that he might die, because it helps me. I'm practicing.

It helps to brace myself, to temper the hopefulness that rises up unbidden and unwarranted. The day before I got back my own second-view mammogram results, I leaned against my kitchen counter and said to myself, nearly out loud, "This is what it feels like to not have cancer." My results came back clear, but I wanted to lock in the feeling of before, knowing that if there were to be an after, I could never return. In the case of my father, it helps to steel myself, to face the inevitable. I am always saying good-bye to him now. Each phone call, each visit, each trip down south. Each procedure or complication. I am recording his voice, his quirks, trying to etch them deep into the wax of memory.

And yet memory is so faulty, such a poor recording device. There's what we forget, but worse is what we realize after the fact we should have paid attention to. And paying attention is exhausting. I find myself paying close attention, but I end up feeling like a blinkered horse, with full vision cut off, the world a tunnel. Experience is fundamentally altered, too. Nothing just happens or is felt: it all has to be named, quantified, and measured on the scales of joy and sorrow, hope and pain, impending grief.

I TAKE DAD to the hospital for his surgery, a two-hour bursectomy that will have him home by afternoon. I'm allowed to escort him as far as pre-op prep, and while the nurse takes his vital signs and checks off the anesthesiologist's questions, Dad tells her the names of the magazines I write for. I'm allowed to help him change into a gown, and then I am exiled.

In the waiting room, I choose a chair that faces the reception desk, away from the general seating area and its droning television suspended from the ceiling. I fan the pages of magazines and dig for the blue cheese, bacon, and chicken in my takeout salad. Will my father's heart, with its leaky valves and overtaxed reserves, the chemo, the years of heavy drinking and too much lard, hold up under the strain of anesthesia? Will the doctor approach me with that somber Marcus Welby face, the bearer of the worst imaginable tiding?

Dad's procedure takes exactly two hours. Afterward, the orthopedist, a specialist in upper extremities, comes to sit by me. He has kind eyes.

It went well, he says. *I think we got all the infection. The issue now is how well the elbow heals.* The next couple of weeks will be crucial, the test of whether surgery worked. *We don't want to go back in.*

He speeds through the recovery protocol at such a clip I keep hoping someone else has all of this written down. Still, I take notes on the edge of a manuscript I am supposed to have been editing. I phonetically approximate the names of the two antibiotics he mentions, then note their dosages and which one he's already started Dad on. I note that I'm to call the oncologist and see if she'll let Dad take another week off from chemotherapy, to give his immune system a leg up. The doctor shakes my hand and leaves, and I sit for another half hour, forty-five minutes maybe, before being led into the recovery room. My intolerance of anesthesia must have trickled down maternally. Dad is awake and aware and hungry after fasting for the last twenty hours. His arm has been rigged to a flat board so that it cannot bend. When it comes time for him to switch out of the gown and back into his clothes, the nurse accompanies him into the wheelchair-accessible changing room. Then Art appears.

Art was Dad's roommate fifty-five years ago, a member of the same housing cooperative where my parents met. He's a good guy: well-meaning and generous, but occasionally obtrusive and endlessly talkative. A mensch, but a bit of a noodge. He's also still at sea after losing his wife a couple of years ago. Once widowed, he moved back to the Philadelphia area to live with a daughter and a grandson in a nearby suburban town. He is fond of my father, game to visit and watch TV, come down to the farm, go anywhere. He is a specimen of health: tennis-playing, Prius-driving, bran-eating. As we wait for a dressed Dad to emerge, Art waves a book in the air, a convalescence gift: *Anti-Semite and Jew: An Exploration of the Etiology of Hate*, by Jean-Paul Sartre.

We talked about it, Art says by way of explanation.

DAD SITS AROUND the furniture-choked Waverly apartment, his arm pillowed up and splinted into a *Heil, Hitler* as it heals. When I'm unavailable to chauffeur him to doctors' appointments and chemotherapy, Lois and I urge him to take taxis or arrange transportation through the Waverly shuttle service. He ignores us and drives himself.

I'm fine, he says even when I offer to give him a ride. *I drive slowly and it's not far.*

I recall driving-school propaganda I learned decades ago. "Most accidents happen within twenty-five miles of home." I do not say this to my father, only that he should let me know if I can be of assistance.

Dad's surgery follow-up exam indicates less than optimal healing, and he lands back in the office of the infectious disease specialist, who advises ratcheting up the antibiotics to an intravenous drip of the more powerful vancomycin, two hours a day for the next ten days. Insurance technicalities and a lack of space preclude my father from going into Muirfield, Waverly's 60-bed nurse-staffed wing, and so two weeks after the outpatient surgical procedure, he's in a hospital room, gowned and bored. I pay a visit, stopping first at Waverly, at his request, to pick up his cell phone.

> Daughter Lesson #1: Do not try to make Dad feel more at home with snacks and books and pajamas. *This is not home*, he says.

> Lesson #2: Bring snacks anyway. Salted peanuts a guaranteed home run. Take leftovers home.

> Lesson #3: When the radiology intern comes in during your visit to explain to Dad that he'll be having a port inserted under the skin of his arm, so as to make the constant IVs and blood tests and chemo easier to administer, ask her whatever you want, but only after asking Dad's permission.

The next morning, the port goes into his right arm, halfway between elbow and shoulder. I suggest we go to Georgia as soon as he's let out of the hospital and given clearance by surgeons and specialists.

Dad seizes upon this notion, consulting datebooks and projecting estimated drug course completion times. He hands me his cell phone. *Call Troy Eugene Johnson. Let him know we're headed for Big Foot Country.*

My sisters and I compare schedules and entertain scenarios. The leaves are turning across Philadelphia, a chill has seeped into the night air, and mums bloom vigorously, boasting their hardiness. Fall is passing us by.

The elbow surgeon is conservative. At their next meeting, he advises Dad to stay in town at least until the first of October. Dad expresses no regret, no disappointment. Neither do my sisters and I, in front of our father, but among ourselves we are forlorn.

October comes and also begins to drift away, until the 18th, when Dad gets the green flag. "Lois said she is ready to go as soon as Lise could arrange the trip," he writes in a group e-mail to his girls and to Jackie, "and I, Yours Truly, is champing at the bit. The sooner the better."

WITH THE HELP of airport attendants able to push two wheelchairs at once, I escort Dad and Lois to Georgia at the end of October. They'll have only a month here, until some of us come for Thanksgiving weekend and take them home at its end. This abbreviated fall visit is fine with Lois, who would rather be in their apartment, her paid companion in every weekday and her four children nearby.

Dad has indeed contracted Troy's neighbor, Claudia Andrews, to come be with Lois at the farm each day. In low-voiced conversations and clandestine phone calls, Lois, Diane, Margaret, and I agree that Claudia's meal-fixing, laundry-doing, and general watchful presence are essential for Dad, too, even if he doesn't see it.

On the first full day of their visit, Dad expects Claudia at 7:30 A.M. She does not show up. You could not ask for a worse start with my father. He calls after a time, and it turns out he'd told her to come later and she had been just sitting around waiting. Dad will blame her, but I've seen him slipping enough lately to know that the miscommunication likely stemmed from him. Claudia shows up minutes after his call. She must have run to her car.

I leave the next day and call in regularly to check on how things are going.

Leesee. I made a list this morning of all the things I want to do and I lost the list.

Ha. So . . . Claudia seems to be working out.

Yes. So far. She's willing and seems competent.

And is sharp.

If you say so. I'm waiting for the other shoe to drop.

Why?

Because if it is mechanical, it will malfunction, and if it is human, it will err.

What will you do when it does?

You have to stay on an even keel and seek calmer waters.

Dad, I can't keep up with these metaphors!

Well, I told you I lost my list.

HALF OF THE TIME when I call, Lois answers and Dad is out. Within a few hours he'll return the call, explaining that he's been picking up pecans or feeding the fish or going to the barbershop.

Whaddya have to report? I'll ask, a line I learned from him. Or, *I'm just calling to check in.* These are our signal greetings, justifications for calls that are about nothing but calling.

We talk about the usual stuff: local politics and the lack of progress on Funderburg Park, which Dad now attributes to misuse of funds, or, as he begins to refer to it, "malfeasance." When farm- and health-related topics are exhausted, I bring up my ace in the hole: my niece Phoebe, now eight years old. Dad barely knows how to talk to his only grandchild, although you can feel the desire for contact bursting from him whenever she's around. If we're at some family event where my relationally skilled mother is present, I see Dad try to sit by the two of them, lapping up the easy rapport grandmother and granddaughter have had since Phoebe's birth. Dad asks about her always. *Have you seen the Phoeb? Got any stories of the Phoeb?*

I mention that at Thanksgiving, I'm going to try to pass on to Phoebe my fish-catching luck. Previous efforts to teach her how to fish have been fruitless—not even one bite on record—and bouts of impatience and self-hooking have only complicated the matter. Dad jumps on board, and Phoebe's angling becomes a regular portion of our phone calls, mostly discussions of which bait or lure might be more successful or easy to handle. One day, I retrieve a voice message:

Leesee, darling? I think I have solved your problem about Phoebe catching a fish. The catfish have been responding to my throwing the kibble out there. Now they make noise and come up and, uh, entertain ya as you stand on the dock and watch 'em. So what I think you should, uh, anticipate is one, you gotta gotta gotta, uh, somehow acquaint Phoebe with throwing the line out, and you and somebody else can, uh, work that out, I'm sure. Then you gotta shorten the, uh, distance from the bait to the, uh, whaddya call it, the little bubbly, the-the-the cork, to about twelve inches. So when you throw the kibble out, you cast out among the kibble with this shortened, uh, bait, uh, shortened line. And you're guaranteed to catch a catfish! And it may be a big one! So I'm excited about the possibility and, uh . . . you can work out the details and I will just be the grandstand, uh, spectator, uh, cheering you along. Bye-bye.

* * *

AT THE START of Thanksgiving week, Dad leaves several messages each day to discuss how we're going to keep the *Caja China* pig cold between the time it's delivered and John arrives to cook it. On Tuesday, Dad calls to say that Lois suggested we use the *Caja* as a cooler, embedding the pig in bags of ice. We did this for the first pig roast, and I don't call back. Enough already. I am busy with work, trying to minimize how much the upcoming trip will set me back.

On Wednesday, I call to check in. Dad is less peppy. The butcher from the Piggly Wiggly delivered the pig earlier today but Dad sent it back. We aren't cooking till Friday, and Dad figured the supermarket's refrigeration would be better. Dad mentions in passing that the Isuzu wouldn't start so he went up to Covington Ford, across from Ingles, and bought a new truck. I ask for details.

It's a Ford Expedition, 2002.

What color?

Brownish color.

Something's off: I've heard him be more enthusiastic about a new brand of supermarket coffee. He used to purchase his work cars by telephone, surprising the salesman when he turned down offers of test drives. But this is a farm vehicle, and decisions associated with the farm are usually savored. Maybe he's just put out that the Isuzu finally quit after all these years. Maybe he's got precompany jitters. I've seen him get wound up when he's anticipating guests, and John and Phoebe, the newest additions to the family, still inspire Dad to impress and entertain. Maybe he's just distracted.

Holiday traffic and delayed flights plague the Philadelphia contingent, which consists of Margaret, her husband Greg, Phoebe, John, and me. Diane has opted out of this trip, choosing instead to accompany our mother to see her side of the family in Minnesota. We spend most of Thanksgiving Day in transit and pull up to 354 Fellowship Road at 6 P.M., taking up a good portion of the driveway with our supersize SUV rental, the only thing that would fit us, plus Dad and Lois, on the return trip to the airport.

We find Lois and Dad in their usual spots. He's anchored to his chair at the kitchen table, in the middle of things and almost blocking traffic in and out of the door to the garage. Lois is in her recliner in the sunroom, reading a book she holds with gloved hands. Her hands are always cold.

SUPPER'S READY, Dad says as we come in the door. *Please serve it.*

Margaret and I drop our bags in the dining room and go to the kitchen to see what's there. At Dad's urging, I'm sure, Lois has orchestrated a Thanksgiving meal using Claudia's services. We find a turkey breast sitting dry and lonely, in Lois's clay baker, sided by macaroni and cheese. Our cousin Carolyn has come down from Atlanta and arrived just minutes before us.

After Carolyn's initial period of shock about Jackie, she had grown curious, and once the time line clarified that no hanky-panky had happened behind Aunt Ruthie's back, the news seemed to threaten no one. Carolyn and Jackie talk on the phone and Carolyn has come to visit and spend the night in her—their?—grandfather's old house on Funderburg Drive at least once. This weekend, Carolyn is open but not gushing. Jackie announces their siblingness at every turn. *Where's my favorite half sister?* she calls as she comes through the door.

Carolyn does feel like a fourth sister to Diane, Margaret, and me. She was trained by the colonel, Dad's younger brother, Charles, and so when my father commands us to get the food on the table, she responds instantly.

In the kitchen, everything is broken or breaks at a touch. The oven doesn't work; the dishwasher's jammed; I pick up the coffee thermos and it falls, in pieces, onto the floor. When it comes time for dessert, the ice-cream scoop breaks in half. Someone mentions the new truck. Dad says, *It won't start.* Dad himself won't start. He barely moves from his chair, gives no golden handshakes of welcome, and shows none of the sparkle he's had in recent phone calls. His voice, when he does speak, is gravelly, and not once during the evening does he refer to Phoebe as "Granddaddy's darling," his usual refrain when she's within earshot.

Friday morning promises a sunny, pleasant day. Claudia comes at seven-thirty to make Lois breakfast, but some of us have gotten up already, so Lois tells her she can go home. Before leaving, Claudia unburdens herself to Margaret and me.

He gave me a rough time, she says to us more than once, anxious for us to understand what's been going on with our father. We thought Claudia's job was to be a companion and safeguard for my father and Lois. Apparently, he saw her sitting down as idleness. He would order her to do tasks all around the farm, often just before she was to go home. From Claudia's tone, and her repeated use of the word *rough*, I'm guessing Dad was short with her, most likely his signature combination of expecting much but saying little to make his expectations clear. A surefire recipe for mutual disappointment. Margaret and I apologize repeatedly on his behalf. We are used to his clipped instructions and peevish rebukes, but I can't imagine how it would feel to be newly on the receiving end of them.

Dad had a rough time of his own, Claudia tells us, doubling over in pain a week earlier, none of which he mentioned in our daily phone calls. Claudia took him to the hospital. A CT scan revealed gallstones.

I'll find my way home, he said to Claudia, telling her to go back to the farm, where she could be available to Lois. But when Claudia's workday ended, she drove by Jasper Memorial and found him there, finished and rideless. She drove him back to the farm.

Dad's rough time clearly has not come to an end, and Margaret and I whisper to each other and to Lois whenever Dad is out of the room as we try to figure out what's going on. He has been like this for days, Lois tells us. Margaret and I make forensic comparisons of our recent talks with Dad. We pinpoint the change as having begun in phone conversations a couple of days earlier. He suddenly lost his spark. He was less in the middle of things, less picking up pecans, less training the catfish to come when kibbled, less darting about in general. His voice grew increasingly thick, he was home when we called, and he sounded tuckered out.

While we piece together recent events, John fixes the stove (bent door latch), and Greg fixes the dishwasher (clogged drain). Before 9 A.M., Troy comes by so he and John can drive over to the Piggly Wiggly in Jackson and retrieve the previously rejected pig. The house is surrounded by trucks: Dad's old Isuzu and new Ford, neither of which will start; Troy's 1983 Chevy S10, a bantamweight half-ton pickup that's scuffed and scraped and still working hard even as it approaches the 300,000-mile mark; Carolyn's new silver Infiniti QX4, a streak of stuffed Tigger characters hanging from its rearview mirror; two monstrous Fords belonging to the Automobile Association guy and Ford dealership guy, respectively; and our rental, which someone has dubbed "Big Mama."

Both of Dad's vehicles have dead batteries. He left the Ford's lights on, the dealership rep discovers, but the Isuzu's problem is unclear. Both trucks are jumped and charged, and their engines turn over willingly. Troy follows Dad into town, to the BP station owned by Ben Tillman's brother-in-law, so the mechanic can determine if the Isuzu needs a new starter. When Dad and Troy return in Troy's truck twenty minutes later, they are laden with smoked ham hocks from Ingles for Margaret, who has either volunteered or been volunteered to cook collard greens.

We had hoped to get greens from Troy's garden, but by this time of year, most of the crop has been picked, cooked, and eaten.

How do you cook your greens? Troy asks Margaret after he hands her the hocks.

I use smoked turkey legs for seasoning.

What?! Troy exclaims, throwing off a look of mortification. *Where you from? New York City? People down here don't want no turkey in their greens. They want their greens greasy* [gree-zee].

By the time the sun hits its high mark in the sky, the temperature is 60 degrees. The under-seventy set divides and subdivides into fishing excursionists, TV watchers, snackers, and errand runners. Dad gravitates toward whatever action there is, but he doesn't partake. He mostly sits at the kitchen table amid the comings and goings, droopy and slow. He looks sleepy most of the time, his left eyelid half closed.

On his instruction, Carolyn and I drive to the Monticello Pecan Company on Highway 83 to pick up the order he'd dropped off a few days earlier. The company's building is a squat cinderblock rectangle capped by a pitched roof, crouching under the shadow of the town's water tower and up the road from a self-serve car wash. Otherwise, pastures and forests are its neighbors. Barbed wire–topped chain link surrounds the property, a deterrent to any pecan theft rings that would otherwise run rampant. Two piles of husks sit to the left of the entry, the newer mound holding the rust red of the shell's internal membranes and the older one faded to a dull brown.

Shelling machinery takes up half the building's interior. Customers are barred from the shelling room, a Seussian conglomeration of pipes and fans and screens and conveyor belts, as well as square-topped funnels and no less than seven husk-collecting galvanized garbage cans. The noise of the fans and motors fills every inch of air space and cuts through the dust raised from the crushing of the shells.

The cracking and shelling costs thirty-five cents per pound, but Dad goes the whole nine yards, as he calls it. Proprietor Tommy Beasley cracks, shells, and then dries the pecans for three hours in one of his two gas furnaces, which extends the shelf life of the nut meats. He then has an employee who isn't present at the moment—"the girl," as Beasley calls her (Race alert! Sexism alert? Accurate age reference nonalert?)—run the meats on a conveyor belt to grade them, picking out shriveled or rotted specimens and clinging shell remnants. The whole nine yards is what Beasley would have to do to meet state requirements if he were going to sell the nutmeats retail, as he does in good years, portioned into one-pound bags.

Cracking, shelling, drying, and grading brings the cost of Dad's fourteen-pound order to a whopping $8.40. The end product is delivered in a brown paper grocery bag, top rolled over and taped down into a flat, roughly rectangular package, dotted with oil stains. *Gree-zee*.

A handwritten logbook sits on the pecan company counter underneath a shellacked wall plaque featuring a squirrel and the legend "Welcome to the Nut House." The book is open to the page of current orders, and Dad's shows up toward the bottom of the nearly filled page. A few people have brought in as little as six pounds. Maybe they only have one tree on their property, or the kids found them in the wild. Others have brought in hundreds.

Back at the farm, everyone comes and goes in individual orbits. Phoebe sits on the sunroom couch, fixated on the cable television cartoons she doesn't get at her broadcast-only home, while Carolyn sits beside her, talking with Lois about favorite mystery writers.

Margaret, Dad, and I drive into town to mail eight boxes of pecans to people who are either in Dad's good graces or with whom he wishes to curry favor. Because I was the one tasked with boxing and labeling, under Dad's weary but watchful eye, I manage also to add two cousins from my mother's side who happen to love pecans. Dad waits in the truck while Margaret mails packages, her pile framing the clerk's window. Crawford Ezell, a contemporary of my father whose own father, Frank, was the county's sheriff for almost thirty

 years, sees my sister in the post office, then stops by the truck to say hello. Dad invites him to the pig roast. Then we check on the Isuzu, since we're just around the corner from the BP station. It's ready. It needed a battery.

Margaret takes the Trooper, Dad and I take the Ford. We stop at Ingles on the way home, and my father stays in the truck while I shop. I only have a few items on the list, but I deliberate over which cookies, which shelter magazine, which type of yogurt for the picky granddaughter. I stand in line and scan the front of the store. Framed photos of proud managers and associates line the wall, and below them, a long glass-fronted case holds chewing tobacco and snuff. When I come to the end of the case, I see my father. He stares blankly, and I see that the inside of one pant leg is soaked with urine. It takes a million years for the person in front of me to pay, another eon for my handful of items to be scanned and totaled, change made, items packed each into its own sack, a region-specific wastefulness. Dad stands erect, his eyes fixed straight ahead, waiting for me to come into view. When I finally get my bags, I head for him.

Do you want to go to the men's room?

It's too late for that. No rancor, just a statement of fact.

When we reach the new truck, Dad waits for me to cover his seat with plastic bags before he hoists himself up and inside.

Maybe you could help me out when we get back to the farm, he says. *You could put these pants in the wash and maybe they'll be dry in time for the pig party.* His closet is full of pants, waist sizes from thirty-six to forty-four, but these are the ones he likes.

You bet, I say.

JOHN AND TROY COME BACK from Jackson with the pig and two bags of charcoal, one of them Dizzy Dean's Ole Diz Charcoal Briquets, featuring the photographed head of Jay Hanna Dean (1911–1974), who pitched for the St. Louis Cardinals and Chicago Cubs and presumably showed some skill at the grill. His head on the bag is superimposed over a signed baseball, and he wears a fedora tipped slightly back. John also has the pig's head and feet to bring back to Philadelphia for Claudia. He thinks this will be funny. But this is not the sweet Wilbur face he'd envisioned. The head, resting on a yellow tray, has been skinned right down to the turned-up snout and, to John's disappointment, has had its brain removed. The severed ears are laid up against the side of the head, dainty toes poking out from underneath. The eyes have been left intact, plaintively staring through clear shrink-wrap.

The pig's body is shrouded in white, garbage bag–grade plastic, a petroleum product ghost with a pert little tail making a pup tent at one end. With plastic pulled back, the pig is naked to the world, a meat inspector's blue stamp soaking into the flesh near the spine and along a graceful, supple curve that reminds me of the tattooed young college women and men I teach in Philadelphia, mandalas and butterflies peeking out above low-slung waistbands.

John spreads the carcass between the two *Caja China* grids, then uses pliers and wire cutters to snip and twist lengths of wire between the grids, securing the pig inside. He and Troy try to lower the sandwiched pork into the roasting box. The hefty pig won't fit in as is, so they pull it out, lay it on the floor of the garage, and set about cutting off more of each leg joint. They develop a two-step process: first John uses a knife from the kitchen to cut through the meat, then Troy follows him, severing the bones with a hacksaw.

Dad changes into a temporary pair of pants and is ready to execute his plan for Phoebe to catch a fish. He had Claudia Andrews buy three plastic tubs of red wigglers yesterday, on Thanksgiving morning, and now Phoebe, Dad, and I, three generations of Funderburgs, head for the pond, fish-luring kibble in hand. We park as close as possible to the pond's edge and trudge across the beach to the fishing dock. The day is bright, the water glistens. We are surrounded by pine and oak, the Phoebe Funderburg Moore Woods. I look for the heron that sometimes flies across the pond, always east to west, a four-foot-long stream of grace launched by the arrival of boisterous humans. Sometimes we can only hear its call, a cranky sound Holsey was the first to point out to me.

Hear him holler? [Him-ha?] he asked.

Today's soundtrack is a mix of smaller birds I can't identify, and the crunching sound of cows in the woods above the far bank. Phoebe tells me quietly that she wants to throw the kibble out into the water, but Dad has already started. He doesn't see the fun of it. He doesn't know how to engage the girl, to keep her invested and not bored. He doesn't recognize that throwing anything would appeal to the eight-year-old set. Since her birth, practically, I've struggled against the urge to mediate between them, to run interference whenever I see her heading into some sharp word or remonstration. But Dad's been so obsessed with this plan, with how to make it work out right, I can't resist butting in. I tell him she wants to throw the kibble. He obliges. Then he puts the line into the water while she stands by idle and increasingly fidgety, and he holds it there until it tugs. He hands the rod to Phoebe so she can reel it in. She knows she didn't catch the fish, but she doesn't fuss. At eight years old, she has started to treat both my mother and father differently from other adults. She doesn't quibble with them the way she does with her parents and aunts. Her grandparents ask her to do something, she does it.

Margaret has walked down to the pond in time to see this historic event and take photos. Phoebe reels in a ten-inch catfish. Dad is satisfied. Phoebe is well behaved, not beaming the way she does when she feels like *she's* done something. Dad, having done his duty, retreats up to the house. The day is crisp and pretty, but he won't stay. Maybe he wants to be sure the pig party preparations are under way, maybe he just doesn't have the energy.

I stay with Phoebe and we keep fishing. It's cold enough to warrant fleece vests and pullovers, but sunny. I spend less time fishing than I do baiting lines and unsnagging snags—and when that fails, cutting lines and tying on new hooks (a secret handshake of filament twists and loops recently passed on to me from the owner of Monticello Farm & Garden). John joins us, taking up a rod for himself. Not too much time goes by before Phoebe catches her own fish. She holds the rod firmly and reels it in but can't lift it out of the water. Her little rod bends almost in half, and Margaret takes over, dragging the line around to the side of the dock and then along the bank, tugging the fish up onto land and John yelling, *Play it! Play it!* the whole while to uncomprehending ears.

The big cats won't stop feeding on our worms, and we each catch a fish, even the reluctant last arrival to the dock, Carolyn in her Tigger sweatshirt and kitten heels. The catfish croak at us while we try to remove the hooks. Some people describe that sound as belching, others liken it to rubbing a balloon between fingers. I liken it to last words. The fish are scaleless, fleshy, and pliable, and the hooks seem to lodge more vigorously than they do in the bream and the bass. It's tricky to disengage the barb: we're trying to avoid their whiskerlike barbels, convinced by folklore that they contain poison.

By early afternoon, my father drags himself from the house to the garage and sets himself up on his rolling utility stool.

Leesee, he calls.

Yes, Dad?

Get my etching gun from the garage and Phoebe's fishing rod, will you?

This etching tool has marked many a gun, camera, and wine bucket with Dad's Social Security number. Today, while Phoebe watches, he inscribes "Phoebe" along the shaft of the rod she used. In the moment she demonstrates no feeling about this personalization, but in the future she will fish with no other rod.

Troy and John drive up with a picnic table in the back of the truck. John says Troy, who's seventy-five, lifted up his end like it was nothing. One-fingered. The table sits at the edge of the garage driveway and turns, for the late morning and early afternoon of Friday, into a fish-processing station. We have the fish we caught and four more retrieved from the fish trap, a chicken-wire box with a one-way entrance that hangs from a chain off the end of the fishing dock.

Dad often sets it with bait, and by the next day he'll find bream and bass and catfish and the occasional turtle inside. Altogether, today's haul is twenty catfish, an amount that constitutes, technically speaking, a "mess."

John takes on the fish cleaning with Margaret's help. Their approach seems improvised: they cover the table with newspaper and raid Dad's tool bench, picking out hammers, thick nails, pliers, and wire cutters. They commandeer work gloves, a plank of spare lumber, and, from the kitchen, a fillet knife and wooden cutting board.

I find and print cleaning instructions from the Web, much of which are focused on techniques for peeling back the catfish skin. By the time I bring the papers outside, the duo has improvised a system similar to the methods I've collected, although John's extra touch, which he maintains is standard catfish-skinning procedure, is to nail the fish through its head and onto the plank. The live fish. This seems gratuitous, literal overkill, but if I'm going to keep my hands clean, I need to keep my mouth closed.

They end up cleaning all the fish. John does the skinning, gutting, and decapitation. Margaret does the finish work, the filleting. The picnic table has become a testament to ichthyological carnage: blood and guts dripping everywhere, fish heads gasping for air even after their bodies are gone. Entrails fill a bucket: veined swim bladders, chunks of tail, venomous spiny fins, sheets of skin, barbel whiskers now twisted and turned. In a large mixing bowl, freshly individuated filets soak in reddened water.

Carolyn watches from the padded driver's seat of her parked truck, door open, a safe distance from any spill or spray.

John finishes with the fish and moves on to the pig. He strains his marinade, a musky orange liquid, then injects and injects and injects.

I'm going to Ingles, I announce. I'm getting cornmeal for the fish fry and mayonnaise and pickles to make tartar sauce. *I'll come along*, Dad says. He has come up with another fishing instruction idea that requires props. He wants a ball, he says, to put on a fishhook so he can teach Phoebe to cast without risk of catching human flesh. He assumes we'll go to one of Monticello's two dollar stores, but I suspect Ingles will furnish his quarry. Once we're inside, he uses a shopping cart as a walker and I leave him in the toy aisle to go find my ingredients. When I come back, he's found no ball but instead is holding a large dump truck. We walk in silence toward the check-out, and once we're in line, I say, *I'll just go take one more look*.

Among the plastic soldiers and false fingernails, I find a thin wooden paddle with an elastic string stapled to the center of one side, and a soft pink ball secured to the other end of the string.

Perfect, Dad says when I return. He takes the paddle from me, and I head one last time to the toy aisle to put the truck back.

SATURDAY TURNS OUT to be a colder, grayer day. In the morning, John takes Phoebe and Jackie's same-aged granddaughter down to the pond. Dad recruited John into conducting the pink-ball-casting lessons in the driveway the night before, and the instructions may or may not have paid off. He and the girls stay down for hours and he comes back exhausted, describing tangled lines, hooks in cloth-ing, and lots of casting and reeling in but little of the in-between of waiting for the bobber to be pulled down. Somehow, each caught a fish or two.

I spend an hour on the treadmill to counteract impending pork consumption. Lois passes by on her way to the bathroom, herky-jerking along on her walker.

I think your dad is depressed, she says, *because he worries he'll never feel well again.*

Dad solicits a ride into town. He wants to stop by Eddie Ray's to see if Leon Tuggle is inside so that he can invite him to the pig roast. Leon Tuggle is a white man my father's age. More than once I have heard that as a child he bloodied my Uncle Owen's nose and was consequently punished by his mother, whom, for this reason, Troy still describes in reverential tones.

She was a nice lady, he'll say, whenever Tuggle's name comes up.

Leon Tuggle is also the grandson of a local legend, a farmer named John S. Williams. In 1921, white farmers around Jasper County still practiced an indentured servitude that was indistinguishable from slavery. Like most white farmers, Williams relied on black labor for keeping his crops planted, tended, and harvested. Some farmers, including Williams, relied on peonage. They would offer bail to men who'd been jailed, usually for a trumped-up charge, in exchange for the prisoner's labor. This was supposedly better than ending up on the chain gang, a fate my grandfather had warned my willful young father against many times over.

My father didn't have to be told about chain gangs. While he was still in elementary school, he sat on his front porch and saw the chain gang working on the road in front of his house. This was decades before the road was paved and before my grandfather successfully lobbied the town into pouring sidewalks, and so the convicts were clearing the washed-out gulleys on either side of the road and resurfacing it with white clay that compacted, sort of, into a drivable surface. There was Mr. Couch, the same neighbor who'd asked Grandfather for help in opening a savings account. Mr. Couch had been caught making corn liquor and was sentenced to twelve months. Now he was one of the convicts rebuilding the road, convicts who had to ask permission to urinate or defecate by saying *Number one, Boss,* or *Number two, Captain,* then had to bring back evidence of their functions on the end of a stick.

One Christmas during my father's childhood, the doctor who normally treated chain gang prisoners had gone out of town. The prisoners had been given alcohol, a holiday treat, presumably, and a fight had broken out. One convict was hit across the face with a shovel and the guard called my grandfather, who decided to take my father along.

My dad remembers that when they arrived at the camp, far out in the countryside, they were led into a cabin where bunks were stacked in threes, scarcely any space between the beds. A prisoner called Long John stretched out on a bottom bunk, bleeding from the cheek and nose.

I can't treat him here, Granddaddy said. *I need more room.*

Get up, Long John, the prison guard commanded.

Gettin' up, Cap'n.

Walk, Long John.

Walkin', Cap'n.

Long John walked into the mess hall and lay across one of the wood tables. Granddaddy tried to clean blood from the wounds, but Long John fidgeted.

Be still, Long John.

Bein' still, Cap'n.

As a result of the same dubious accounting practices that kept tenant farmers beholden to landlords even after abundant harvests, laborers on peonage farms couldn't seem to work off their debt. Sometimes a pretense was made that the laborers had incurred new obligations through housing or food costs, but at the farm of John Williams, it seems no pretense was made at all. Williams and his grown sons carried guns and showed no reluctance to use them. In an unusual move, they even allowed Clyde Manning, a black field hand who had grown up on their land, to be armed. The black parolees were intimidated, whipped, and locked in their quarters after dark, with doors bolted and windows nailed shut no matter how hot the night.

The practices of the Williams farm might have gone unnoticed, except that one farmhand escaped and took his story to the Georgia Bureau of Investigation. In February 1921, two agents were dispatched to investigate. They interviewed Williams, the overseer, and the hands. Williams denied any wrongdoings, and not one of the black laborers uttered a word of complaint. But after the agents left, Williams, presumably for fear of what might come next, disposed of the evidence. Under his direction and by his own hand, eleven farm hands were murdered in the space of two weeks. They were shot, buried (possibly alive), axed to death, or, lured by the promise of going home, driven to and then thrown off area bridges, chained to rocks meant to keep their thrashing bodies from rising to the water's surface.

Williams's crimes, eventually discovered by bureau agents who'd been dissatisfied with those initial interviews, made the national and regional press, white and black. My grandfather had to have read about this in articles published mere months before he moved to Monticello.

I USE DAD'S TUGGLE-SEARCHING TIME in the barbershop as a chance to look for printer cartridges on the square. Dad has asked me several times to print out photos of this weekend for Lois. He likes to show her what's going on in the world beyond her chair, and to supply materials for the photo albums he's always trying to get her to make, and which she seems to hold on to the notion of making, although for years now there's been no indication this will happen beyond her throwing away unwanted shots. Neither the Radio Shack nor the stationery store has the right cartridges, which is not surprising, given the limited customer base. Only big-box stores thirty and forty miles away would keep such a comprehensive inventory.

When I come back to the barbershop I stay by the car. I am hoping to avoid the proprietor, who tends to hug a few seconds longer than I'd like and stand a few inches too near. Sure enough, though, Eddie Ray comes out and close-talks me.

Your daddy left me a surprise, he whispers in my ear. *He left me two fish.* I back away and try to appear joyous.

Oh, good, I say. I remind myself that he used to call Uncle Holsey every day, just to check in and say hello. Every day.

Y'all take care of me, Eddie Ray whispers. *I got enough for a fish fry now.* Every day. Without fail.

THE PICNIC TABLES, Troy's and ours, are set up in the garage, and the fully cooked pig is laid out on one of them in its crispy, cross-hatched glory, diamonds of pig candy skin waiting to be eaten. As soon as food is set out on the kitchen table, my father sits at the opposite end from his usual seat and eats. He seems oblivious to the lack of other guests. He eats more robotically than usual and doesn't look up until he's done.

The first guest to arrive is Jerry Goldin. Actually, he arrives twice. Several hours early to drink beer and stand around the box with John as John arranges and rearranges the coals. Then again, to stand around with John and a plate of food. I have taken to inviting him every time we come to town, disregarding the fallout from the Happy Debacle, glad to have Jerry's good-natured wisecracking nearby. Rain pours down through much of the afternoon, and the turnout is poor. In the end, only about thirty people show up, a third of whom are the hosts.

Eddie Ray is invited to the Pig Party, but he doesn't come. Neither does Claudia Andrews, nor the Howard twins, nor Leon Tuggle, whose path Dad did manage to cross. We don't know who else Dad has invited, but they don't come, either. Less than a third of the pig is eaten, even though John has tweaked his marinade to perfection, so perfect that Troy, who never asks for anything, asks if John has any left over. Troy beams when John hands over a quart-size mason jar, filled to its brim. Once again guests are pushed to take copious leftovers. For Jackie, we fill supermarket bags with pork and pies and most of the fresh fruit and vegetables accumulated over the last few days. She adds into her bags the unopened sodas and various chips and nuts, opened and unopened.

I want those Häagen-Dazs, she announces, heading for the freezer.

I might want some before we leave, Margaret counters.

Okay, Jackie says, *but I'm coming back for that ice cream.*

We leave the next day. But not until late, plenty of time to indulge in a few more sessions of fishing fever.

You want me to cast for you? Phoebe asks me. *I'm pretty good at it.*

Indeed she is. At one point in the afternoon, under a sun that has returned to glisten over the water, her well-cast line goes taut. It's a big one. So big she can't reel it in, so big her parents, together, can barely drag it onto the shore. It's a gigantic cat, a full fourteen pounds. It's half her height. Phoebe doesn't realize how unusual this is, that no one's ever caught anything close to it on any of Dad's ponds. No one knew such big fish lived in them. But it is only the third fish she's ever reeled in, including the Dad-engineered catch, and so to her it might as well be standard fishing fare.

We take many pictures. Phoebe pointing at the fish laid out in the grass. Phoebe standing next to an adult who holds up the fish. Phoebe lying on the driveway next to the fish. The fish has only one possible destiny.

That's a month of breakfasts, Troy says when he comes to pick it up.

MONTICELLO

I KNEW MY FATHER'S FATHER, Frederick Douglas Funderburg, in the last two decades of his life. He was already seventy when I was born, a distinguished but shrinking man. Pictures indicate that in his prime he was robust, arguably obese, but in my time his button-down shirts hung loosely from his frame, tucked into perma-press double-knit pants held up by suspenders he referred to as "galluses."

When I knew him he ate a banana every morning and checked his blood pressure each day with a kit left over from his days as a practicing physician. When he came to visit, or, later, when I visited him, he turned his entire attention toward me, undistracted by other cares or obligations. He taught me how to play cards: pinochle, casino, and gin. He was patient when I forgot a rule or flubbed an attempt to bridge while I shuffled, but he could not give away a great hand. As he threw down his victorious last card, he'd offer a sympathetic shake of the head and drawl, "Sad and touching. Sad and touching." In the time it took him to pick up the winning trick, he'd paraphrase a poem by Frank Lebby Stanton, the southern homilist:

> This old world we're a-livin' in
> Is mighty hard to beat;
> With every rose you get a thorn
> But ain't the roses sweet?

Once in a while, pretending sympathy, Granddaddy employed the expression that I thought for a long time had originated in my family, a locution that conveyed disappointment or bore witness to tragedy or simply asked, *Can you beat that?*, its accent laid heavily onto the first syllable, the next two descending in equal measure, likes steps down a staircase:

"Mm-mm-mm."

He lived to be ninety-seven. In the 1980s, five of his last birthday dinners were held at my father's house in Philadelphia, where Grandfather cooked or supervised the cooking of one of his specialties, roast leg of lamb. The keys to the dish's success were slivers of garlic slipped into deep cuts made across the surface of the meat, Campbell's cream of mushroom soup stirred into the drippings to render a gravy, and plenty of mashed potatoes.

Lois, back then a zealous family archivist, conscientiously attempted to make recordings of my grandfather, using a low-fidelity cassette recorder from an office supply store. The "on" button was pushed and left alone until tapes ran out, so there was as much of the business of eating—at one point, my father turned the pepper grinder twenty-five consecutive times—as there was of my grandfather's life story.

There was also a lot of my father. Although no one seemed to dispute his position as host, master of ceremonies, and general shot caller, he reasserted it constantly. He cut off Granddaddy's reminiscences: "Hey, Dad, we went over that. . . . That was not the story I was trying to prompt. . . . I think we've imposed upon you enough."

He challenged his father on points ranging from what year something happened to how to pronounce *irrefutable*:

"Think so, Dad? . . . Are you sure about that, Dad? . . . You want to defend that position you're taking?" At times, he was cloyingly solicitous. "Say something for posterity, Granddad . . . Tell me, what do you think young folk ought to do today?"

And he regularly interrupted whoever was speaking, no matter what the topic, to offer more food. "Is there anyone else that I can cut just a sliver of lamb for? Just a sliver? It's mighty, mighty good."

Despite his tendency to challenge in the name of accuracy, my father did not tolerate correction well. At one point, he was describing how Granddaddy's patients paid him during the Great Depression. "There used to be four and five wagons lined up in our driveway on Saturday," Dad said. "Two chickens. A bushel of corn."

"Not a bushel," Granddaddy said. "*Bushels* of corn."

"Well, whatever. Your fees weren't that high, so what the hell are you talking about?"

In the last recording, taped just months before Grandfather died, my father's slurring suggests more wine than usual. Grandfather was delighting the married couple who had come for dinner, the center of their attention for a time. Perhaps too much time. My father said to the woman, "My father has a photographic memory, and he bores you with it sometimes, reciting chapter and verse. My father can recite to you every door number, every birthday, everything that went on in the city of Monticello since nineteen hundred and twenty-two."

The guest seemed impressed. "Write it down," she encouraged my father. "Do you get him to write?"

"I don't get him to do a damn thing," my father said, " 'cause it bores the hell out of me. I don't want to hear it."

Despite the limited technology of these recordings, not to mention the obliterating clatter of plates and cross-talk and my father, I can still piece together twenty years later the texture of my grand-father's life and the world into which my father was born—so fittingly a breech baby, a newly minted nonconformist determined to hit the ground running.

GRANDFATHER WAS BORN in Anniston, Alabama, in 1889, thirty-three years after the United States abolished slavery. Anniston was a town of ten thousand, hugged up along the Alabama-Georgia border. Grandfather was the first of four boys. His father, George Washington Funderburg, was a foreman at Anniston's soil pipe foundry and a bootlegger on the side. His mother, Ophelia Blass-ingame Funderburg, was a homemaker known for her nonstop cooking ("That's what killed her," one of her in-laws once told me, "too much cooking.") and a forceful personality attributed, both disparagingly and admiringly, to her being half Creek.

As a child, Grandfather attended school sporadically. When he finished the equivalent of seventh grade, he went to teach in a one-room country school, then tried working in Alabama's coal mines. But he didn't want to end up like the undereducated, strug-gling blacks who dominated his community in Anniston's Furnace Hill section, where the shotgun shacks lacked even the basic southern amenity of a front porch. "The intellectual and cultural and social environment did not magnetize me in any sense of the word," he declared in one birthday dinner recording. "I left. I did not want any more life in Anniston or the coal mine. I moved to Atlanta. I went there a stranger."

It was 1906 when he made the ninety-one-mile trip. He was seventeen years old and nearly penniless, asking a cab driver to suggest a place where he might stay.

His first job was as a bellhop. He detested it. "I hated for the man in charge of the front office to tell me I had to clean the cuspidor. Damn it, I just didn't like it. I resented it like hell." When an acquaintance opened the Silver Moon Barber Shop and offered to teach Granddaddy how to barber, he didn't hesitate to make the move.

"That was 1911, and I worked there 'twelve, 'thirteen, and 'fourteen. The happiest years of my life I lived in Atlanta. There was a bridge club in the vacant room upstairs over the barber shop. There was a poolroom on the corner. I could go when business got dull to the matinees in the afternoon. When the grand opera came, I got employment up at the auditorium in the hat check concession so that I could hear [Enrico] Caruso, Frieda Hempel, *Lucretia Borgia,* and [Antonio] Scotti."

The Silver Moon was on Auburn Avenue, which guaranteed a passerby clientele of professional black men. Around the time my grandfather came to the city, one-third of Atlanta's 155,000 inhabitants were African-American, and Auburn served as their professional and commercial center. Several institutions on the street anchored black Atlanta's life: Big Bethel A.M.E. Church, the Odd Fellows building and auditorium, and Ebenezer Baptist Church, in which both Martin Luther Kings, father and son, preached. The entire street smacked of firsts: the first black-owned office building, the office of Atlanta's first black optometrist, the first black-owned drugstore, and the first black life insurance company. "Sweet Auburn," as it was known, was the "richest Negro street in the world," according to the civic leader John Wesley Dobbs, who lived in Atlanta from 1897 until his death in 1961.

The social structure in black Atlanta was said to be like a pie with no filling: there was an upper crust and a bottom, but no middle class. As a barber, my grandfather befriended railway workers, postal clerks, and doctors. He partnered in bridge games with a West Indian statistician who worked for the life insurance company, shot pool with Auburn Avenue habitués, went to house parties with college graduates, and played tennis with young men and women of whom much was expected. Even though he presided over the Silver Moon's prestigious first chair, Grandfather grew dissatisfied with his prospects amid the strops and razors, the witch hazel and bay rum.

"In the spring of nineteen hundred and fourteen," Granddaddy said on his ninety-second birthday as the rest of us ate lamb and potatoes smothered in gravy, and pressure-cooked green beans seasoned with cubes of fatback, "a friend came into the shop. He was bell captain at the Alabama Hotel. He had gotten married, saved enough money to make a down payment on a house, and moved his bride into it."

The news pushed my grandfather into a funk. When, he wondered, would he ever be able to do the same on the wages of a barber? He ruminated for days on end.

"I sat down and assessed my assets. I never had a hundred dollars above my needs. I lived and moved in the upper echelon, but I saw no potential there to acquire what I would need to have in order to live and interact on that plateau of society. I decided, finally, that I would strive for the attainment of my first love. Whatever the cost, I would tie up the broken threads of my aspiration and do what I saw a black man doing in my home when I was a child: practice medicine. Barbering was not my realm. I was going back to school and whatever the price, I was going to pay it to become a doctor."

A fine plan, but Granddaddy hadn't finished high school. A doctor friend helped him solve the problem: they manufactured a résumé that included a high school degree. His deceit, told to me not by Grandfather himself but by my father after Granddaddy's death, won him admission to a two-year premedical program at Raleigh, North Carolina's Shaw University, the oldest black college in the South. He paid his way through, barbering over the holidays and working for the railroad in the summers. He graduated and applied to Columbia University's College of Physicians and Surgeons in New York. Again he was accepted. Eleven years after leaving Alabama, he joined Columbia's incoming class of 1917, the first to admit women and in which he was most likely the only African-American, a point of information he may have hidden from the school.

He managed Columbia's coursework through the fall term but ran into trouble with chemistry in the spring. He worried that he would fail the course and be expelled, so he weighed his other options. World War I was still on. Grandfather knew that there were advantages to joining up rather than being drafted: as a volunteer, he could specify in which branch he'd serve. He headed for a recruitment office on Manhattan's lower Broadway. The U.S. military was and would remain segregated for another three decades. Pay scales were set accordingly, so it mattered that the recruitment officer never asked my fair-skinned grandfather his race. The recruiter did say, at one point, referring to the wiry texture of my grandfather's hair, "I've never seen a white man with black hair." My grandfather said nothing. Later on in the interview, the recruiter repeated his comment. Again, Grandfather said nothing.

Granddaddy shipped out as part of an all-white medical corps stationed in rural France. He saw no battlefields, and the armistice was signed shortly after his arrival, so his enduring memories were of Gallic cooking and gardening techniques.

When he mustered out, he transferred to a black medical school, Meharry Medical College in Nashville, Tennessee. He also proposed to Ethel Maude Westmoreland, a woman six years his junior. They met while Fred, working at the Silver Moon, was renting a room in the house of Ethel's sister Mamie. Ethel, the tenth of eleven children from a top-crust Atlanta family, had lost her mother at the age of twelve. She was raised by another beloved sister, Eva, and watched over by siblings in between. Ethel continued to live with Eva while waiting for Fred to finish his studies, even after the couple married.

In June of 1922, my grandfather's fate, and thus my father's, and thus mine, was cast. Four years before my father's birth, my grandfather stood on a corner of Auburn Avenue, having just

stepped off a train from Nashville. With a diploma he'd received at the end of May, he was freshly graduated from Meharry with, as he would point out even seventy years later, the second-highest average in his class.

He was thirty-two years old and ready to begin a residency that would equip him to carry out the school's mission, which was to care for underserved minority populations. His career stood ready to take off, and his personal life held equal promise. Ethel had given birth to their first child, Frederick Jr., on the thirteenth of March. My grandfather couldn't attend the birth. He pawned his gold watch to pay the obstetrician's fifteen-dollar delivery fee, and the last of his funds were reserved for paying off school accounts, a prerequisite for receiving one's diploma.

He had planned this June stopover between graduation and another summer of railroading, but the visit could not last long. Like many preprofessional African-Americans of the time, my grandfather earned relatively good wages as a Pullman porter, carrying luggage, cleaning shoes, and making beds for well-to-do white passengers on their way to summer retreats in the Adirondack Mountains. He performed the tasks well enough to make ends meet during medical school, and in fact well enough to curry the favor of one passenger, a Mrs. Chase of the Manhattan banking family, who gave him a small subsidy for school expenses. School was now over, his professional life was about to commence, but the income from railroading was too certain to ignore.

My grandfather started across Auburn Avenue, but a landau blocked his path. The horse-drawn carriage held four doctors, men my grandfather knew, some whose hair he'd cut. The men exchanged amenities with the young graduate, then invited him to climb up into the carriage.

"Get in and go with us!" one doctor entreated. "We're going out to the cemetery to bury Turner." The deceased was a black doctor who had practiced in a rural town sixty-five miles south of Atlanta.

Grandfather had heard of Turner: the nation's entire pool of black doctors consisted of fewer than thirty-five hundred people. But Granddaddy knew him only by reputation, that Turner was from an island in the Caribbean and had graduated from McGill University Medical School in Canada. Because Grandfather was going to meet his wife and new baby, he declined the carriage-borne doctor's invitation. Some days later, Grandfather again stood on Auburn Avenue. This time, he ran into his old bridge partner, the statistician.

"Funderburg," the man asked, "what are you gonna do this summer?"

"I'm going to New York and railroad, to work for the Pullman Company as I've done in past years. Then I've got an internship coming up in October," Granddaddy told his friend, "on the basis of the second-highest average in my class."

"Awww," the bridge partner said, "your days for railroading are over. What you ought to do is to go down to Jasper County and break into the practice of medicine. You've taken the board already.

Break into the practice of medicine and acquire Turner's library and office equipment.

"I'm co-executor, with his wife, of his estate," continued the partner, who, like Turner, was West Indian. "I'm going down this weekend, and I'll make arrangements for you to stay with her." And so my grandfather went.

MONTICELLO, IN THE CENTER of Jasper County, was a bustling farm town of 1,900 people, even though the county itself ranked as the state's poorest and most rural. On the ride down, my grandfather would have passed lush fields of spring wheat, acres of cotton planted by farmers who still hoped for profit despite the boll weevil's recent devastations, and orchard after orchard of peach trees, leafed out and verdant. The land was neither mountainous, like the Appalachian and Blue Ridge sections of north Georgia, nor flat, like the gulf and coastal plains further south and east. Instead, it was fertile, rolling piedmont, and it boasted several waterways. The Ocmulgee River, to the west, served as the area's major trade route until railroads came along. Murder Creek ran to the east, and the 4,700-acre Jackson Lake, created by a dam built in 1910, anchored the northwest corner of the county.

Monticello formed around the intersection of several highways. Routes 16 and 212 ran east-west, and Routes 11 and 83 were roughly north-south, creating a spider with the town square as its belly. A hotel, drugstores, groceries, banks, and the large department store, Benton Supply Company, framed the square. In the center stood a statue paying tribute to the Confederate fallen. Numerous memorials had been erected since the Civil War, but this particular style, a spiking obelisk topped by a lone soldier, had close likenesses in town squares across the South. All were erected around 1910 and funded by their local branch of the United Daughters of the Confederacy. The impetus was most likely no particular anniversary of a battle or invasion but rather the desire to pay homage while one or two of those being honored might still be alive to receive it.

Turner's widow had a house on Colored Folks Hill, at the top of Warren Street. The neighborhood was next to a well-to-do white section, physically separated by the rail line that angled into town from the city of Macon, forty miles away. Upon his arrival, my grandfather had to assess not only what the Turner estate had to offer, but also what kind of life Monticello would provide. He walked the town's streets, introducing himself first to the white leadership.

"I went to see the lawyer, the leading physician, and then the sheriff," he remembered. The lawyer was pleasant enough and the town's gregarious white physician, Francis Belcher, urged Grandfather to fill Turner's shoes.

"Funderburg," Belcher said, "your people need you. I hope you come."

Grandfather finally got to the sheriff, Will Persons, a man who was at that point only halfway through thirty-three years of holding his position. Grandfather spoke first.

"Sheriff," he said, "my name is Funderburg. I'm down here looking over Turner's field with the idea of coming to practice medicine."

Sheriff Persons wore a broad-brimmed black Stetson on his head and a six-shooter in his holster. Over six feet tall, he towered above my grandfather, who was only five feet eight inches. Persons responded to my grandfather's introduction by launching into a story of his various political contests.

"I ran for sheriff two terms and won," he told my grandfather. "The third term I lost. The fourth term I won. And the morning after the election, I met Turner on the street, and Turner said to me, 'Sir, I wanna congratulate you on your victory,' and shook his own hand. He was a good nigger. He knew his place."

* * *

WHEN HE TOOK LEAVE of Persons, Grandfather wandered off the square and into the black neighborhoods.

"I went among the black people, and they were most importunate. I can see the old lady rocking on her front porch . . ."

At this point in the tape, he switches into an unschooled country dialect, a way of speaking he resolutely avoided in the twenty-eight years I knew him, except for when he recited the sly vernacular poems of Paul Laurence Dunbar. Otherwise, Granddaddy veered in the opposite direction, toward a painstaking and baroque articulation. He was the king of the dependent clause, and he never, according to all available records, dangled a preposition.

"I jes' don' know whud I'm gon' do fuh a doctah," the woman said to him.

My grandfather took over Turner's practice. It was to be temporary, a way to get his feet on the ground. Then he'd move Ethel and baby Fred up to West Virginia, where a fellow doctor promised

there was money to be made by the baleful, where Granddaddy could be worth a hundred thousand dollars in just ten years, for him a fortune almost beyond imagining. But that's not how it turned out. As he built his practice and responded to the call of the destitute, trampled population around him, Monticello became home. And the family grew. Ilon Owen and Mary Hannah Howe Chase were born in the first two years. Two years after that, in the spring of 1926, my father arrived. The last child, Charles Edward, came along in 1930.

My grandfather held the curious position of heading up black Monticello's leading family. For many years he was the only black resident with either a college or postgraduate degree. He held one of the only jobs besides undertaking with a guaranteed income stream. Actually, since patients were often too poor to pay at the time of service, or in cash, or ever, it would be more accurate to say he had a guaranteed clientele. Still, the Funderburg house was two and three times the size of most neighbors' shotgun shacks. My father and his siblings never went hungry, and throughout my father's childhood my grandparents hired a neighbor named Annie Chapman to assist with the washing and cooking and cleaning that filled each day.

But the family's affluence was relative. In the separate-but-equal world of Jim Crow, the leading black family was still a black family. My grandfather received some privileged treatment. He was light-skinned and educated; he paid his bills and bank notes early rather than on time; and he made a point of conducting himself in a manner beyond reproach. As he said on one birthday, "I practiced medicine for fifty years in a rural community and boasted of the fact that no one had ever smelled liquor on my breath, and no one had had a drink of liquor with me. I had a bar in my house. Self-discipline."

His self-discipline would have meant little if a conflict were to arise or a spiteful accusation made. He was still the "nigger doctor" and therefore without recourse. As a consequence, he strove to protect his family from exposure. He forbade his wife to enter white-owned stores for fear of what could happen. It was bad enough that the youngest stock clerk would call her Ethel, not Mrs. Funderburg, but if she were insulted or threatened, Grandfather would have had to retaliate. If that happened, the family would have to leave town. Immediately.

He had to negotiate his own safety as well. In one incident, as he backed his sedan out of an angled parking space on the square, a white woman rear-ended him. She was in the midst of apologizing when a white policeman came along.

"Not so fast," the policeman said, and he began to recraft the incident with the fault falling to my grandfather. While my aunt Chase watched from the front seat, her father stood silent as the policeman carried on, insulting and threatening, finally permitting him to leave. He drove home humiliated, only to be greeted by a ringing telephone. It was a different white man, the manager of a store on the square who had seen the interchange. The manager had talked the policeman into backing off the threatened charges, and now worked to mollify Grandfather so that he wouldn't pack up the family and leave.

Whites had a vested interest in having a black doctor around to keep their labor pool healthy, and some benefited directly from his expertise. For many years, Granddaddy's only white patients were men who came knocking on the kitchen door, late at night, seeking treatment for venereal diseases. But when a flu epidemic hit the region in 1938 and temporarily put the white doctor out of commission, white citizens had no choice but to come to Dr. Funderburg for help. He built a reputation as a skilled diagnostician, and not all the white patients wanted to leave him after the flu crisis subsided.

Fitting an integrated patient roster into a segregated world was no small challenge. He devised a strategy that he first tried out in the town of Eatonton, which was thought to be somewhat less racist. When it worked, he brought it to his Monticello office, the former Odd Fellows' lodge he'd bought a block south of the square. In the front portion of the small building, its footprint no more than forty feet square, he made a rectangular waiting room, each half a mirror image of the other. Same art, same chairs, same flowers in the same vases. Mrs. Freeman, the office manager who kept the room spotlessly clean, made sure each day that even the ashtrays were positioned correspondingly. Grandfather put up no signs designating which race should sit on which side. He didn't have to. When patients came through the door, they segregated themselves. The left half would be white one day and black the next.

Grandfather took an active civic role, which included serving on the school board for decades, in both its segregated and integrated versions. Early on, he and his cohorts attracted well-trained teachers from Atlanta by reducing living costs. An empty building on Warren Street was converted into a dormitory, furnished with beds and cooking utensils, and offered free to the new hires, all young women. Beyond such efforts, Granddaddy also lent his reputation. In a town where blacks were expected to clear the sidewalk whenever a white person approached, where a black man had been shot for waiting outside a store for his wife longer than the proprietor appreciated, and where a black woman was slapped in the face for not calling the butcher "Sir," the simple act of buying provisions could be perilous as many of his postprandial stories showed.

> *None of the girls had any money when they came down to start teaching school. I would take them to Benton's Supply and ask the manager to open an account for them and make myself responsible for the paying. Well, bringing in five schoolteachers was giving them some business.*
>
> *Benton's had a country boy clerking in dry goods. One new teacher went in and she bought this and that and the clerk said to her, "Anything else?"*
>
> *She said, "No." And then she reflected a moment, "Oh, yes. I want some kerosene."*
>
> *"Have you got the can?"*
>
> *"No. I haven't."*
>
> *He said to her, "I'm a white man. Don't you say yes and no to me. You say 'Yessuh.'"*

Well, he frightened the girl. She came to the house and told my wife. My wife told me. I didn't want a community affair over it. I didn't want anybody taking revenge on her or on me. I finally evolved an approach. The man that ran the store was a very fair-minded Christian man. On a certain day, as he stepped up on the sidewalk out of the intersection, I stepped up on the sidewalk. Spoke to him. I said, "Mr. Malone, I have come to believe that hate is a destructive force. Destructive not only of the person towards whom it is directed, but also for the person who feels it." Now, that was the introduction. I said, "Your young man in the grocery department hates black people."

He looked at me superciliously. I recited the incident. He said, "Well, now, I'm surprised, Doctor. What happened to him over the counter is nothing more than what happens to me back at the office. I'll handle that."

Ten days later, I went in the store and he said, "Doctor, I looked on the books to see if that boy was selling those girls as much merchandise as he'd been selling them in the past, and I've sat here in the office and watched him when your teachers came in to see if he tried to avoid them. And I haven't seen any change in him."

Well, I wasn't quite satisfied with that. The girls got their paychecks. I went to them and said, "I want you to pay your bill, ask for receipts, ask that it be marked paid in full, and then when you get your bill, ask the clerk to close your account." All hell broke loose then.

That was, say, Thursday. Saturday I was in the store. The manager of the dry goods department was there. He stopped selling merchandise, came over to me, and said, "Doctor, I've been here X number of years and I've never lost any business." He said, "This boy was wrong. 'Yes' and 'no' is the English language. If you'll help me get that business back, I'll wait on your teachers myself."

What went around, came around. When Will Persons, the unwelcoming sheriff, grew too old to run for office, the alcohol control board threw a patronage job his way, a position with the office that tracked down moonshiners. Persons was breaking up a still one day and stepped on a ten-penny nail. "The irony of fate came into play," my grandfather exulted. "He had to come to me for treatment."

Because my grandfather never left, practicing medicine in Monticello for fifty years "to the day," as he would say, the place incorporated itself into his blood and the personal histories of his children and the two generations that have followed. Years after Granddaddy retired, after old age and frailty took him away—reluctantly, by then, because his memories lived there, the path and pace of life worn and familiar—he still marveled at how he had ended up with that town as his geography, how he had struggled to fulfill dreams and feed his family when the patients he treated earned no more than a dollar a day.

"When I found that I had let down roots," he said on his ninety-second birthday, "I often wondered what I had done to displease Almighty God to cause him to locate me in this godforsaken place."

8.

WEARING THIN

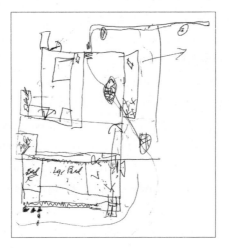

I T WAS A GOOD SUMMER and fall, full of improvements and abilities regained. Nothing was sweeter than taking Dad down to Georgia in October, watching him spurn the walker and cane, and head off to various putterings with a confident gait. For three or four months he had only gotten better. But Thanksgiving feels like a car thrown into reverse. We bring Lois and Dad back home at the end of the holiday weekend, and my sisters and I know that his run of luck is over.

Part of me will die when my father dies. I will exist less. I've always wrestled with wanting my father to know me even as I struggled to put up a front that would be acceptable to him, that would please him, that wouldn't aggravate him or spark his ire. Now I see that when he dies, there is a way in which the world will stop knowing me. There will be an end to a singular place I hold in another person's heart, all the more precious in how constant it's been despite his despotism, his unattainable and shifting standards.

In the week after we return, I stay by the phone for hours, hoping not to miss a call from Dr. Schnall, the oncologist, the doctor my sisters and I like the most, the one who alludes now and then to her late father, how he was difficult, too. She speaks so quickly that we have trouble following. Dad doesn't even try. He just offers to ship her peaches from Georgia and asks after her husband and daughter, when he can remember their names, names he's written down at least a half dozen times, names that I find peppered throughout his pocket calendars and address books. Schnall speaks with con-cern and dedication, affection, even, and none of us have trouble understanding that. She gives him a peck on the cheek before she releases him from her exams. She gives us her home telephone number and tells us to call anytime. When we crowd into her examining room to ask our questions, then apologize for taking her time, she gives us the same refrain: *You only have one dad*. That we understand.

We don't, however, get what has happened to our father. We have faxed questions to Schnall, and when she calls to respond, she agrees that in his post-Thanksgiving checkup, Dad wasn't as perky as he has been. Thinks we ought to check out his head, see what's going on. Has given him a prescription for a CT scan. Suspects a small stroke.

Stroke. This would explain the drooping on one side of his face, captured in every picture I took in Georgia. This would explain the sudden downturn: the increased confusion over appointments and logistics; more missed pills, days taken out of order, the compartments of his seven-day pillbox emptying in a random pattern, a blood thinner left behind here, a potassium pill left behind there;

increased loss of bowel and bladder control. The flatness of him, pleasure and irritability both blunted. Schnall's explanation offers up relief by giving it a name and by being something other than cancer-related, even as it opens up a new frontier of complications and demise.

After talking to Schnall, I talk to Dad, who says through his fog that Schnall gave him a prescription for pain medication. I don't contradict him, but I mention, as if in passing and to make conversation, that I know he's also got a CT scan coming up.

Diane visits him, seeing him for the first time since October. When she gets home, she calls Margaret and breaks down. She'd asked Dad if she could do anything for him, she tells Margaret. *He said, "Make me well."*

Margaret reports this to me. I wish she hadn't. I can only bear to feel what's going on in small doses. It's too hard to switch from the comforts of the last few months, our father mobile and relatively pain-free. I have to ease back into this dying thing. I have to gear up for what's to come.

MY SISTERS AND I fall into step in the face of our father's increasing frailty. We come up with tasks and apportion them among ourselves. We call one another with updates and to compare notes: what we've seen, what we've heard. It's his confusion that's hardest for me; his loss of a sense of command. In the same way people talk about relatives with Alzheimer's and schizophrenia, sometimes I don't recognize him. He's gone missing.

While we're waiting for CT scan results, my father calls and leaves a message. He thinks I have the flash to his camera, and he can't find instructions for it. I have no flash and I'm guessing the instructions are filed away somewhere in that assemblage of boxy, claustrophobic rooms that make up his and Lois's two-bedroom apartment. I listen to all of Dad's recent voice mails. I have been saving his messages for years. I used to tape-record them. I wanted evidence of his oddities and expectations and random mix of humor and peevishness. Now I save them in case they turn out to be evidence of his life. The difference pre- and post-stroke is stunning. Verve and vim in the earlier version of him, a parade of devilishness and playful tones and put-on accents. Then, post infarction, his voice turns molasses and craggy, phlegmed and dragging. He'll talk, but the wind is out of his sails, and there are no more conspiracies, no more elaborately crafted plans. No more *Yellow Fever, Yellow Fever, This is Sunshine, over*, the greeting we borrowed from his days in the Korean War, when he heard a radio operator use the phrase.

I call a social worker from Waverly about expanding my father's durable power of attorney to include one of us daughters along with Lois. This is with both Dad's and Lois's consent, and because my sisters and I are hypothesizing a scenario in which Lois might not be available, physically or mentally, to make a health care decision on Dad's behalf.

But my sister Diane, the social worker informs me, is already listed along with Lois. Once I know this, I'm ready to hang up. The social worker feels there's more to discuss. At length and repeatedly. How to make decisions on a loved one's behalf. How to make decisions not based on what we want but on what our parent wants. By the third round of instruction, I'm tempted to disagree, to say that after a certain point, it's not about what they want at all. The children and spouses are the ones who will have to live with themselves, with their actions, with the tied-up or unraveled or frayed ends of the ailing one's life. But the call has gone on too long as it is, with only one of us doing the talking.

The social worker emphasizes, again, that even though it's a difficult conversation for some people to have, we should make sure we know what my father's intentions and desires are, what kind of quality of life he holds as a minimum. Basically, what he wants. Basically, I want her to shut up.

The day the CT scan results are scheduled to come in, I drive across the river for Dad's appointment with his Waverly physician, Dr. Battaglia. Out of respect for patient privacy, I'm kept in the small, tidy waiting room during Dad's examination, a room differing from other waiting rooms I've seen recently only in the geriatric bent of its brochures and the increased incidence of wheelchair scuffs along the walls.

Eventually, a nurse leads me into the exam room.

Sit up there, Dad says, nodding at the examination table. I do.

Battaglia has seen the test report and confirms a subacute infarction, in other words, a not-fresh stroke, which jibes with the change in behavior we've pegged to a week and a half before Thanksgiving, give or take a day. Probably a frontal-lobe stroke, Battaglia elaborates, which affects the personality: overall affect, ambition, energy, concerns, and also speech. Check, check, check, check, and also check. Dad seems like a dulled knife, hypervigilance replaced by the barest awareness of what's going on around him.

Battaglia tells Dad not to drive, probably because Lois called Battaglia before this appointment to rat Dad out. She attempted to express her concerns to Dad directly, but he brushed her off. Lois rarely leaves the apartment and so hasn't been in the car with him for months, but she thought his new confusion over medications and chronologies and his inability to stay awake during the day weren't good indicators of his ability to maneuver a two-ton vehicle on public streets. And no one can tell how much he sees or doesn't; no one's been able to tell for months.

Not until the confusion clears up, Battaglia says.

I ask him to explain this driving sanction so that Dad can hear the reasoning. If workmen were on the road unexpectedly, Battaglia says, and traffic patterns changed and a kid crossed out of line all at once, that might be too much to react to and somebody, Dad or somebody else, could get hurt.

So don't you think not driving is a good idea? the doctor near-shouts at Dad, as if his hearing's gone bad or maybe to wake him up, as Dad looks like he's nodding off when he's not being directly spoken to. It's a grasp at buy-in, transparent as water.

No, Dad says. I find this dissension reassuring, familiar. Potentially dangerous, but comforting.

The doctor writes "No Driving" on Dad's medical chart.

In classic form, also unchanged by stroke, Dad has not mentioned to the doctor the consuming problem he's having with incontinence. Dad spends hours in the bathroom these days, wears diapers day and night, and still soils clothes and bedding so that each has to be changed at least once each day. I tell this to Battaglia. He suggests physical therapy. *The stronger you are, George, the more it might help you control yourself and get to the bathroom on time.*

Use it or lose it, I think. The diuretics Dad takes to keep his heart from having to circulate extra fluids aren't helping the matter, Battaglia concedes. Those are some strong doses the cardiologist has prescribed and probably bear most of the responsibility for the incontinence.

Next, I pass on Lois's news that Dad hasn't been eating. Battaglia rubber-stamps the obvious concern. *You gotta eat, George,* he says. *Even if it's Boost or Ensure.*

I ask for a recovery prognosis. Battaglia can't say. And then, even though my father is right there, I ask the doctor if Dad knows what's happened, knows that he's different from before. Battaglia says probably not, then turns to Dad and raises his voice.

Do you feel different, George?

No.

Do you feel like something happened to you?

No.

Apparently, according to the protime (prothrombine time) blood-clotting test Battaglia's office administered on Dad's return, Dad had not been taking his blood thinner, Coumadin, in Georgia.

If he had, the clot would most likely not have formed and the stroke most likely would not have happened.

How amazing. How amazing that someone like my father, with financial resources, abnormally high levels of medical care, and attentive family members, would be so out of sync with the medications he needed. I blame Dad. I blame his stubbornness and his intense need to be in control and free from others' scrutiny. Someone else, with a different ego, I suppose, might have recognized the missed or dropped pills as a problem that needed solving and assistance, rather than as a sign of weakness that needed to be masked or ignored.

I blame him without hesitation. It's comforting and exonerating to remember how much of his world, good and bad, is his doing. If he were easier, we could have stepped in earlier. The problem is, we're all learning about this aging and dying and the inversion of parent-child roles as we go along, sometimes a half step ahead and often, as is the case here, a crucial half step behind.

MY CAR IS PARKED outside the doctor's offices and I offer Dad a ride to his building, on the other side of Waverly's campus. He says yes, then changes his mind.

Would you like to have breakfast? he asks.

I don't want breakfast, and I'm worried about the time and the work that's waiting for me at home, but he hasn't been eating. So we walk down the maze of corridors connecting Muirfield, the medical wing, to Waverly's Coffee Shop. Dad moves slowly, leaning into his walker and stopping every ten paces or so to straighten up, arching his back and then pausing before rolling forward. We pass resident mailboxes, a wall of resident watercolors and pastels, and a small side table that, more often than not, holds a picture and framed notice of the most recent resident death. *The Amen corner,* Dad calls it.

When we reach the coffee shop door, he stops in front of the daily special board.

I can't see too good, Leesee, he says. *Read it to me.*

Every action is information, every motion or lack thereof a barometer. He winces with certain leg movements but denies feeling pain. He walks slowly but goes through the food service line and waits for his order instead of aiming straight for a table. He lets me carry his tray but eats everything on his plate and mooches a strip of bacon from mine.

Just as I made an album of our first pig roast, I've made one of the Thanksgiving weekend. I've brought along the pocket-size flipbook, and he looks through it with great curiosity once he's finished eating, no sign that he remembers any of the scenes he sees pixilated onto paper. If he sees them.

I'll lend it to you, but don't be trying to steal it, I joke. *Don't forget to return it to me.*

I get it, he says. My teasing has missed its mark.

I can make you one of your own, if you like. But I don't want to tread on Lois's territory.

Lois isn't doing anything, he bristles, then softens. *Anything you could do would be much appreciated.*

After breakfast, he sends me on ahead so I won't rush him. I leave him at the coffee shop door, walk back to the medical wing, drive my car around and past the town house he and Lois lived in for eleven years, park in a visitor's space in the back of their tiered apartment annex, call Lois from the outdoor intercom and wait for her to buzz me in, then take the elevator to the third floor. My father's route is a short pathway, elevator ride, and single corridor. I still beat him to the apartment. Lois is in her recliner, and her favorite aide is by her side, looking through catalogs for the pair of pants Lois wants to order. While I wait for Dad to get back, I look for his camera flash and instruction book, the equipment he thinks I have but don't. I find a Spanish version of the manual, but that's as close as I get after going through closets, drawers, shelves, and camera cases. Search complete, I turn to his computer. He can't keep up with his e-mail these days.

It's all yucked up, he'll say whenever I ask and so I go through his in-box, deleting the multiple *New York Times* digests, Morehouse College alumni bulletins, and DVD rental alerts. Three messages survive the cull, and I print them: a polite e-mail from my mother thanking him for pecans; an update from a self-appointed good-government group in Monticello that calls itself the Taxpayer Watchdog Committee and whose activities Dad follows with great interest even though he has noted repeatedly that a disproportionate number of the elected officials they critique are black; and a Web link from my brother-in-law to a photo album he has made of Granddaddy's Darling in Georgia, picking pecans in the grove, rolling down the driveway on Dad's utility stool, posing in front of her Phoebe Funderburg Moore's Woods sign in hip-jutting rock star stances.

The printer cranks out its last page and still no Dad. Lois wants to compare notes before he arrives, to hear the doctor's comments and to fill me in on her concerns. She wants her companion to show me the centralized distribution system she and the Waverly nurses have worked out. It's a big blue plastic organizer divided into the days of the week, four sections per day. The nurses have used round Band-Aids as labels, pasted over the box's preprinted time intervals and then written on to indicate Dad's schedule. The ink has already started to rub off. One of the handwritten times makes no sense. When I point this out to the aide, she takes the box back to the nurses' station. I find a permanent marker and some white stickers in Dad's desk and I cut out labels for each compartment lid. Monday 9 A.M., 1 P.M., 4 P.M., 9 P.M. Tuesday 9 A.M., 1 P.M., 4 P.M., 9 P.M.

I run out of stickers halfway through the week—in Dad's pre-cancer and pre-stroke world, there was never a shortage of office supplies—and try to imagine if Dad's stricken brain will be able to extrapolate the pattern beyond the labels. According to Lois's aide, he took his first and second doses at the same time this morning. What is to be done?

When Dad finally makes it back, I don't leave. I help with whatever odds-and-ends tasks he can devise. I have given up on a short visit, especially since Dad has chemotherapy later today.

Could I drive you to chemo? I ask, as if he'd be doing me a favor. *But then you'd have to take a cab home.*

That would be good, he says.

I finish placing an online order for a replacement camera manual and call the local camera shop for a flash attachment, per Dad's instruction and with his credit card. What's another two hundred dollars, I figure, of his money, if it satisfies some urge? The missing items are probably in Georgia, but Dad doesn't know, and these are the things that occupy his mind. Whenever he's ready, I suggest, we can pick up the flash on the way to the oncologist's.

I'm ready, Dad calls out from the bathroom, then doesn't emerge. A few minutes pass, and I check on him. He's lying flat out on the stripped bed, today's soiled sheets already in the wash. His eyes are closed, his arms overhead. I watch to see that his rib cage is rising and falling. It is.

We should go pretty soon, I say.

Okay, he says, opening his eyes briefly. I leave the room and chat with Lois. Another ten minutes pass. I return. He is sitting on the edge of the mattress in his T-shirt and diaper, transferring the loose change and pocketknife and billfold and Kleenex wads and datebook from one pair of pants to another, sometimes taking something out of the first pair and putting it into another pocket of those same pants.

I watch through the filter of before and after. Before, he would make a mistake or misstep once in a great while, the typical ravages of aging and human fallibility, and he'd belittle himself for it, curse himself out loud. *How stupid can you get?* he might say. Now he doesn't register that it's a mistake.

Here, I say, taking one pair of pants and bringing them to his feet. I help with the pants and slide his shoes onto his feet, noting that his ankles are swollen again. Good thing he's going to the cardiologist soon. Maybe going back on Coumadin, the blood thinner, will help. I'm tying one shoe, and I see that the laces are wearing thin.

You're going to need new laces soon, I say.

I have another pair, he says. *In Monticello.*

Well, there's a reason for us to go to the farm.

Right.

WHO CAN KEEP UP with demise? You think you've got a grip on pulmonary embolism, leaky heart valves, metastasized prostate cancer, the conditions themselves and their attendant therapies, and then boom, you've got subacute infarction. There are new Web sites to hunt down, many from socialized medicine countries, Canada and the United Kingdom, telling you what life will be like once the patient is no longer "in hospital." You plod through Web pages on diagnosis, symptoms, prognosis, recovery, and recurrence; you assign the pertinent information to Dad's story, building a case file, a series of concerns to take back to his doctor; and you craft reassurances to give his wife, yourself, and your sisters. And him.

In early December, the best news I've heard since Dad's downward tilt is from Margaret, reporting on a visit to Waverly.

Guess what? she asks. *He was grumpy.*

Get out of town!

Lois was trying to get him to take his pills, then Diane was trying, and then he started to give that stare.

The one where he looks like he's going to kill you?

Exactly.

How great!

I know!

It is great that he's coming back to himself, although the idea of stroke-prompted disinhibition had its appeals. So what if he has begun to make questionable financial decisions, buying replacement cars when batteries die? Has threatened to buy the abandoned dollar store on Funderburg Drive with the idea of turning it into a funeral home to be run in partnership by Marshall Tinsley and Jackie, whose undertaker education he's willing to finance? So what if he talks about selling the farm to the twins if they can come to mutually agreeable terms? Seems newly obsessed with making farm "improvements," such as his plan to obscure the front door of 354 by building a rain-protective carport, which he refers to as a porte cochere and claims came to him in a dream? Has the idea, illegibly rendered on a piece of paper, for a second-floor addition to 354 that will have views from all sides? So what if he spends all his money on such frippery? Would that be so horrible? What if Dad's personality were to have changed, but only in the kinder and gentler direction? What if he became consistently docile? Compliant? Patient?

Not from this stroke. As the first weeks of December show, we are back to wrestling with him over every missed dose or medical concern. On Battaglia's orders, my father had a poststroke physical evaluation. The absence of paralysis put him far ahead of many other stroke sufferers; he was told that he was in great shape. Dad interprets this as documentation of his capacity to drive, a point he plans to bring up with Battaglia as soon as Battaglia calls him back. Dad says he's left messages, which means he's stalking.

Whaddya have to report? I say when I call to check in over the next week.

The doctor still hasn't returned any messages, Dad tells me each time. *I suppose he's busy,* he says, unconvinced. I can imagine my father leaving multiple messages at both of the doctor's offices. Finally, the doctor telephones to say Dad should have his driving assessed by a special facility several towns away. Dad sets up the appointment instantly.

I TAKE DAD to his cardiologist. I go along to keep him from driving himself, but also, a butting-in daughter should be present. Sure enough, Dad goes through the examination saying everything is fine, mentioning neither stroke nor incontinence. When the cardiologist asks how Dad's ankle swelling is, up or down, Dad says down. I look at him, incredulous.

My daughter's grimacing, he says to the doctor, whose back faces me. *Maybe you should ask her.*

The swelling seems to be up, I say. The doctor checks. He guesses Dad is holding about fifteen pounds of fluid in his ankles alone. They are like sausages. The skin is taut and bloated around the joint, pouring over the edges of his shoes.

The doctor explains that if Dad takes his Coumadin as prescribed, it should prevent new clots from forming, which will prevent more strokes. He ups the dosage of one of Dad's two diuretics from three times a week to daily, and he reminds Dad to drink fluids only when thirsty. Dad should weigh himself every day, and if he can't bring his weight down in a couple of weeks, the next step will be three or four days of hospitalization to give a stronger diuretic intravenously.

The exam ends, and the doctor hands us a sheet for the checkout desk, stipulating a return visit in four weeks. On our way out, I stop at the desk. I turn to my father and, in the most casual tone I can assume, point out a restroom across the hallway.

I don't need it, Dad says. He sits in the waiting area, among the other cardiologically challenged, the thick-lensed, wheezing, overweight, and aged. I arrange appointments, blood work, and refills for four medications.

We take the elevator one flight down, and Dad sees a men's room.

I'm going to stop in here, he says, but the door is locked. I check the ladies' room door. Locked also. I am about to suggest we take the elevator back upstairs, but then the occupant of the men's room emerges, Dad goes in, and I leave to get my car.

I deliberate where to station my car, close to which door, whether I'm coddling or comforting him, whether he should have the use-it-or-lose-it exercise that comes with the extra twenty steps he'd take if I were to keep the car at the valet stand, our customary pickup spot. Instead I choose the medical annex door from which he'll most likely emerge. I wait longer than I should, then see through my rearview mirror that Dad is at the valet stand. I swing the car around, and when I get a full view of him, I see the crotch and one leg of his off-white jeans are soaked. I think about whether I should offer him some plastic barrier between his pants and my car's cloth upholstery. He wouldn't be offended. He endorses conscientious up-keep whether he's telling us to keep our hangnail clippers sharpened or testing our understanding of prime lending rates. *With assets come responsibilities,* he says.

I think about the story my father tells of the calf:

> *Your granddaddy started off with a horse and buggy and then he got a 1928 Chevrolet, which he drove for many years through the Depression. Until 1935, I guess. People would pay him in produce and livestock and I remember one time they put a calf in the back. The doors were so shabby—the locks had failed and the doors were rotting out—that he had those hooks from screen door latches to hold the back doors closed. And the calf defecated in the back 'cause farm animals defecate whenever they feel like it.*
>
> *Who cleaned up the car? I'd ask.*
>
> *I don't know. Anybody. Hell, it wasn't a big deal. Just wipe it up, hose it down, douse water on it. It was just like sweeping out the barn. One of the things we kids would ex-*

*perience was stepping in cow plop. And we went barefooted
in the summers. We'd be in the pastures or around the barn
and you don't always look where you're stepping and the
cows don't always give you notice about where they're leaving their piles of feces. You had to clean your feet off, but of
course that didn't hold up anybody for any length of time.*

I forgo a seat covering.

I didn't make it, my father says as he lowers himself into the passenger seat.

That's too bad, I say.

It's a pain in the ass, he says.

We get to Dad's apartment, and after a long stay in the bathroom, he emerges.

Wanna buy me lunch at the coffee shop? I ask. Hopefully, he'll eat,
too.

I guess so, he says. I have never heard him hesitate at a daughter's
invitation to anything.

Shall I get something and bring it back?

That would be good.

I stop at Muirfield first to make the change in his diuretic orders.
At the coffee shop, I ask the woman tending the grill for a "Texas
Tommy," a hot dog with al dente grilled onions.

Funderburg, right? the cook says.

How'd you know? I ask. *Is he the only one who orders this?*

She nods. *And he'll have two pickles, no chips,* she says as she pre-
pares his plate. What doesn't my father try to control?

Back at the apartment, I'm setting out lunch and a Waverly employee comes to the door with a package.

Hello, daughter, the man, a complete stranger, says to me. *I can
see that you're his daughter,* he says several times. *Yes, you are.*

Dad shuffles into view and says he's going to get a drink and some
mustard from the kitchen. He brings a glass of soda to the table,

leaving the mustard behind. No big deal, right? Everyone leaves things behind, forgets what he was doing, slips up now and again. Not my father.

He sits, slowly, and I set a medicine-filled ramekin before him and aim for cheery, lighthearted.

Here are your pills, I announce. He doesn't take them. He sits at the table and downs his diet cola in one long gulp. I am thinking of his ankles. I get up for the mustard he left behind.

Get me another Coke, will you, Leesee?

I don't want to fight him, to tussle over every health infraction. I want him to feel good instead of belittled, which is how he seems to take even the most gently delivered reminders and cautions. I will pick my battles, I think, as I pour the soda. Besides, cola has caffeine, and caffeine is a diuretic.

By three o'clock, my skin is beginning to crawl. I am mindful of all that is not getting done at my own home. My last task for Dad is to submit Phoebe's big fish picture for publication in the *Monticello News*. Our chances are good: we're competing with front-page headlines such as "Eagle Is Spotted Here," and "Australian Man Cycles Through Monticello." I call the newspaper's office, and once I tell the woman on the other end what it is I'm after, she says how funny that is [ee-iz] since they just ran a similar picture in the last issue. We swap specifics and finally ascertain that we are discussing the same little girl and the same big fish. The photo has already run.

Maybe you could go to the mailroom to see if the mail's in, my eavesdropping father says before the receiver has hit its cradle, before I've said good-bye. He's been a *Monticello News* subscriber for decades.

I've got to get back to work, I say, the only no I think he'll understand. He doesn't protest, but he edges toward a wheedle. He's not afraid to sound pathetic, if that's got the best odds.

Okay. Forlorn. *I'm sure you're busy.* Resigned. *Thanks for everything.* Helpless.

I traipse down three flights of stairs, across the brick walk and under the overhang of ancient, perfectly manicured oaks, through the dining hall corridor and to the mailroom. The box is empty. The day's mail hasn't been delivered. I return to the apartment, report the failed mission, and gather up my coat and bag. Before I leave, more on reflex than hope, I shuffle through the piles on the coffee table, only to find an unread issue of the paper underneath other neglected mail. There is the picture, large and captioned. Dad rises from his chair, fairly quickly, and takes the page into his office, the second bedroom. He presses the power button on the side of his stone-tablet-era photocopier, perhaps the first "desktop" model produced and big enough to cover the surface of a double-width filing cabinet. He hastily folds the pages over to something close to letter size and makes cockeyed copies.

Here, Dad. I'll do it. Dad steps back from the machine, and I refold the article so that the paper's name, date, and page number will also be copied. When I finally extract myself, I am laden with photocopies of Phoebe for familial distribution, various office supplies Dad says he no longer needs, and communiqués for my sisters.

Over the next week or so, Dad leaves me at least one message a day. I'd recently mentioned that my teenage stepson, Jason, was wondering whether venison makes good jerky. Dad has been on the trail of deer meat ever since. *Elbert Howard has reported seeing Jason's venison walking around,* Dad says in one message. *He should have it in the cooler by the weekend.*

Later, Dad calls to report, although he's already told me this, that he has finally heard back from Battaglia, who is referring him to a special facility that conducts driving tests. In another message, he says he's thought of a way to taste the hard cider he's heard that John is making in our garage, which would be to have it with Peking Duck Dad could bring for lunch, maybe over the weekend, he proposes. He points out that he and the duck would both need to be picked up, since he's not allowed to drive. He calls again to discuss the duck and also mentions an idea he's had about my neighbor Claudia who's such a good cook (and Jewish, I believe is the subtext).

This is the time of year that synagogues have that meat, that cut that gets cured, what's it called, and those potato pancakes, he says. *Maybe she could be persuaded to cook some of that meat.*

Brisket, I say, a day or so later, when I call him back.

Brisket, he repeats, savoring the recovery of the word.

Calls bounce among the three daughters, and in the end we come up with a get-together plan for the upcoming weekend that will celebrate Margaret's mid-December birthday with the duck and the cider. Brisket sits out this round.

DAD WANTS TO GO to Georgia desperately. He latched on to my shoelace offer proffered after the stroke diagnosis, my idea of giving him a future to hang on to. Hang on he did, asking and asking. When my sisters propose January's Martin Luther King weekend, he latches on to that. Then he starts mentioning, announcing, bringing up apropos of nothing, that he's thinking of going down on his own beforehand, for anywhere from a few to twelve days leading up to when my sisters would arrive. On his own. I suggest instead that I could go down with him a few days before the weekend. Diane tells him no, straight to his face.

Part of me isn't willing to infringe on this solo voyage idea, even if it's delusional. He has the right to create his own disaster. He has the right to script his own death. Where do we need him to die, anyway? What does it matter if it's drivable? What does it matter, considering the misanthrope he is, if he's alone? If I got everyone to agree to let him go down unprotected or he just went anyway and then died, alone, in a fall or in his sleep or in his truck or by the pond or in the field, would I feel like a murderer? Would I miss him so terribly and for so long that letting him go would reveal itself to have been shortsighted?

What would I give for one more, six more, twelve more months of him? How do I know if that's more important than giving him what he wants? What he wants is so elusive . . . to fish or not to fish? But nothing is clearer than his desire to be at the farm.

The Monday after our duck/cider/birthday gathering, I come back from walking my dog to find a phone message. Dad's received the replacement camera manual.

It came on Saturday. But, he adds with his usual under-oath precision, *I picked it up from the mailroom today.* He also mentions that he'd missed his opportunity at Margaret's birthday dinner to make clear to everyone that it was John Reynolds Howard and not he who had taught Phoebe how to cast in the 354 driveway. He is refuting the caption in the *Monticello News* stating that Phoebe's grandfather had taught her how to cast a line. The newspaper, lacking the budget for fact-checking, had not identified John, who was in the photo with Phoebe and the catfish, suggesting by implication that John was Phoebe's grandfather. No one on the planet cares about this, except for Dad. But he does care, so he looks for opportunities to set the record straight, and when he misses his chance, it plagues him. He mentions it in his message and then again when I call him back hours later, after avoiding the call for reasons I can't quite figure out, except that I don't have enough to offer him, no amusing stories or Phoebe reports or travel itineraries for Big Foot Country.

Before I dial, I check my calendar for his doctor's appointments and see only Battaglia on Thursday. When we speak, Dad tells me he's also got chemotherapy on Wednesday, he doesn't know what time. I assume he has no appointment at all, but I say I'll call to check the time, and maybe I'll take him there, to spring him from one ride in Waverly's transport van or one episode of waiting for a cab. Dad missed his regular blood workup recently, the one used to calibrate his blood-clotting levels and therefore his appropriate dosage of blood thinner. The appointment was written everywhere, on Lois's blotter calendar and on Dad's computer, desktop, and pocket calendars. And still they missed it. So I have inserted myself, sometimes inserting additional confusion. Calls volley back and forth to Lois and to the oncologist's office once I suggest his chemo schedule is out of whack. It turns out Dad was right. But then I notice that the next week's chemotherapy is less than two hours before a urology appointment. I ask how long chemo takes. Dad says three hours. I suggest this cuts it too close, and if he'd like, I could call and reschedule the urologist.

No, he says. *My first reaction is to leave it like it is.*

Okay, I say. *But if you have a second reaction, call me and I'll help you out.*

Historically, every aspect of this interchange would have been forbidden: the daughter butting in, the daughter suggesting he change plans, the daughter raising the possibility that he might come around to her way of thinking. To suggest he alter his plans would imply I knew better. And he, in turn, would not have allowed me to finish the sentence. He would have rebuked or berated. Traditionally, if I were to have said, "I thought it might be easier for you," he would say, "You weren't thinking."

I've gotten more of a voice as I've gotten older, as I've constructed a life of my own, built on my own disappointments and successes and no small amount of talk therapy with a person I've come to call "the Rocket Scientist." When it's not just my ego at stake, when it's his health or his safety, I can't stay silent, even though I still flinch inside as the words come out of my mouth, anticipating. It's amazing we don't carry weaponry, his daughters. His wives, too, for that matter, current and ex, all of us bearing wounds, some healed over, some scars that still itch, infection not just burrowing but settled deep into the bone.

MAYBE MY FATHER IS DYING now. Really, imminently dying. He is as close to the brink as I've ever seen: his husky voice a warning bell, every aspect of his person chipped away at. Maybe he knows he is losing or he's given up or the cancer's winning. Or some combination of it all. I wonder if Dad plans to die in Georgia, if this is embodied in his declaration that he's going to go down before any of us daughters can join him. Or if he just can't stand the closing-in walls of his apartment, filled with Lois and her companions watching TV together and ordering Lois's knit separates and 9AAAA shoes from catalogs, can't stand the women's watchfulness over his pills and appointments and quantity of fluids consumed.

Whatever's prompting this proposed solo voyage, I can't imagine he'd function well on his own. He won't eat well, he'll drive when he shouldn't, he'll miss medications, he'll fall and break his hip and lie on the floor for hours before Troy or Marshall comes out to check on him, worried that he's not answering the phone. At that point, Dad will either be dead or in terrible shape, in which case he'll go to a hospital where he won't recover, proving the Georgia oncologist's claim that breaking a weight-bearing bone kills people more often than the cancer does.

I think of the pets we had as children, how when they were lame or dying they'd go off by themselves, crawl under the porch to heal or die. Did they do that to keep themselves from being sniffed out by predators, to save themselves the indignity of being shredded to bits for another's meal? Do instincts defend against insult?

WITH THE START of the New Year, Margaret and Diane have begun weekly paperwork visits, sorting Dad's mail and paying bills while he sits with them, making conversation or accusing them of conspiring against him. If they call me with a question during one of these sessions, it is inevitable that all three of them will dissolve into peals of laughter, usually after my dad accuses one of us of losing his papers or creating confusion that even he knows he has created. While my sisters plow through the mess Dad has made in the six days since their last visit, he sits back and receives their questions and instructions like a king giving audience. He basks in the attention, the swirl around him, even though he can't follow it.

I don't know, is his frequent answer. Or, *Wherever you put it the last time you were here*.

Dad continues to deaccession. During one of the bill-paying sessions, he tells Diane to divide some troy ounce gold coins between herself and Margaret. A few months earlier, he gave the coins to Diane just for safekeeping.

Is there a reason you're not including Lise? Diane asks.

Lise, too, he says. He makes these decisions in the blink of an eye. Diane estimates that we've just been given about seven thousand dollars each. Sometime later, we ask Dad why he bought the coins in the first place.

I bought them when I was still concerned with building an estate, he says, a lesson he credits his Wharton education for having taught him. *And I wanted to be able to fill out every portion of the federal tax return, to be a fully participating member of the economy. I believe gold was worth about a hundred dollars more per ounce then than it is now.*

That's a precipitous drop, but valuation isn't his problem anymore, it's ours. Less and less is his problem now. He got rid of Martha's Vineyard, the island home for a man who can't swim. He got rid of the cows he and Bubba took on together. He cares about his wife and his progeny, as far as I can tell, and I think he has a soft spot for my mother, but beyond that he has no siblings, few friends, random associates. Maybe he worries about his health. I can't tell. I can't tell what he thinks. He lies to every doctor I've seen him talk to. He says he can't see, then he drives his car or finds something in the paper to tell me about. He denies feeling any pain, even when caught cringing or groaning in what seems unmistakable agony.

I don't know why old age treats me this way, he allows now and then, and yet his answer to every doctor's question is *fine* or *great*. No elaboration, no mixed response. No complaints, no reports, no chronologies. He asks questions only of Ellis, the urologist, who does not pussyfoot around. Ellis's bedside manner has earned him several shipments of Georgia peaches, ordered telephonically each spring.

What's your advice to the lowly patient? Dad asks at his January checkup, before he submits to his monthly shot of Plenaxis, the testosterone-blocking hormone for patients whose prostate cancer is advanced and symptomatic.

Well, Ellis says, looking directly at my father, not breaking his gaze once, not until he's done, at which point he looks at me, a combined offering of sympathy and apology for what I've had to hear. *Live life to the fullest because you may pass away from this. You may have many years, but I'd guess more like two. So every day you wake up feeling good, take advantage of it. You're not going to have those days every day. They're going to be parsed out.* He makes a chopping motion with his hand. *It's hard to have this conversation with your daughter here, but it's better to be honest.*

She can take it, Dad says. *We're farmers.*

Okay. You're probably going to die from this, but you should wake up every day and live your life. But you're doing that, by God. I have to give you an A-plus in how you're dealing with it. You really know how to live.

After the talk and the shot, while we're sitting in Ellis's waiting area for the requisite thirty minutes of postinjection observation, a withered old man wheels past us, hunched over his walker and taking glacial-melt steps.

His two years are almost up, Dad says. On the way back to Waverly, I ask Dad if he would mind if I stopped for coffee.

Do you have time for me to do that? I ask.

Sure, he says. *I've got two years.*

Dad also has to see his eye doctor this week, and next week he has the monthly cardiology appointment and the driving test. I would guess that the only appointment he cares about is the last, his last shred of autonomy, his last escape from the carpeted prison of the apartment. I hope Dad will feel good enough to get to Georgia this month. Lois won't be going with him. She's done with travel, she says to my sisters and me. She doesn't yet say this to Dad, who either wishfully or perfunctorily includes her in talk of visits to the farm. On this next trip, we will implement a rotation plan proposed by Margaret, who has a gift for solutions, for seeing through the jumble of displayed anxiety to the core need. I'm sure she's always had this ability, but maybe having a child has honed it. Whatever the source, it is coming in handy.

According to plan, Diane will take Dad for the first weekend, I'll fill out the week, and then Margaret will go for the second weekend and bring him home. He gets a good ten days or so out of the deal. We girls will lack the benefit of one another's company, but we don't need as much solace as we used to. We don't need people to cry with, off in a bedroom or on another floor, safely away from his lashing words. His lash has lost its power to completely devastate. He doesn't have the energy, maybe, or is too indebted to us now. We are good daughters. Everyone tells us this, we know it's true, and even Dad has begun to tack onto every good-bye the phrase *Thanks for everything*, and it stops me in my tracks every time, its tone so heartfelt, so naked, so loving. We are his entertainment, his nurses, his accountants and entertainers, his jesters and devoted gophers. We are his jailbreaks.

9.

CREEP CREEP

Injury to the surfaces of the frontal lobes can result in a variety of cognitive and neurobehavioral disturbances; cognitive disorders frequently associated with frontal lobe injury include distractibility, loss of abstraction skills and problem solving abilities, a lack of organizational strategies and a dependence on external structure, impaired initiation of action (despite intact ability to verbalize the need to take action), and impaired mental flexibility. Neurobehavioral disorders often resulting from frontal lobe injuries include impulsivity, disregulation of affect, a lack of insight or awareness, and inadequate self-monitoring or self-control in a social context.

—"Traumatic Brain Injury: An Intellectual's
Need for Cognitive Rehabilitation,"
Camilia Anne Czubaj, *Education*, 1996

THE EYE EXAM TAKES PLACE on a foggy, drizzling morning in early January. I'm running late. I panic as I drive toward Waverly, pushing the limits of safety on the wet roads, breathing slowly to counteract the thumping of my heart.

Must have been a bad accident, Dad will say to a tardy daughter before sliding into a reproachful silence that lasts hours.

It's a crapshoot whether I'll find my father ready and simmering or sitting undressed on the edge of his bed. I swing my car around to his parking garage, and there he is, fully dressed and standing at its edge. Pre-stroke, this would have been a likely rendezvous point, him outside and ready five or ten minutes ahead of the appointed time, standing alert with either cane or walker. Poststroke, I encourage him to wait in his apartment so I can check for missing essentials in the multipocketed sportsman's vest he wears like a portable desk, its pockets overflowing with checkbooks and calendars, passports current and expired, camera and mobile phone, penknives and rubber bands, medication lists and spare diapers.

I try to anticipate his neurobehavioral pattern and take precautions, but the change in him is still too arrhythmic to grasp. Too Alice in Wonderland, upside down and backwards. We'll plan something, he'll seem to understand, and then everything gets bollixed up. I've started to call when I'm leaving my house. It's an alert that I'll be there in twenty minutes, to get him started on dressing if he's lost track of what to do, to remind him of which doctor we're going to see. I'll call again when I've exited the highway, a five-minute warning.

I wasn't supposed to be here. I've tried to be more selective as trips to doctors multiply. I don't go with him to chemo anymore. I don't go to the dentist, and I wouldn't be going today, but no one called Waverly's transport service in time and Dad threatened to drive himself, which got Lois all in a tizzy and prompted her to call me. I've already taken him to the cardiologist and urologist this week, and yesterday I picked him up from the oncologist's to take him to a community tennis center that might be a model for one he suddenly wants to build in Funderburg Park.

But the eye doctor is important. Dad's old glasses don't work at all, he says. He needs a new prescription. When he takes his poststroke driving test at the beginning of next week, we want him to have every advantage.

I AM ON A CAMPAIGN to assess and rehabilitate my father, neither of which I'm qualified to do. But our family boasts an above-average tendency toward unlicensed medical and psychotherapeutic practice. Diane tells me her reading of Dad's brain-scan films corroborates his doctor's analysis of the infarction. Margaret suspects a link between chemotherapy and Dad's obdurate incontinence. Dad even suggests I lance his pus-filled elbow at home so we don't have to bother setting up an actual office visit. However, my practice is theory-driven, not hands-on, and I demur, as I also do when he suggests I express an irritating pustule on his back, which he gets Margaret to do, filling her dreams with viscous imagery for days afterward.

I am new to neuropsychology, a term I came across during a half hour of Internet reading. Theoretically speaking, I'm collecting data in order to build a template for understanding the constraints that now frame Dad's life. Practically speaking, Dad makes for a difficult case study. He has no paralysis, no aphasia. Such physical impedance is measurable, but the disinhibition of a damaged frontal lobe, Dad's likely manifestation, would be easier to perceive if the patient had previously exhibited any signs of inhibition.

For example, is Dad's recently expressed desire to have a menagerie at the farm (corralled so that the animals can be viewed from the sunroom window) pathological or the deadline-conscious desire of a terminally ill farm-loving man? Considering his six-week rooster rental some years ago, so that Lois could hear its morning cock-a-doodle-doos, it seems possible that this is just Dad.

In my desire to understand my father's brain, I do not protest when he heads for the driver's side of his car on the morning of the eye exam. I want to see how he drives. Surely his 3,500-pound luxury sedan is the best possible car to employ for the task. Surely it did well in crash tests. Surely I will be buckling my seat belt.

I am, after all, riding shotgun with a man who needs new glasses, has had a stroke, and may have his license confiscated in the next five days. Consequently I observe his technique behind the wheel with considerable interest. In the first mile, his speed is reasonable, if a little slow. He steers without veering or swerving, and he seems confident in his actions. A blinker stays on too long, but the error is so minimal it gives comfort. This isn't so bad, I think. People do worse all the time.

Don't tell Diane I let you drive, I say. My oldest sister is a force to be reckoned with, as dogged as he is, especially if she feels bolstered by reason. *I'm afraid of her.*

I won't, says my coconspirator. *I'm afraid of her, too.*

Once we're on Route 30, the four-lane spine of the Main Line suburbs, my right foot starts to work a phantom brake pedal. Dad stops at red lights, then begins to inch forward, three, five, seven feet into the intersection. Other cars make wide turns to get past him, and he is oblivious. Every muscle in my body flexes.

Dad, I finally say in a mock cranky voice, *you'll never pass the driving test if you creep creep out like this during red lights.*

We're already running five minutes behind, but this man who spent the bulk of my lifetime being so punctual that on time was considered late decides to go the wrong way. It's not pure confusion, my initial assumption: he's trying to pace the journey between Waverly and another retirement place farther west.

In ten minutes we'll turn around, he says when I mention his eye appointment a second time. I watch the dashboard clock, the shifting LCD display.

Dad. The eye exam is at ten-thirty, and it's now ten-thirty-five. I'd say we're at least ten minutes away. I'm lying. It's more like twenty.

I guess we should turn around, he says.

At the next traffic light, without signaling or looking behind

186

him, he crosses two lanes to make a U-turn, unaware of the large truck barreling up from behind. I am phantom flooring it at this point, hoping we'll get out of the way in time. We do, but now I see deficits everywhere. He can't hold the car still at lights or stop signs—are his leg muscles too weak to keep the pedal depressed?—and when we finally get to the medical complex garage, twenty minutes late for his appointment, he disregards the yellow arrows and heads up the down ramp. Even as other cars come toward us, he's unfazed.

This is the wrong direction, I say.

That's okay, he says, and keeps motoring slowly upward against a current of oncoming SUVs. The drivers gesticulate and make faces at him, mouths moving behind their windshields, and I do my best to catch their attention. I hold up my hands and give an exaggerated shrug, then I point to the handicapped placard hanging from the rearview mirror.

We hit no one. No one hits us. Dad finds an open spot and pulls in at a confident speed, narrowly avoiding the car to his left. But he doesn't clip it, and we start for the elevator. Rather than bring his walker, Dad uses me as support. He puts his hand on my left shoulder and holds fast, his grip more iron than affection. He begins to steer rather than follow, which is not a problem until he tries to direct me into the path of an oncoming car.

We are thirty minutes late, and we wait another forty-five before seeing the doctor. Plenty of time to observe the waiting room's furniture, aggressively ugly even for a waiting room, and its occupants, all old people with canes and walkers, plus one bricklayer who got something in his eye while on the job. Finally, Dad is called.

Should I stay here or come along? I give him as many choices as I can.

Come, he says, and I lead the way, his hand clamped onto my shoulder. Unlike other medical appointments I've been to with Dad, I say nothing during this exam. The doctor starts out jocular. Hail fellow. The kind of guy who'll crack wise on the golf course and make rousing toasts at family gatherings. Pictures of his kids hang on the walls of the examination room, and there's a framed, illustrated alphabet citing twenty-six reasons he's such a good dad.

But when my dad becomes confused, the good doctor turns snippy. The doctor wants my father to look through a viewer while he switches lenses, relying on Dad's evaluation of which lens best sharpens the projected image. Perhaps the doctor thinks Dad is intentionally uncooperative, but I can see that the instructions come too fast, and Dad has trouble pressing his forehead against the headrest while viewing the eye charts and answering the rapid-fire question of which lens is better or worse.

> *. . . distractibility, loss of abstraction skills and problem solving abilities*

Sit forward, the doctor commands a third time.

> *. . . a lack of organizational strategies and a dependence on external structure*

I can't see what Dad sees in the better-or-worse portion, but I suspect he is trying to say what he thinks the doctor wants to hear, repeating back whichever word the doctor himself has given more emphasis. I suspect this doesn't follow an ophthalmologically supportable pattern, because after a while, the doctor just starts saying, *No.*

> *. . . impaired initiation of action (despite intact ability to verbalize the need to take action)*

At a certain point the doctor gives up. He moves on to a chart posted on the wall opposite my father's chair, and he asks my father to read it. With his left eye, uncorrected, Dad accurately reads only the top row, the largest two letters. He keeps going, though, misreading several more rows with confidence.

. . . and impaired mental flexibility

Somehow the doctor gathers enough data to make a determination. He returns to a sunnier self, guaranteeing my father that the new prescription will make for great improvement, that Dad's weaker eye, now legally blind, will see as well as the stronger eye had been seeing, and the stronger eye will see even better than that. In fact the glasses will help, but not much, and in the next few months Dad will ask to be tested for cataracts when he hears that Mom has had her eyes done. He'll have copycat surgery on one eye, which will help, but not much.

For now, Dad hitches his hand to my shoulder and steers me back to the car.

I think I'll sit on your side, he says as we approach.

I HAVE SEEN, FIRSTHAND, Dad's diminished abstraction skills and impaired mental flexibility manifested, and yet I hope he passes his upcoming driving test. I offer up small bargains to the universe: He should pass as long as he never hurts anyone else. It's okay if he kills himself. He's dying anyway.

Driving is one of his last recreations. It gets him out of the apartment. He doesn't drive fast and never far, only to the post office or bank or hardware store. It has been months since he last made the nine-mile journey to the neighborhood in which my sisters and I live.

I tell my neighbor Claudia that he's being tested as a result of the stroke. *I hope they take his license away*, she says, and instantly I reflect on what an impulsive driver she is, how many narrow misses I've seen from her passenger seat, how many pedestrians have been put at risk by thinking they had the right of way while she was behind the wheel.

MARGARET TAKES DAD to his test. A stroke rehabilitation facility conducts the exam, using exercises that test brain function as well as knowledge of traffic laws and ability to steer around parking lot cones. Dad fails everything. He can't do any of it. He can't do the part where he's supposed to look up at the clock every fifteen seconds while also copying simple shapes on a piece of paper. Margaret tells me later that he never looked at the clock, even after the test administrator's repeated reminders, and at a certain point he just started filling in the shapes, not reproducing them. In the on-the-road portion, he apparently got stuck in a parking lot behind a truck. The truck wasn't going to be able to move unless my father got out of its way, but my father did nothing. Finally the tester told him to put the car in reverse. Dad did that, but then didn't move the car. He just sat there in the requested gear, foot on the brake. Was he just being literal? Waiting for the next piece of instruction, the one that would instruct him to actually propel the car into motion?

Margaret hears about the driving portion from the test giver. She wasn't allowed to ride along and Dad, upon his return, says only *I think I did pretty good.*

The testing staff gives him the results on the spot. To ensure his compliance, they point out that it would be pretty bad for him if he got in an accident now, after both his doctor and they have given him the thumbs-down. They appeal to his sense of liability, which seems to sink in. The next morning, Dad types a note to Troy, a note with none of the Mavis Beacon accuracy he painstakingly developed when he first got hold of the computer age:

Dear Troy Eugene Johnson,
Yesterday the dreadful day of drivers test failure arrived,

not only that they charged me $295.00 to do it. The DOT representative for PA gave me a failing grade on a drives test. This means that we will transfer the Izusu title to you sometime next week while we are in Monticello as we have previously talked about. This is a short leeter as it does not make one feel good to write it.

    Best wishes,

    G Newton Funderburg

MY FATHER'S WORD WAS LAW when I was a child. Even into adulthood, his instructions were to be followed to the letter, without question, and immediately upon dispensation. Even now, when I'm in charge, driving him to doctors' offices where I'll know more of Dad's medical history than he does, where I have to urge the doctors to look at Dad rather than at me when they speak, I am in the habit of obeying. Dad has lost his sense of time, and so even if we're running late he'll instruct me to swing by the post office on the way to mail some letters. Before I speak, I brace myself.

I'll do that, I say, *but I don't think we have enough time before our appointments*. He says nothing, his acquiescence more painful than the expected barb. He's not all there, but he's not all gone. He records appointments on the right date of the wrong month and dials Social Security numbers on the telephone. He's been robbed of his ability but not his desire to get things done, and more often than not, because this is only partial intellectual depletion, he is cognizant of the gap between intention and follow-through. That betwixt-and-between state infuriates him, spilling into above-usual testiness, particularly toward Lois and her aides.

A week after the eye exam, we implement the inaugural daughterly rotation plan to Monticello. A predeparture checkup with the elbow surgeon and his infectious diseases colleague determines that Dad's elbow was not fully cleaned out during surgery, that this superbug infection, resistant to practically every antibiotic out there, is still present. Another intravenous course of vancomycin, the powerhouse antibiotic, is their first line of attack. If it fails, more surgery.

Rather than cancel the planned and ticketed nine-day trip, and despite our calamitous experience with the Covington chemotherapy, I arrange with Jasper Memorial to administer the vancomycin while we're in town. Doctors' approvals are secured, nurses are consulted, prescriptions are faxed. Each daughter will shuttle Dad to the hospital every twelve hours for a two-hour drip. The drips have to go slowly, we're told, because administering the drug too fast will cause "red man syndrome," a system overload that turns skin the color of cooked lobster.

In Monticello, the vancomycin sessions shape our days. While Dad lies on a bed in one of the hospital's four emergency rooms, he thinks up errands for whichever daughter is in attendance. We are given lists: to cash checks at the bank drive-through, drop off forms at the tax assessor's office, pick up paper at Monticello Mail & More, do anything that crosses his mind. If we are delinquent in our return, if we pull into the hospital parking lot to find him already released, standing by the emergency entrance, we will be in the doghouse. We will get the silent treatment or trip land mines in every interchange.

Did you get more photo paper?

They have it on order.

So "no" is the answer to my question.

Diane, whose weekend with Dad leads off the relay, forewarns me, the second shift, of his irascibility. Diane is less enamored with Monticello than I am, and more exhausted by her job as a middle school teacher. For her, the trip is a gift to Dad, exacting a steeper cost, scarcely any pleasure beyond knowing that he is happier here than anywhere on earth, even in his crankiness. We don't see each other for the baton handover—Dad is alone for an afternoon while we are both in transit—so her report comes by phone. She sees red man syndrome during his first drip. From that point forward, the nurses extend the infusion time by a half hour. Sometimes, if there's an emergency in an adjacent room, the nurses won't get started for twenty or thirty minutes. Some have trouble accessing the port implanted in his upper arm, and there are differing views among staff as to the appropriate size or make of needle to be used.

Bearing up under Dad's short temper is hard. One can only muster so much resilience and good humor and perspective and tai chi–like bending in the face of force. Bearing up under his dependence may be harder still. His desire to get things done is in full swing, only now he needs someone else to drive and to execute. What proves most exhausting is to be in such proximity to his treatment, a fellow traveler: the waiting for infusions to start and end; the constant parade of people who care or don't care, are good at needle sticks or aren't, who can or can't manage Dad's efforts to banter with and humor the people whose hands he's in; the lost faxes; the unreturned calls about what manufacturer made Dad's port; and the red LCD display at the top of the IV stand that shows how much time remains before the bag of vancomycin will be depleted, at which point the irritating but welcome bleat of an alarm blares until a nurse comes to shut the damn thing off.

Night drips are easier, Diane tells me, and so they are when I am there for my weekday stretch. Offices and stores are closed, he falls asleep, and I bring knitting or reading or a portable DVD player with movies rented from Ingles, where the blockbuster-only selection perfectly suits my desire for simpler plot lines, easier laughs, and happier endings. When I fall into bed each night, I fall with a thud, and I sleep soundly until the alarm clock clangs, or Dad knocks on my door with his desire to go for breakfast before treatment, or, if he has been feeling particularly energetic, I smell coffee.

Lise Funderburg

* * *

IRRITABILITY IN MONTICELLO IS one thing. Irritability back at Waverly is unmitigated by room to stretch out, be by oneself, escape, even for a moment here and there. Dad comes home with Margaret as planned, and instantly his confusion and inability to remember conversations, actions, and details increases.

Tax season approaches. Once again Dad counts on Diane to organize his records and submit them to his accountant. She stopped accepting pay for the work some years ago, specifically so that Dad would have to adapt to her timetable. This year he can't bide his time while she fits the work into her schedule—his sense of time is broken. He does not care that she is also paying his bills, keeping track of his accounts, and that the aggregate is too much for her on top of her job teaching in an overcrowded and underresourced public school. We daughters each have our strategies for skirting Dad's wrath. Diane's has been to give minimal notice prior to her visits, to name the day but not necessarily the hour. He cannot bear this. He tries the wheedling and the affectionate doggedness and then naked insistence.

Diane is feeling her way around the boundaries of his stroke damage and diminished eyesight, as we all are, identifying what he can and cannot do for himself, what we can and cannot do for him. She proposes that he help by writing checks if she leaves the pile of bills out, opened and stacked. She can't do it all, she tells him. At first he says he'll try her idea, but within a day he rejects it, becoming obsessed with getting her to do things his way.

She is already driving to see him one Sunday, intent on helping with finances for several hours and with Margaret in tow, when he leaves a message on her home phone.

Oh, Diane I'm calling because the last uh response to my request kind of uh upset me a little bit and I don't really uh

194

uh agree with it and uh I'm going to try to persuade you uh to change your position but if I can't I can't. And I'll just have to take some other route.

My position is that I don't want to write any checks. I don't want to do anything. I want you to do it all. If you can't do it all, I'll just have to make some other arrangement. And if you want to visit Monticello you're going to have to go on your own nickel. And you can forget about golden handshakes and other accommodations. Bye-bye.

As soon as my sisters walk in the door of the 80-degree apartment, into the cocoon of aging, Dad calls out from the bedroom, his staging area between the bathroom and life, and asks Diane if she has gotten his message. When she says no, he calls her into the room to say, in private, that when he asks her to do something, he expects her to do it. He explains no further. He doesn't mention that he has telephonically threatened sanctions.

My sisters spend the next eight hours working on Dad's bills. They only scratch the surface, especially now that he's in an apparent spending frenzy. Two days earlier he telephonically purchased a horse, which came on the heels of buying ten goats, two turkeys, four geese, fifteen chickens, a jackass he calls Papa George, and an affectionate, pregnant donkey he's named Georgie Girl. As a direct consequence, he'll require a larger corral than the one he has just had the twins build in the upper pasture, labor costs already sounding to the tune of $4,200.

Diane gets through the day with him, working hard to remain unruffled, only to get home to his voice mail threat.

I don't even like going to Monticello, she says that night after replaying his message into the telephone receiver for me. *I only go to be supportive of him.*

* * *

FOR THE NEXT SIX WEEKS, unable to drive and increasingly less inclined to walk, my father hibernates in his apartment. He has not lost his will to dial, though, and his telephone use evokes the shower scene in *Psycho* or, alternately, lab monkeys trapped in newspaper-lined cages, relentlessly pressing levers to release crack cocaine. Dad keeps his cell phone clipped to his shirt pocket and sits within arm's reach of the landline, either at the small dining table that was once uncluttered but now fills with papers that tumble onto the floor, or in the wing chair in his spare-bedroom office. On the cell he tends to use voice dial, which we set up at the hospital during the hours of antibiotic drips.

Dad still struggles with aspects of wireless communication, such as retrieving messages or managing multiple-choice automated response lines. But voice dial he has down cold. *Howards' cell,* he commands when he wants the twins. *Jackie's cell.* On the landline, if he gets a busy signal, he stabs at the redial button until the line clears.

I spend a day at his apartment, determined to finish updating his computer-based address book, taking out the dead people and inching Dad's entries toward alphabetization and correct spelling. I volunteer for this after noting that every time I visit, it seems Dad has again failed to print out the seventy-page file. The printer jammed halfway or he had the second side upside down. His multiple failures pile onto tabletops and spill out of trash cans. He is deforesting the planet.

Dad scribbles corrections or crosses out obsolete entries wherever he sees them. He corrects his own address book, Lois's copy, and the misprinted versions that lay in stacks around the apartment and that he refuses to throw away. Occasionally he also inputs changes directly into the computer. I try to explain that his method is too decentralized, but this concept does not penetrate.

I yucked it up, he says when I ask what the problem is. As with so many things these days, he seems content to turn over tasks to whichever daughter is willing. On inspection, I see that the most redundant entries are those people or businesses with whom he has the greatest contact. Often the redundancies vary by one or more digits of the address or phone number or by the description he types into the notes field.

"She is held in the highest regard for integrity by me," is one entry for Donna Coe, the woman who bought the horse and donkey for him and who has been entered into the book five times. "He drew up our wills," is another person's notation. "Lies sometimes writes for *Oprah* magazine. She is a good writher," comes after my name. In the job title section of my husband's entry, Dad has typed, "Son-In-Law."

Keep me company, I say to Dad before sitting down at his computer, several address books gathered onto his desk.

I'm comin'. I'm comin'. I'm comin'.

Before I can get to the project at hand, Dad has a request.

Leesee, he says. *I wonder if you could help me write a letter to the attorney general.*

To my father's mind, Funderburg Park has been egregiously yucked up. The design plans were complete and ready to be acted on five years ago. Then they were lost. Funds seem to disappear. Scheduled work seems impossible to complete. Subcontractors seem to overcharge and underperform on a regular basis. Dad is convinced of foul play. He doesn't know who, locally, he can trust, and so he's determined to take his concerns to the highest available authority.

With him in his wing chair and me at his computer, we communicate the facts as we know them (his idea) and heartstring-targeted mentions of Granddaddy's service to the community (my idea), as well as Dad's sense of urgency as prompted by failing health (also my idea). While I work, Dad sits behind me making calls. He leaves no less than four messages for Jackie: some generic *Call me*'s, at first, eventually replaced by a scolding advisory for her to listen to her own outgoing message, which he deems too long, too fluffy, and as is the case whenever there's the slightest mention of God, as in, "Have a blessed day," too offensive. It strikes me that even the most succinct message would reveal shortcomings if listened to so often.

He tries the Howard twins. No answer. Dad calls Monticello's county agent to invite her to the lamb roast he has decided to have over Easter, once John agreed to come and cook the meat for him in the *Caja China*, temporarily redubbed the Lamb Box. Dad asks the agent to bring her husband, kids, and grandkids, if she has any, since his family will be there in multiple generations. Then, his largesse knowing few bounds, he tells her to invite one of the people in her office. The county agent must ask about a second staff person.

That religious woman? Dad responds. *Hell, no, I don't want to invite her.*

He dials my mother to follow up on a call he made a few days ago that seemed to her to have no purpose. They are not, after all, great buddies. Civil, yes, and cooperative over anything concerning their offspring. But not pals.

Do you think, my mother asks me later, *that he was just calling to chat?*

In their first phone call, my mother filled the awkward pauses with references to Phoebe. Mom mentioned that she had gotten horse books from the library for Phoebe, in anticipation of Phoebe meeting the new quarter horse Dad had Donna Coe purchase for him. Dad's call today is to see if Mom has given Phoebe the books and how Phoebe has responded. Mom doesn't answer. I wonder if she has caller I.D.

Dad calls Troy to discuss whether a fox or a buzzard killed one of the new roosters in Dad's expanding menagerie. The expansion requires continuous purchase: chickens and ducks and geese seem to die off or disappear on an ongoing basis. Jackie and her husband, Eddie, are in charge of the animals but seem unable to keep the population stable. Troy argues for fox, since the rooster's bones were not picked clean. Dad and he discuss the progress of the electrician's efforts to light the new horse corral; the need for Marshall Tinsley to come fix something on the farmhouse roof; and whether Troy knows anything about Eddie's ability to slaughter a lamb. Troy says he'll ask Hard Time. Hard Time, we've recently come to find out, is Eddie's nickname, although we don't know its provenance and speculations vary as to whether it's something he gives people or something he served.

I am trying to stay out of the whole lamb business, its purchase and preparation, but my father has other ideas, ideas that keep changing. First he told me that we might go with Troy to pick up the lamb the week before Easter, when Dad and I will be at the farm alone. The rest of the family comes for the holiday weekend. The rest, that is, except for Lois, who's been having dizzy spells, and Diane, who has told Margaret and me she will never go down again. Even our mother has agreed to come along, after countless invitations from Dad. She's curious to see this place, and perhaps this visit will set to rights his refusal throughout their seventeen years of marriage to take her home with him, claiming the dangers of being an interracial couple in the South, making her feel left behind. Even my sisters and I were allowed to come when they were still married. We flew down without either parent, when I was seven or eight, to visit our grandfather during a school break.

It would be a new adventure, Dad said of the lamb-retrieval plan.

Sure, I said, *sounds great*. But then he called again. He dispensed with a conventional greeting, instead opening with, *I stuck my foot in a bucket*.

Uh-oh, I said. *How so?*

Well, Leesee—

His use of my name signaled trouble. As did the muffled guffaws.

—we may have to slaughter the lamb ourselves. I thought the twins could do it, but turns out they don't mess around with that kind of stuff.

Squirrel they'll mess with, since it's their favorite meat, and the way they clean fish together—silently, lightning fast—is balletic. But not lamb.

When you say "slaughter," what does that entail?

Killing it, eviscerating it, draining the blood, things like that.

When you say "ourselves," who does that include?

Us. You and me.

But I might lose my appetite.

No! It will only whet your appetite.

I crossed my fingers for Hard Time.

DAD DIALS WHILE I SIFT through the bits and pieces of address book I've harvested. I attempt to merge disparate electronic versions that somehow coexist, separate and unequal. Two hours after I've intended to leave, I am completing a third and final round of alphabetizing and proofreading. I managed to cut out about thirty entries, thanks to redundance and death, and the total is still over four hundred–plus contacts. Dad occasionally offers unsolicited computer support advice. *Go to "Properties,"* he says, apropos of nothing. Or, *Call them up!*

I am given to offering unsolicited advice of my own. *Why don't you call Claudia Andrews and invite her to the lamb roast?* I asked a week ago. During Claudia's Thanksgiving stint as Lois's companion, she was competent and conscientious, prompt and full of common sense, but not braced for Dad's bullying. She has declined to work for them again.

To hell with her, Dad responds. *She abandoned me.*

A frontal lobe stroke apparently impairs short-term memory. Dad doesn't remember giving Claudia a rough time. Then again, even if he remembered their interactions, he might have thought his behavior appropriate. Only after several instances of him suggesting that he could hire her again as a helper had I let on that she probably wouldn't work for him again. Now he spins that into abandonment. In the course of Dad's calls and my collation, I bring up the invitation idea again, but this time using what Dad calls my "slickster talk."

I think you should invite Claudia Andrews to the lamb roast for two reasons, I say as an opening gambit. As a man who prizes careful reasoning, even if he can no longer muster it, he has to hear me out. He waits to see what comes next.

First, with the goal of you spending as much time as possible in Monticello, I think we should keep open as many support channels as we can. I wait a beat or two for that to sink in. *And if we don't invite Claudia Andrews to the lamb roast, she might not send us a Christmas card.*

I've got him. I've appealed to his basest desire, spending time at the farm, and I've used his own platitude—in this case, one he inherited from his father about why you have to keep up good relations with people in a small town—against him.

He looks up Claudia's number, misdials it several times, then gets Claudia on the phone. He invites her and her "husband or boyfriend" to "a Sunday reception."

Easter Sunday, I specify.

Easter Sunday, he clarifies. She tells him she'll come and at that, he says, *We'll see ya. Bye-bye*, and hangs up.

WITHIN THE WEEK, my father commits to and then retreats from purchasing a mutton, commits to purchasing two lambs, agrees to sell his last piece of investment property, a wooded lot on Martha's Vineyard, and who knows what else. When he calls to tell me about accepting the offer on the lot, he says, *Maybe now I'll get a pickup truck. Every farmer should have one, especially a farmer with horses.*

I don't point out how obscene it is for a man whose driver's license was recently recalled by the authorities to purchase a third vehicle. Instead I recollect another season of pickup fever, a good decade ago, when Dad went around test-driving trucks for weeks before talking himself out of the purchase. I doubt, in the current climate, in this spendaholic season of disinhibition, that Dad is likely to be stopped. Plus, until his spending threatens to get him and Lois bounced from their cushy retirement home or forces him to buy his chemotherapy on the street, I don't see much harm. Waste, yes, but not harm. So I aim for damage control.

What a great idea. Why don't you trade in the Explorer for a pickup? I don't like the Isuzu's replacement. Dad struggles in and out of its high-riding seat, and comfort features seem to have wedged out functionality. *We'll always have a rental car on hand,* I point out, *since we use them to get from the airport to the farm.*

His eyes glisten with pleasure. He looks at me lovingly, approvingly.

Good thinking, he says. *We'll just have to test-drive a few when we get down there.*

10.

MAUNDY THURSDAY

W HEN TROY STEERS THE ISUZU, now his Isuzu, into the driveway of the sheep farm a few minutes before 4 P.M. and three
days before Easter, we see no signs of life. Human, that is. Sheep fill
the pastures and corrals. It must be lambing season, since new- and
recently born sheep tumble around the fields in multiples. They
bleat and cavort and knock one another about while never straying
too far from their mothers. Our arrival creates a wave in the flock:
with one liquid, unified move, they flow away from our vicinity. An
aged Great Pyrenees barks at us from inside an old livestock trailer

parked at the edge of the barn. The dog is ragged and hoarse but committed to defending its flock, even from its makeshift pen.

Troy parks close to the barn and next to a hulking Deutz DX90 tractor and a beat-up golf cart. The three of us step out of the truck and wait. The first person to appear is a gray-haired white woman, statuesque and well coiffed, wearing a blue dress and windowpane check emerald jacket, tan stockings, bright red lipstick, and terry cloth house slippers. She hurries toward us from the main house with small careful steps. When she speaks, her voice is a mix of whisper and urgency.

I tried to call you, she says before we've had a chance to say hello. *I left you two messages. Mr. Lawson was going to cancel. We didn't know where you were, and he doesn't like the sheep to wait too long. You were supposed to be here at four.*

Even if our watches are slow, we're still on time. No one points this out to her. Instead, we introduce ourselves. She introduces herself. *I'm Margaret*, she says. *Mr. Lawson's wife.*

She repeats her story of the phone calls, possible cancellation, and timing concern, but I still can't make sense of it. She is addressing me while my father and Troy wander, taking stock of the operation. I smile and nod sympathetically, hoping we'll get to leave with the two sheep Dad ordered.

Mr. Lawson comes down from the house to where we're standing. His gait is hampered (stenosis of the spine, he'll tell me later), and he is thick around the middle and in his fingers. He wears farmer gear: oilcloth Carhartt jacket, misbuttoned; baggy Carhartt overalls; half-laced work boots; and a camouflage-patterned bill cap turned backward. Except for the fact that he's white and in his late seventies, he has a hip-hop aesthetic down cold.

Mr. Lawson does not pick up where his wife has left off. Instead he greets us and launches into his selection process for our order, how he hopes the sixty-pound, three-month-old sheep he's picked out are big enough. Technically, a spring lamb should be somewhat heavier and twice as old, but he thinks ours will do just fine.

We'll get you some chairs to sit on, Mr. Lawson says, and Mrs. Lawson, Margaret, hurries back up to the house.

We'll get in position, Mr. Lawson continues, *and Little Joe will be here in a minute.*

Little Joe, the couple's youngest son, is doing the butchering. This is an eleventh-hour development for which I am exceedingly grateful. Dad had been unsuccessful in finding a butcher. As late as Tuesday, two days ago, when he and I flew down, the matter was unresolved. I was beginning to think Dad and I—and Troy, who wouldn't leave us stranded—might actually have to confront, in a visceral way, issues of sheep anatomy and morphology: innards, in other words. But Mr. Lawson's son was able to get off work early, and he's agreed to take on the task.

When Mrs. Lawson returns, she carries two white plastic lawn chairs and has a small bundle of printed matter tucked under one arm. She puts the chairs down and approaches me.

We're Christian, she says. *We celebrate tonight. We don't celebrate Easter. We celebrate Jesus' death: the sacrifice he made, not his resurrection. Are you Christian?*

There's meat at stake.

I was raised Christian, I answer.

Oh, she says. *I thought maybe you were Jewish.* Then she makes a noise, a hurried giggle that I decide over the course of the afternoon is a tic, a closed mouth *hm-hm-hm* that finishes most of her sentences.

Dad takes the plastic seat that's offered, but Troy, man of action, demurs. Little Joe strides up, a solid six-footer in Carhartt jeans, blue T-shirt, and brown galluses. Joseph Lawson III is square-jawed, sandy-haired, muscular, and handsome, maybe thirty-five or forty. He says hello, shakes our hands, and unrolls a brown hand towel he's set on the seat of the golf cart, revealing a sheathed butchering knife. He lays a hacksaw and a pair of red-handled pliers alongside the knife and then, with his father, goes into the stable to fetch the first lamb.

TODAY, THE DAY the Lawsons celebrate, is Maundy Thursday, aka Holy Thursday. For Christians it commemorates the Last Supper and Judas' betrayal of Christ in the Garden of Gethsemane, which resulted in the son of God's crucifixion. Maundy stems from the Latin *mandatum*, meaning "command," and refers to Jesus' bittersweet instruction to his disciples on that fateful night that we should all love one another.

I love my father, but we are not speaking. Not more than we have to, at any rate. I am furious at him for getting furious at me for taking too long when I went to help Marshall Tinsley get his e-mail working yesterday.

I don't think you understand your role, he said to me when I finally got home from Marshall's trailer, having missed a visit from Donna Coe, the horse broker Dad had, up to that point, only spoken to by phone and I'd never spoken to at all.

I am the host and you are the cohost, he said from his chair, his pop-eyed glare burning holes through my head. *And anything that interferes with that focus is not appropriate.*

Dad, I said. *You supported my going to help Marshall when we talked with him about it this morning.* Dad said nothing. I thought of how Marshall had taken us out in the rowboat earlier that day, lifting it off its sawhorses by himself, despite his crumbling spine and bum leg. How he rowed the three of us around the big pond, all of us in life jackets per Dad's insistence, all of us trying to fish, Dad's line irreparably tangled inside of a minute. How Marshall had driven the ribs up to Philadelphia for the wedding. How he stopped by whenever we were in town to pay his respects or take us on a tour of the county or take us to catfish and grits breakfast in Eatonton or at his brother's place. *And besides, Marshall's always very nice to us.*

What the hell did Marshall ever do for us? Dad lashed back.

In one instant, every good thing I'd ever done seemed to disappear from the deposit column of my father's scrupulously attended ledger. Even this trip—taking days off from work, making travel arrangements, taking care of the shopping, the cooking, the laundry, the medications, the dressing of the yet-again reopened elbow wound, the lamb party preparations, the stepping and fetching at my father's ceaseless beck and call—had been erased, nullified by a couple hours of my absence when he wanted me close by.

The full force of his disapproval occupied the room at that moment and nothing, neither past nor future, diluted his condemnation. I, on the other hand, was filled with thoughts of before and after. Especially before: before the cancer's return had brought, until that moment, a seemingly mellowing dependence; before I took on the architecture of my own life, before I learned that relationships didn't have to be predicated on power or the lack of it, that some people love without penalty, that not thinking fast enough or saying "um" or forgetting to stand straight didn't automatically constitute a lapse in character. Before, I didn't know there were people in the world who would love you and encourage you to be whatever you wanted, even if you were never the best at it.

You should have known to come home in time to meet the horse lady.

I was apparently not the best caretaker or daughter or mind reader. We spent the rest of Wednesday night in near silence.

Did you return your sister Margaret's call? he asked at one point.

What do you want to drink with your pills? I asked at another.

This morning started off as stonily. He made what I suppose was an attempt at reparation. As I filled the coffeemaker, he sat at the kitchen table, his back to me, and explained in overly enunciated words what, his tone suggested, any idiot might have understood.

I think, he began, measuring each word before loosing it upon me, *that our differences are rooted in a lack of comprehension of our respective roles, and that by understanding them, we can proceed with clarity. I am the host and you are the cohost. Our sole purpose is to provide our guests, especially Maggie and Phoebe, a good time. Nothing should interfere with that focus. Your job is to help me, and if you have time left over, you can work on my address book, because it's incomplete.*

Time left over? As if I were in some way sloughing off, taking it easy, derelict in my duties. Address book incomplete? Immediately after my day of working on it in his apartment, he mixed fresh pages with old versions I had neglected to throw away. Of course he'd found errors right and left, but they were on old pages. I saw the same people die, the same businesses close, the same friendships fall away. The **M** section disappeared, but **J** showed up twice, once after **I** and once after **P.** Mr. I-Never-Throw-Out-Anything. Mr. Stroke Brain. Mr. The Best Defense in the Face of Diminishing Control Is to Keep Everything, Make Copies of It, and Make Copies of the Copies.

He finished his speech and waited for me to bring him coffee. I tried to see his side of things. As those of us around him do, around by choice or by birth, I tried to come up with a rationale for his behavior. It's Mom, I thought. He's extra nervous because Mom is coming. It's her first time, and for whatever reason, his ex-wife's experience matters. And Phoebe, I thought. Dad's been concocting this menagerie to engage her, which entails riding lessons, which entails Donna Coe. I brought his cup around to him and sat down, facing him, looking at him. He stared at me, poker-faced.

Can I still go fishing?

If it doesn't interfere.

Then it got murky. It always gets murky at some point. I said something and he said something, and maybe I said something else, and then I know I told him he was being harsh and disrespectful and treating me like an idiot. Then he responded with some belittling comment or snort or gesture that hurt my feelings.

Dad, I said in my steadiest voice. *You're belittling me and hurting my feelings.*

He laughed. He laughed at me, just as he had once or twice before in my life, decades before, at other times when I tried to stand up for myself. He laughed the way I'd seen him laugh at my sisters and at Lois, when they were upset, when they were at their most exposed, belly up, armor down. I managed not to cry. I managed to keep some shred of composure even as I told him he shouldn't laugh at me, that it was wrong to do so.

Now you're talking to me like I'm an idiot, he said, mocking me. I stopped speaking, went into the kitchen, emptied the rest of the coffee pot into my mug, and then rinsed out the pot. Why couldn't he just have asked me to be there for Donna Coe? Why couldn't he tell me he would feel uncomfortable without help, without someone who could get refreshments and make small talk and take the full burden of exchanging pleasantries from his shoulders? I wiped down the countertops, lingering at the range, where only the scrubby side of the sponge would break apart the crusts that ringed each heating element. Was there no limit to his expectations? Did he believe that we, his daughters, owed him everything? Was I a fool to have made myself so available, so open, such an easy target? I could not stay where I was, but how far from him could I get? I would never abandon him completely. His need was indisputable, great and only growing.

Dad remained in his seat, sipping his coffee and doing nothing else. Finally, I walked back into his peripheral vision. *I will help you,* I said.

This time, he added without turning to face me. We both knew I'd left the sentence incomplete.

Yes. This time. But if you're not careful, you'll run out of daughters to bring you down here. Diane already won't come.

MR. LAWSON HAS SPRAY-PAINTED red and blue stripes on the backs of the sheep he's selected, and he tells Little Joe which holding pens they're in.

I don't like to make them wait too long, Mr. Lawson says, explaining, I guess, his wife's anxious calls and reproachful greeting, although we weren't late, so none of that is any clearer. *If the adrenalin starts running it changes the flavor.*

Little Joe cradles a fidgeting sheep in his arms and gently lays it down on the ground, on its back on the grass and in front of the tractor. My father sits, watching, and Troy stands close, ready to help.

Under Mr. Lawson's instruction, Little Joe folds the sheep's forelegs against its chest and Troy pins the hind legs, stepping on one to secure it to the ground. Mr. Lawson bends down near the sheep's head, holding his son's sharp, curved knife. The killing is slow and gentle. The men speak only in soft voices and only the slicing of the neck is swift. Although the Great Pyrenees' view of the proceedings is obscured by farm equipment, he bays in our direction.

He doesn't like it when we mess with his sheep, Mr. Lawson says. *We can't let 'im out when we're slaughtering 'cause he gets too upset. He won't bite us, but he'll get pretty upset.*

I wouldn't be embarrassed to turn away from my first slaughter, but I am not horrified or nauseated by what I see, even though the blood pooling on the ground is a brighter red than I could have imagined, and the sheep's last struggle to break free of his captors is unmistakably sad. But the Lawsons do their work with a reverence for the animal, handling him tenderly even as they cut his throat and slice off his testicles. I am not repelled, although I do feel a twinge once they hang the ram by his back legs onto a two-pronged meat hook hitched to the arm of the tractor, and the animal twitches and kicks several times even after Mr. Lawson declares to Troy that he's gone.

MR. AND MRS. LAWSON stay for the entire procedure, throughout the slaughtering and butchering of both rams. It's a tough call as to who's more entertained, us by them or them by us. Mrs. Lawson's armful of papers turns out to include a photo album of former customers: a Jordanian family that did its own slaughtering under the shade of trees down in the pasture, and an African king who was seven feet tall and made his pregnant wife stay in the car throughout his visit to the farm. He wanted the largest ram they had, Mrs. Lawson tells me, as a ransom for his unborn child. I think she means something like a baby dowry, since the imminent heir was right there at the time, in utero. Mrs. Lawson shows me Polaroids of the sheep shearers who came for two or three weeks each year. They were itinerants from Australia and New Zealand who, like migrant fruit pickers, worked their way from Florida to Canada.

The giggle ends every new piece of information, every show and every tell. *That was when an African king came hm-hm-hm. These were the men who came to shear the sheep hm-hm-hm.*

The Lawsons don't need shearers since they switched over to woollies. Now they breed Katahdin hair sheep, a relatively new variety named after the highest peak in Maine. Katahdins are known for docility, for not needing to be sheared, for exceptional mothering instincts, and, of particular interest to me, for excellent lamb chops and meaty carcasses.

Little Joe is still working on the first carcass when Mr. Lawson takes me out for a spin on his golf cart. What's left hanging from the bifurcated meat hook as we drive past is a Y of hind legs and spine. The rest has been sliced or sawed into sections and layered into one of the two coolers Troy brought, waste-filled entrails carefully segregated into a separate tub.

We bump over the fields in the cart, which holds a homemade feeding machine in back. A blue plastic drum is filled with corn and is controlled by wires and rope the driver can tug on each time he wants to release an allotment of grain.

The sheep know what's coming when they spot us. They fall into step behind the cart; we are a magnet plowing through a field of metal shavings.

There's a good little sheep sheep, Mr. Lawson intones in a loving falsetto. *There's a good little sheep sheep.*

We drive in a big circle, the sheep now our contrail as some linger to clean up this or that pile of corn. Mr. Lawson points out a lamb born this morning, standing with its mother a good thirty feet from the rest of the flock. He circumnavigates a feeding station he's made for lambs ready to wean. Wooden shipping pallets and widely spaced wire mesh form the pen's fence: lambs are small enough to slip through the pallets' slats, but their mothers are not.

Before Mr. Lawson and I return to the slaughter, we tour an enclosed pasture next to the house. This is where rams are kept until breeding season. The alpha ram is a three-year-old with horns that curl almost twice around in lazy spirals. Several of his sons and grandsons hover at a respectful distance.

I wouldn't want to be on the receiving end of those horns, I say.

Well, they can really go at it when they're trying to determine a pecking order, Mr. Lawson tells me. *Sometimes they'll butt each other so hard that one or both rams' necks will break.*

Oh, my goodness.

That's the way sheep do.

When we rejoin the group, Little Joe, with Troy's help, has killed and skinned the second ram and both men have a hand inside the abdominal cavity, reaching through a belly-long knife slit. The viscera hang together inside a membrane that the men carefully pull out into the air, and the sac of guts dangles there for several minutes, attached by muscle and the digestive tract, which Little Joe carefully cuts so as to avoid any backflow of waste onto the meat we plan to eat.

Meanwhile, Mrs. Lawson shows me issues of *Border Collie* magazine, including one from the early 1980s containing a profile of her husband, examining his dog-training methods and the resultant field trial champions, particularly Mr. Lawson's beloved Mirk, a sheepherding dog of unparalleled skills and named after a legendary Scottish champion.

BEFORE WE LEAVE, Mrs. Lawson gets me to write down my name and address and my husband's name and our phone number in her guest book. Dad's and Troy's signatures sit on the lines above mine, and I antic-  ipate that I will start receiving religious tracts, possibly before I get home. Troy and Little Joe pose for a picture in front of the last two halves of sheep, fully cleaned and hanging from their hooks. The men shake hands and look into the camera the way politicians and award winners and guest lecturers do, except that Troy, with his other hand, is steadying the side of sheep that keeps swinging into the flannel sleeve of his extended arm.

Troy turns to face the golf cart. Dad leans on it with one arm, and on his cane with the other. Mr. Lawson sits in the cart's seat, his arm resting on the steering wheel. Troy spreads his arms out in a gesture of accomplishment. Ta-da.

There's your lamb, he says. *There's your lamb.*

Perfect. Perfect. Perfect, my father says.

Yeah, we never would have done that, Troy declares.

213

No we wouldn't have, Dad agrees.

No way, Troy says. *No way.*

Troy packs the coolers into the back of the Isuzu, we shake hands all around, and I fill out a check from Dad's checkbook to cover the sheep, two hundred dollars, and Little Joe's butchering, a mere forty more. We start on the fifteen-minute drive back to the farm, leaving the Lawsons and two pools of poster-paint-bright blood in their lawn. Troy speaks first.

No way, he says again. *No way we could have done that ourselves. No way, no way, no way. I'm gonna say that all the way back to Monticello. No way.*

We are flush with the success of the trip, the mission accomplished. I try to savor the pleasures of the afternoon slaughter, aware that an evening alone with Dad lies ahead, one more night of silence and misunderstanding before my relief, the rest of the family, arrives.

BACK STORY

3517 HAMILTON STREET

THE FOUR YEARS THAT separate me from my oldest sister, Diane, have evaporated over time. We are on opposite sides of fifty, but both so close to it that we fall into the same generational slot. We both remember where we were when JFK was shot and when the World Trade Center was hit. And whether nurture or nature is accountable, we also share traits that mark us as Funderburg Girls. We both have a weakness for buttered toast, an overdeveloped sense of responsibility, a genius for trash picking, the ability to tough out crises, and a fidelity to the thought, anyway, of regular exercise. The enduring difference between us, the demarcation line that will never erase itself, is that she remembers when our parents were happy together. She remembers my father planting a big smooch on my mother's cheek. She remembers him taking my mother in his arms to dance her around the kitchen. I don't recall them ever having a conversation.

MY PARENTS BOUGHT THE HOUSE on Hamilton Street in 1960, when I was one, and our family lived there together until the summer of 1971, when I turned twelve and my father moved out. We occupied the house's first two stories, small backyard, and crumbly basement. The third-floor rental unit typically went to a tenant who taught or studied at the University of Pennsylvania. The house had windows on three sides. The fourth side was a solid masonry wall connecting us to another house, a common Philadelphia building style called a twin (versus the less desirable "row" and the more desirable "single"). Some twins were architecturally identical; ours was more fraternal, which provided us with a private front porch facing onto the sidewalk.

Along the windowed side of the house was a walkway, separated from the next house's walkway by a low wrought-iron fence that had a gate at about the halfway point. This gate was in constant use as my sisters and I traipsed back and forth to play with the three Oshana girls, who lived with their mother, Julie, in the three-room first-floor apartment. It was possible, we found out, to connect a tin-can telephone from my second-floor bedroom to the Oshana girls' bedroom across our adjacent yards. Lauren, the middle daughter, and I were convinced we could hear each other when we pulled tight the connecting waxed string and put ears and mouths into the empty cans.

Side yards were for birthday parties that featured homemade cakes and cone-shaped hats. Backyards were for digging to China, mud pies, and attempts at urban orchards that invariably failed. On our side of the fence, we tried sour cherries, apples, and grapes. On Lauren's side, a peach tree yielded for a number of years, then gave up under the various assaults of dogs and cats, children, cold winters, and meager air circulation. Once my family brought home Storm, a German shepherd whose unchecked protective instincts led to heavy confinement, our backyard became his trampled, grassless kennel.

When my father was at home, I steered clear of him. This was mostly in the evening, since he worked every day of the week, and it mostly meant staying out of the living room, where he would sit in the wing chair and watch the evening news or read the paper.

My mother, on the other hand, prompted no such detours. I can picture her in every room of the house: ironing in the back, fixing meals in the kitchen, showing me how to foxtrot to the Ink Spots in our dining room, where the small portable stereo played only when my father was out. *I love coffee, I love tea. I love the Java jive and it loves me.*

In my parents' bedroom, I would rummage through my mother's dresser drawers, to pull out my baby book or to play with her jewelry: antiwar pendants and tortoiseshell earrings, seed bead necklaces and tiny cast-metal llamas from her mother's trip in the early 1900s to visit a missionary brother in Peru. If my mother came in while I was trying on her crocodile pumps, she might stay to show me other saved treasures, like the wasp-waisted dresses and skirts from before she lost her figure, which loss, she maintained, was the direct result of my birth.

DIANE NOT ONLY has different memories from mine, she also has supporting evidence. Black-and-white photos of parents and

firstborn all together on the front stoop, on a picnic, changing a diaper. I say I don't recall our parents ever having a conversation, but I'm sure they talked. I don't remember overt silent treatments. I also don't recall laughter or debate or teasing or disagreement. I don't remember them ever touching, ever—except once.

My parents didn't fight in front of us, but one night they were arguing behind closed doors in the second-floor spare room that separated their bedroom from the bathroom. My sisters and I huddled together at the top of the stairs, a few feet away. Maybe I was nine, which would make Margaret eleven and Diane thirteen. We sat there, pushed up against one another, crying, tangled up into a ball.

Something must have escalated. Maybe my mother cried out or a tone changed or my father raised his voice. I extracted myself from the knot of sisters, walked to the spare room door, and opened it. My father's hands ringed my mother's neck. He dropped them to his sides as soon as he saw me.

"Why can't you love each other?" I cried out. Maybe I pleaded, maybe I wailed.

"Everything's okay," my father said. "Go on back out."

"Don't leave," my mother said.

OTHER THAN THIS ISOLATED INCIDENT and the general absence of interaction, I have no firsthand information on my parents' marriage. Only in my teenage years did the truth begin to leak out, including Diane breaking the news to me that my mother was pregnant with her when our parents married, and my mother allowing herself the occasional snide comment about Lois.

Lois had lived on the same block of Hamilton Street, across the street from us in a large detached single that accommodated her, her husband, their four children, and an ancient collie named Thor. Lois helped my father start his real estate business and then worked with him there, even though her husband ran a competing realty company serving the same neighborhoods.

Lois and my father left their families within a year of each other and bought new houses a block apart and in the next neighborhood over. At first, I didn't make anything of it. And it was left to me to make sense of things: my father said nothing to me or my sisters about what was going on. If Lois had wanted to say anything to us, I'm sure my father forbade her to do so.

The summer I turned seventeen, my father took Diane and me to a family reunion in Monticello. We would have cousins to pal around with, fishing to do at Granddaddy's little lake on his little farm, and meals that always lived up to the promise of plenty more in the kitchen. I don't remember whether Lois arrived separately or traveled with us. At some point she showed up, unannounced, as part of our contingent. My father did not discuss or explain her presence, and I could see only that my aunts and uncles were on familiar terms with her. In many of the photos taken that weekend, I am not smiling.

Eventually, my mother, my only source of information to this day, relaxed her self-imposed silence. Peyton Place had nothing on us: Lois and my father would go off to the movies while my mother sat home, pregnant with me and minding two toddlers; Lois would host parties for Dad's business at her house, parties my mother was not allowed to attend but could look in on from the street; my father switched beneficiaries of life insurance policies from my mother to Lois while I was still a baby; and he and Lois started to invest in properties through a jointly owned corporation named after Diane and Lois's daughter, D & W Associates. My mother says she asked repeatedly for a divorce, and repeatedly, my father rejected the notion. Finally, my mother told him she couldn't go on living with the way things were. He acquiesced. Perhaps he decided not to be responsible for half-orphaned children.

In the summer of 1971, when my mother told us that our father would be leaving before school started, I cried only once, more shock than sorrow. She cooked a big meal on his last night, a turkey with all the trimmings. The four who were left behind reconfigured the house's atmospheric properties. We began to talk at meals, to sulk openly, to whoop and holler and argue and laugh, to have friends over whenever we wanted, to say what was on our minds, to breathe.

11.

JOSEPH'S COAT

A T THE LAMB PARTY, Troy eats no lamb. He makes no bones about his dislike, his aversion to the smell of it roasting, the very idea of eating mutton, but he helps at every point. He and Dorothy spend much of the Easter event talking with my mother, becoming fast friends within minutes of having been introduced. They find common interests: I pass by and overhear discussions of travel and gardening and walkers, since Mom recently got a new hip and Dorothy's ninety-nine-year-old mother recently broke hers.

Now I see where you girls came from, Troy says. *Now I see.*

My mother collects stories about the Funderburg family and the old days from the Johnsons, regaling us with them later. She hears from Troy the story of Dad with his pocketful of nickels. She finds out that Dorothy worked in my grandfather's office for years, that he put her on a diet when she was a teenager, and that he would close the office some days and take her fishing with him, a pastime that could last for hours if he were catching, but that would end immediately if Dorothy were the only one having any luck.

Time to go, he'd say to Dorothy if she caught the first fish. That didn't mean in a minute or in five minutes. That meant straightaway.

My mother tells us these stories with pride at her sleuthing. My father has been as much a mystery to her as he is to any of us.

 The day before the party, we make a family field trip to Horsetown, a western-wear store that seems to be housed in an airplane hangar and has an extensive taxidermy collection that includes bears. Dad offers to buy everyone boots, Mom included. Inside the store entrance, we disperse, like a cluster bomb, all of us except for Mom, who stays close to Dad, worrying about whether he needs help getting to the bathroom and sitting with him on a bench in the shoe section while the rest of us shop.

Easter is a rainy day, so we bring picnic tables into the garage and most people congregate there, where the air is cool but not cold. The white couple who own Monticello Farm & Garden show up— I'm not sure when Dad invited them—and they are as pleasant as can be, easily flowing among the guest contingents that include the Johnsons, Dorothy's brother Howard, and Jerry Goldin.

The lamb roast, for me, turns out to be the most enjoyable *Caja* event to date. Maybe it's the reinforcement of the troops: in the brightness of Phoebe and the novelty of Mom, Dad's attention is captured and I can retreat. He wants to watch Phoebe's every move: how fearlessly she wanders among the chickens and goats, how quickly she can climb the horse corral fence to give out carrots and apples and peppermints. He can't believe that Mom walks the quarter-mile path down to the pond.

Go get her in the truck, he commands. *She can't walk up that hill.* But of course she can, and she wants to, and she meanders around the pastures and pathways with a pleasurable pointlessness that neither Dad nor Lois has ever practiced.

Margaret is my savior. She goes out of her way to respond to Dad's incessant summonses, to run interference for me.

He really orders you girls around, Mom observes within hours of her arrival. Then she pretends to do the same.

Get me a cup of coffee, Leesee, she says.

Not funny, I say. For a while after my father moved out of 3517 Hamilton, Mom took to bed, spending so much time in her room that it scared me. For all I know, it was one day or one weekend, but it knocked my world out of its orbit. After some months, maybe years, she started to date, still a striking woman at five-foot-ten, with long legs and a nice figure (despite her accusations about my birth). When men came to pick her up, I was pouty and crossed-armed, glaring at them from a corner of the couch.

She had adventures, built up her sizable and international coterie of friends, continued to participate in Powelton Village organizations, but she never found a second partner, never remarried. She continued to be a public school teacher through to retirement, and so Dad and Lois's increasing wealth seemed, now and then, to annoy her. It wasn't so much what they could buy as where it could take them. As they got older, they started taking trips to places she would have loved to see. Spain. Italy. China.

It always seemed to me that my mother was the wronged party, the one disadvantaged by the divorce. If my father weren't part of the equation, he would have rooted for her, the underdog. What goes around, comes around, and it's hard not to relish the wonderment he now shows at Mom's physical prowess, at her relation to

Phoebe, at her ongoing ability to drive, to live on her own, to take care of herself.

I AM DETERMINED to bring my mother, a longtime gardener, to see Dorothy's flowers and Troy's vegetables.

Miss Dorothy, I say when she answers the phone on the day after our lamb roast, *is it okay if we come over now?*

When I'm in Georgia, I try to address older familiars with the honorific of *Miss* or *Mister.* I had always thought of it as a segregationist custom, one in which black people of any age had to show deference to white people of almost any age. Miss Scarlett, I think. Miss Ann. But in the course of trips to Monticello, I began to notice when people, white and black, would call my father Mr. George. It was typically another adult, someone younger or whose business he was patronizing. Ben Tillman called my father Mr. George. Jackie called Bubba Mr. Bubba, and everyone called Dorothy's mother Miss Sarah. There was no rancor or resignation in anyone's voice. This version paired affection and respect. More often than not, however, I can't make my mouth form the combination. I do pretty well for a while, then I fall back into my lifelong habit of first names only, and I hope my respect shows nonetheless, that I'm not seen as rude.

Is now a good time? I ask.

Come on, come on, Dorothy says.

Dad does not accompany us, and as we tour the gardens by their house, I cue Troy and Dorothy to tell my mother some of the gardening gospel they've shared with me over the years. Don't overspice the pickled peaches. Kentucky Wonder green beans keep better in the freezer than in a jar. Collard greens picked after the first frost taste sweeter, and if you want to keep the birds away, move your plastic snakes to new locations at least once a week.

Thanks to Troy's harvests, I have tasted collards that came to the pot less than an hour after being plucked from the ground, and so

I can now bear witness that proximity to the source transforms the eating experience: tomatoes are juicier in Monticello and rutabagas earthier. Peaches burst onto the tongue and the watermelon is so sweet it makes you want to cry.

I've lived my life in cities and have eaten accordingly. I pay a premium for freshness and flavor, but even now, in the surge of farmers' markets and farm-to-city arrangements, I am guaranteed neither. I rarely have access to food that is picked and served the same day, and I would hardly know how to identify its characteristics. But I have glimmers. When my grandfather, who was widowed the year I was born, grew too old to live on his own, he moved from Monticello to Philadelphia and lived with my father. We would go food shopping together, Granddaddy and I, and he taught me to pick out each green bean individually, no matter how many other waiting shoppers harrumphed, anxious to scoop their indiscriminate handfuls into plastic bags. We looked for succulent pods, bright green preferable to gray. We never took a bruised or marked bean, and if they were generally too withered and dull, we passed entirely and went on to the next vegetable. At home we strung the beans by hand, pulling off the fibrous spine that grows along one seam of the pod before snapping it into bite-size sections.

I didn't realize the origins of Granddaddy's fastidiousness until I started spending time in Monticello. People still eat produce in season as a matter of course rather than fashion. They still cherish the fresh over the exotic, even though Ingles and Piggly Wiggly now carry Brazilian clementines and Washington State apples. Monticellans still live close enough to the land to witness its fierce majesty. In my world, the earth is measured in units of thirty-three feet by sixty feet, a common city house lot. Gardening is a precious hobby, and my neighbors and I grow plants in blatant zone denial, coddling those that need to be dug up and embedded in peat moss and garaged over the long, cold winter. In Monticello, people seem less inclined to rebel against the time of year, which is marked not by calendars but by changes in the skin of the earth. Early spring lays billowing clouds of green pine pollen in a fine dusting over every rock and path and car. Late summer, especially during drought, is cracked red clay at the edges of roads and irrigated fields. Winter ends with swaths of tawny, bristled fields, the recently shorn hay rolled into enormous bales.

In such close and realistic relationship to the land, Troy gardens a half-acre plot on the far side of his garage, minicrops that include row after row of okra and collards, netted trellises for beans, and a full quarter of the ground reserved for tomatoes. If he were twenty-five years younger, he says, he'd plant the adjacent meadow. But he and Dorothy keep busy enough with what they already grow, freeze, and can.

The Johnsons and many of their siblings went north for most of their working lives, which pulled them, as it did my father, into the second wave of the Great Migration. Troy and Dorothy spent their working lives in Hartford, Connecticut, she at a bank and he at a textile mill, where he eventually served as the union representative. Troy's garden there was even bigger, a full acre, and he ran a de facto truck farm before and after work. He dropped off boxes of vegetables to the porches of neighbors, also from the South, who paid ten dollars per week to take whatever he delivered. When it came time for the Johnsons to retire, like most of their siblings they came home.

In Monticello, the garden's scarecrow wears the overcoat Troy bought in 1947 to face those northern winters. It has a head made from a white pillowcase and features cut from black tape. Troy says the pillowcase confuses the birds.

They never seen a white man in this neighborhood before. But then he points out the scarecrow' hands, one made of a green rubber glove, one made of a black glove. *The green one's for the garden,* he says, *and the black one's for picking cotton. That's who picked cotton. Black hands.*

Dorothy canned in Connecticut and she cans now. She puts up

the fruit and vegetables using handed-down recipes, sharing the outcome among extended family. She'll make sweet pepper relish and pear relish, which she says is good with meat or field peas but definitely not fish. *The flavors kill each other.* She makes peach and strawberry and fig preserves; pickled peaches and watermelon rinds; and beets that she simply boils and peels.

I think I'm the last generation to preserve things, she tells me. *Kids today are satisfied to get it all out of the jar.*

So that Troy can plant according to need, Dorothy keeps careful records of how much she puts up each year. The goal is to make the preserved food last until the next growing season, both for themselves and for select siblings and friends. This year she will can thirty pints of beets, forty quarts of tomatoes, forty half-pints of relishes, and about thirty quarts of pickled peaches.

Nothing goes to waste in the Johnsons' garden: Dorothy's canning cupboard is a doorless defunct freezer on the side of the garage. A salvaged concrete bench bears the initials of the Future Farmers of America, a group that was whites-only when Troy and Dorothy were children. Old oven racks filter the irrigation system, discarded lumber and cedar branches entwine into bean trellises, and the path between two work sheds is laid with asphalt roofing shingles.

It's like Joseph's coat of many colors, Troy says of the larger shed's patchworked roof. A recent year's drought was so bad he has turned to container gardening on every side of the central planting bed. "Containers" are anything that holds earth, including eviscerated washing machines laid on their backs and the drums of discarded clothes dryers.

You'd see my boots out here if they were big enough, he tells me.

I taste resourcefulness in the food they grow, in this respect for the land, this working in partnership with it. At Monticello Farm

& Garden, seeds are stocked in open wooden bins. You buy by the scoop, and you can pick from three varieties of collards and dozens of beans. The desire to grow, to coax bounty from the land, is infectious. The earth below your feet is just waiting to have its power tapped, as Troy does with his melons and asparagus, corn and sweet potatoes, strawberries and cucumbers, plums and peaches, grapes and rutabagas, and squash, and mustard greens, and three kinds of tomatoes, including a firm-fleshed Rutgers, developed in New Jersey for Campbell Soup.

My mother, herself only one generation removed from a family-farm in Holland, Michigan, fully appreciates the Johnsons' garden. Then she tours the house: the huge aquarium, Dorothy's teapot collection, her McCoy pottery picked up for pennies at yard sales during the Connecticut years, and her nascent collection of glass salt and pepper shakers from the first half of the twentieth century, hardest to find because of their glass (not plastic) screw-on tops. From the way my mother asks questions about the shakers—*When were they made? Do the tops have to be glass?*—I can see that the quest for them will become part of her routine thrift store investigations and I am not

surprised when, within a couple of months, she has found a pair to give Dorothy, whom Mom will stay with when she returns to the farm a few months later, roped in by her love of travel and her desire to be with, if not her ex-husband, at least the rest of us.

12.

DEBT SERVICE

IN THE FALLOUT of the Easter trip, I abandon my father. He knows it. I can tell in his voice when we speak on the phone. He's not clipped, but he's distant. I am no longer in the inner circle. This propels me into some deep-cushioned blame. Blaming him. He is the one who has been so mercurial, so punishingly demanding. What have I ever done but try to be good? To speak up or be quiet, to succeed but not show off, to receive politely but not grab?

I drive to Brooklyn one afternoon to do some reporting, and in the extra half hour I have before my interview, I stop into a shop, one I happened to patronize when I lived there a decade ago. It's a narrow little storefront with no name, shoe racks dragged onto the sidewalk, the single aisle choked by stuffed-to-bursting clothing racks that barely let one person pass through at a time. I ask to see a pair of Earth Shoes.

Do you know the story of Earth Shoes? the owner asks. *Do you know how they work?*

In fact I do, I say.

They first showed up in the 1970s, she says, apparently not having digested my answer. *These people realized that the healthiest stance for your posture was when you were standing in sand.*

I try again. *I actually know about this. My father read an article and made my sisters and me each get a pair.* Not only did I have to read that article, but over the years, I had many a chance to explain, to justify, that the butt-ugly footwear was a defense against a poisoned environment over which we have little control, and that by mimicking the native Brazilians' footsteps in the sand, in which the heel falls lower than the toe, I was not only approximating the yogic Mountain Pose, but I was encouraging my own graceful natural stride. I wore those dark brown clodhoppers throughout the mid-1970s (they were impossible to wear out), and with everything: vintage dresses, low-cut extra-wide-bell Landlubber cords, and the Quakerly gray and blue kilts my sports teams wore on game days. Earth Shoes were expensive back then, and even though my father hadn't yet joined the ranks of what he calls "New Money," he splurged on a pair for each of us. Their style then was Early Corrective, and the pair I try on in Brooklyn is only slightly aesthetically elevated.

I have stopped calling my father because suddenly I am busy. I've snagged or fallen into more freelance assignments than I've had in years, and one involves a few days a week of commuting to New York. I'm busy with household improvement projects and, following Dad's mantra that *real estate is a great hedge against inflation,* managing a miniature empire of two rental houses, which John and I see as our hedge against a destitute old age, but in the present moment is a source of constant irritation, thanks to the responsibilities that ac-company assets. John and I are also facing a wax in my now twenty-year-old stepson's waxing and waning presence, and while we voice support of Jason's burgeoning independence, we love when he comes over to do laundry and we can feed him meals and pack up food for him to take back to his apartment. And I haven't called because I don't feel like calling. I don't feel like becoming embroiled in Dad's endless acquisitions. I don't feel like trying to make him let me in. I don't feel like managing him or myself in every interaction. It's tir-ing, all of it.

Of course, I haven't completely deserted him. I'll see him tomor-row and then a few days after that when I take him to his doctors. And when I do, we will observe the established protocol. He will treat me with love or disdain, depending on whether I'm on time, how I open the door for him, how I drive, where I park, what I say to the doctor, when I speak appropriately or out of turn. When he wants me to convey his symptoms, when he wants me to be silent.

I'm like those wobbly blow-up clowns, the ones with sand in their bases. Punch them and they'll bounce and sway and almost tip over, then right themselves. But I can't seem to get back to vertical with my father. I can't right myself. I have merely been paying lip service to the truth, it turns out, claiming in these post-diagnosis months to know that he's unchanged and unchanging, that even the stench of his own mortality won't temper him, that my attentions and devotion are stringless gifts. But it's not true. None of it.

In the midst of his dependence and vulnerability and, despite what he claims, debilitating pain, I stole glimpses and stretches of being a loving daughter with a loving dad. I stuck so close, I stood by so reliably, I defended his dignity at every turn. Surely he saw the real me, I let myself think, no longer filtered through his cracked lens.

The Easter debacle merely resurrected the truth, my own dis-torted sight, and I can't figure out what to do with it. But I miss him. I miss the feeling of helping him, of having him depend on me. I miss the gallows humor and his impetuous enthusiasms, stroke-induced as they may be. I heard on the radio this morning that one of the differences between old and young people is that the older ones have lost a lot of their passion. I disagree. This unconquerable drive I see in my father, this urge to engage, however awkwardly, may be tinged with panic, but I find much of it passion-filled and beautiful. This is the thing about my father. He's a study in fractions. He is various parts sharp and funny and kind and generous and play-ful. And he's cruel and baiting and grudge-holding and bitter and broken, broken, broken. I love parts of him. I hate parts of him. I forgive much of him, who he is and what he's done. And no matter how hard I try, I can't get past wanting him to turn on me a gaze of absolute, unfettered love.

13.

REGULAR RHYTHM

I S YOUR HEART *still in regular rhythm?* I ask Dad over the phone, a couple of days after his quarterly cardiology checkup and six weeks after the ill-fated Easter trip. *No,* he says, causing my own chest to flatline for a second, until he speaks again.

When it heard I'm going to Monticello, it skipped a beat.

FOR THE FIRST TIME in a year and a half, according to the octopus sensors of the EKG machine, Dad's heart is beating without hiccups and flutters. His ankles are barely swollen, and while his feet are still chafed and ashy, toenails like claws, the feet themselves no longer spill through the straps of his Birkenstocks.

(Desiree, the urology tech at Dr. Ellis's office, always checks to see if Dad might be developing reactions to the Plenaxis shot she administers each month. *Any swelling?* she asked during Dad's most recent visit. *No,* I told her, *in fact, just the opposite. Look.* Desiree regarded the newly trim ankles with one arched eyebrow. *Sexy,* she said, as she plunged the syringe into Dad's flaccid left buttock.)

During the quarterly checkup, the cardiologist was pleased when Dad said he had stopped drinking glass after glass of water. The reduction of fluids lightened the load on Dad's heart, the doctor suggested; less strain on the motor.

Are you walking? the doctor asked.

Not if I can help it, Dad answered.

Well, the doctor said, looking through Dad's chart as he spoke, *it would be good if you did.*

My wife has this cart, Dad said, referring to Lois's motorized chair that he's been absconding with each night to get himself over to his bed in Muirfield. Dad's been sleeping there since the week after Easter. He had to have a second operation on his elbow as soon as he came back, another attempt to fight the antibiotic-resisting superbug that had taken up residence in the joint. The surgeon's goal, once again, was to scrape out the consuming bacteria that prevented the elbow from fully healing, the wound from closing, the tenderness and pain from going away once and for all, especially now that infection had spread into the bone.

As if metastasized prostate cancer weren't enough.

Vancomycin was once again prescribed as the icing on his elbow surgery cake, an attempt to kill whatever the scalpel missed, but Dad has to stay in "The Loony Bin," as he calls Muirfield, to receive the antibiotic, since his insurance would only cover the six-week post-op drug course if Dad were an inpatient somewhere. This stipulation was one more assault on Dad's sense of justice: he was scandalized that Medicare regulations required him to occupy a hospital bed for treatment he could easily have taken as an outpatient.

That's why Medicare's up fourteen and a half percent! he said when he was first remanded to Muirfield. He says this a lot: when we see that the cardiologist's office has been remodeled; when the urology tech, Desiree, makes us wait after the Plenaxis shot for a doctor to come by, shake Dad's hand, then sign a release form; and when the Waverly van takes what Dad deems the long way home.

The cardiologist—with none of the oncologist's sassy affection or the urologist's goodhearted bluntness or the elbow surgeon's empathy—pressed the point during his recent exam that it would be good if Dad walked more: good for the heart, good for his bones, good for his weight.

What about horseback riding? Dad asked. He was full of the devil that day. I could see it the moment we walked out of Muirfield into the crisp spring sun and toward my car. He leaned on his cane only half the time. Otherwise, he twirled it in the air, the same way I remember Grandfather doing from time to time, with the same saucy grin lighting up his face, the one that announced, Here comes trouble!

I don't know about horseback riding, the cardiologist said.

He's serious, I interjected, afraid the doctor might take a hard line that Dad couldn't ignore. *He just means walking around a pasture on a horse.*

Hmm, the doctor said, which struck me as less than giving his blessing.

What's the worst that could happen? I asked, pushed by desperation for his sanction. *He'd fall off and die.*

Dad laughed.

No, the doctor said. *He'd fall and break his hip or end up paralyzed.*

I said nothing. Dad said nothing. That would be worse. The cardiologist threw us a bone.

I guess it couldn't hurt, he conceded. *If it's something that makes you happy.*

Afterward, Dad's gait had a bounce to it. We headed for the car, and he seemed on the verge of breaking into a jog.

What are you doing? I asked.

I'm walking, I'm walking, he said.

At the valet stand, Dad handed me his wallet so that I could pay, and we waited for the car. Dad sat on a bench inside the hospital pavilion's main doors, and I stood by the curb, in the warmth of the May sun. The attendant took an unusually long time, and my father finally joined me outside. A shiny beige pickup drove by, steroid-pumped fenders and riding high, a trail of testosterone in its wake.

I think I'll buy myself a pickup truck, Dad said while we waited. *As soon as I get my license back.*

MY FATHER HAS BEEN in this state of end-stage cancer for more than two years now, and while he's still dying and, since Thanksgiving, stroke-impaired, he's in the midst of a very good run. He's a week away from his seventy-ninth birthday, and somewhere between the chemotherapy and the Plenaxis, his PSA level has plummeted by 50 percent. It's still a train wreck: 150 points is about 140 above the line between having and not having cancer. But slowing down the disease reduces its assault on the body; there is less gnawing away at the bones. And it seems to mean more spring in one's step. Or is it the upcoming trip to Georgia that has put the bounce in him?

Every farmer needs a pickup truck, he says on more than one occasion.

Margaret and I have arranged a trip down to the farm that will finish up on Memorial Day weekend. She instigated this particular effort, checking calendars and proposing dates, and soon I caved, my Easter wound-licking worn thin. And neither of us could resist Dad's mounting campaign.

I'm going to ride across the pasture, Dad would say out of the blue. *Phoebe and I, saddled up and riding into the sunset.*

I wonder if there are any ripe peaches on the trees, he'd say. Or, *The twins have finished the new boat dock. We'll have to go check it out.* Or, *Troy says the tomato plants are flowering.* Or, *Troy says the watermelon hill is all planted up, right there by the scuppernongs.*

Before we had set anything in stone, Margaret went to the apartment one day to pay bills. She saw that Dad had noted on his calendar: "GNF and Leesee to Georgia." Not that we'd talked about going or that he could have gone then, his arm still in a cast, his life tethered to vancomycin treatments.

Are you and Lise going to Georgia? Margaret asked after seeing his scrawled note.

Well, I'm thinking about it.

Does Lise know?

I haven't talked to her yet, he said.

I visited him later in the week and the notation had been erased. But the campaign was not abandoned.

Hi Leesee, the telephone message began a few days later.

> *This is your dad. I'm calling to see if it is possible for you to, uh, help me get to the airport on the nineteenth after I get a shot at 933 [the oncology office address] which I can get early in the morning and, uh, I'm under the impression that Margaret is going to come for Labor Day weekend, I don't know whether—I mean Memorial Day—I don't know whether you're coming or not but I was hoping so. But anyway, what I'm trying to do is get on a plane to Atlanta sometime on the nineteenth after I take the shot. And the plan is for Jackie and her husband to pick me up and take me to the farm and be*

available for me in sufficiency so that I can stay at the farm
until the other members of the family arrive for the Memorial
Day weekend. So that's why I called. I'm just finishing up my
chemotherapy, waiting on transportation back to Waverly, so I
thought I'd give you a call. Bye-bye.

If that didn't beat all. Dad flying on his own? And what exactly did
"available in sufficiency" mean? I spent days avoiding his calls, trying to figure out with Margaret some overlapping of our schedules
that would give him the most time down there, how many days I
could spare or bear to be with him alone. More than that, I thought
hard about a list of self-preserving conditions I would impose before
agreeing to go, about how to state them, and what they should be.
And then, even though I was still in the midst of these deliberations,
I couldn't bring myself to avoid more calls, and when the phone rang
and I saw it was him, I answered.

What's the report? I asked. He told me that the donkey hadn't yet
had her baby, that the twins were finishing up their projects and said
they'd mail him a photograph of the new dock, an extension of the
existing dock but with a trapdoor-covered boat slip so that someone
unsteady on his feet could get in and out of the motorboat more
easily. Not that the motorboat's been in the water more than three
times in the last fifteen years.

By the way, he said, *the twins say they know someone who used to*
work at City Hall and who says she knows what happened with the park.
Dad is certain that corruption rather than incompetence is at the
root of Funderburg Park's problems.

Really? I asked. *What?*

Well I don't know. They told the twins they want to talk to you.

Me? Why me?

Because of your relationship.

To the twins?

This made no sense. I still couldn't tell the twins apart. I knew one weighed a little more and one talked a little more, but I didn't know which attribute belonged to Elbert and which to Albert. And the few times I'd sat with them long enough to adjust to their rhythm of speech and thickness of accent, I still averaged a comprehension rate of only about 60 percent.

To the entire Howard family, my father said.

Really? A few days after I'd interviewed their mother about pickled peaches, Dad bought a watermelon and had me bring it to her while he waited in the car.

And probably also because you're smart and because I can't get around.

Slickster. He wanted me to join the fight. I don't always understand my father, I often don't like him, I always love him, but there are certain things I know. And I knew he wanted me to climb aboard or, better still, take over this cause of the embattled park. I didn't want to do it. I could see how messy it was, how it could turn into a repository for old grudges and small slights, a magnet for the unwieldy remnants of the town's racist past. Most of all, I knew I wasn't fluent in racial idioms, certainly not the way my grandfather had been. His workarounds balanced dignity with survival, and they made lasting impressions. On one trip to Monticello, I ran into Oliver Barron, the dentist who rented Granddaddy's house for many years and later purchased his Monticello office building, out of which Oliver still runs his practice, even though at sixty-eight, he's past the age at which many people would retire. Some of Granddaddy's medical equipment is still in use, and his portrait, stern and unsmiling, hangs over the entryway door. Oliver, who is somehow related to Dorothy—a cousin, perhaps—told me he'd been associated with my family since my grandfather "pulled him out into the world," and that he saw Granddaddy apply those strategies in every aspect of life.

> *I remember when we used to go to the ice house, the man would say something and your grandfather would say, "That's right." He said, "That's right," to everything the man said.*
>
> *Finally, the white man said, "Nigger, I believe you're saying, "That's right" as a way of avoiding saying 'yassuh.'*
>
> *"'That's right,' your grandfather said.*

At the other end of the line, my father was waiting for my response. I scrambled for one that would be supportive but not entangling.

Do you know who this Deep Throat is?

No.

Well, Dad. I would be happy to listen to the information and then tell you—

And then deliver it to the proper authorities, he interrupted. *You have to be extremely precise in how you go about this.*

Here was my way out. *That's just the point,* I said. *I don't understand the politics of Monticello. They're way over my head. And what if somebody gets mad and shoots me?*

Don't you worry, he said. *If anybody shoots you, I'll shoot them right back.* This from a man who claimed he couldn't see worth a damn.

I know you mean that to be reassuring, Dad, but I'm a little uncomfortable with the fact that I still end up shot. This got a laugh. *Okay,* I said, giving in. *What happens next? Should I wait for the twins to call me?*

No, Dad said. *We just need to tell the twins when you'll come down there.*

What? I have to actually be there in person?

Oh yeah. She won't want to speak to you over the phone.

Dad. Is this a ploy to get me to take you down to Georgia?

No, no, no.

Well, I said, unable to sidestep the topic any longer, *I do want to take you down there, and I want you to be able to go to Georgia as much as you can, but I have to tell you, last time was too hard for me.*

I have to set up a few conditions before I can go down with you again.
Silence. *Dad?*

I'm listening.

First, no big pig parties. It's too much to take care of everything from day to day and set up a party. So for now, I need a break from that. I'll give you a party when you turn eighty and you can invite whoever you want. Okay?

Okay. What else?

I need some time off. I can't go zipping around with you all day long without a break. So whether it's to do my own work or to fish or just sit around, I need to have some time off.

Anything else?

Well, if I'm going to travel with you, I need you to wear pants that zip up.

I don't know about that. On this point my father was unyielding. He'd buy a horse without blinking, but he wouldn't let me or my sisters or his wife buy him a pair of jeans to fit over the diapers. I often wondered how much of this was about not caring what others thought, and how much was about defending his ability to be in charge of himself. Whenever I sensed it was the latter, I let it go. At least until I'd banked a few uncomfortable elevator rides or been tagged by the valet cashier or a nurse one too many times, scolded or whispered at to close the barn door.

DAD HAS TALKED JACKIE into staying with him at 354 Fellowship Road for the week before Memorial Day weekend. She'll cook breakfast and dinner, and she's arranged for a cousin of Eddie's to come in during the day to clean up and surreptitiously provide surveillance on Dad's safety while Jackie's at work. Eddie, who has no car and does not work and is apparently in some permanent state of disability, will stay at the farm day and night, caring for the menagerie.

At first Diane withholds her support for the plan. *I'm not com-*

fortable agreeing to this, she declares, *unless I talk to Jackie first and feel like she understands what she's committing to.*

I marvel that Diane feels the authority to sanction or put the kibosh on the whole thing based on her comfort. Birth order? Over-protectiveness? Realism? She backs down from her stance after Lois calls Jackie to brief her on Dad's deteriorated condition.

Dad arranges for Jackie and Eddie to pick him up at the Atlanta airport, so that after one of his daughters hands him off to a wheel-chair operator at the Philadelphia end he can fly alone. Once the logistics are set, I make his plane reservation, file the appropriate doctor's orders with Waverly, and confirm that my dad will be fin-ished with the vancomycin the day before he leaves, even though Waverly has the termination date noted as five days later. None of us daughters want the treatments to extend to Monticello this time around. That would be too much to ask of Jackie. Or anyone.

Weeks before he's set to go, Dad brings his suitcase down from a closet shelf and sets it on a dining nook chair. He packs, unpacks, and repacks, although the end result is always more or less the same: camera equipment, medications, diapers, and address books. No clothes; he has enough at the farm.

This is a generous commitment for Jackie to have made, even if she was cornered into it by Dad's cajoling and charm. It's a commit-ment she may well regret by the end of the week. But if it works out, it opens up tremendous opportunity for Dad to spend more time at the farm. If all goes according to plan, we, the daughters, will check in by phone and look forward to our weekend with him at the end. In the days before our arrival, Dad will eat catfish and get his hair cut and "stimulate the local economy," as Troy puts it. Margaret and I will carry on with our own lives and commitments. On Friday, we will go down with Phoebe for a short, sweet trip, and on Monday we'll bring Dad back home. If all goes according to plan.

This is a new vista we're facing, this new way for Dad to spend time at the farm without being entirely dependent on us, and "us" has most often meant the flexible-schedule, no-young-children, Monticello-liking me. The new plan is a great innovation and a big relief. I feel replaced.

A YEAR OR SO AGO, my mother instituted a new tradition: weekly family dinners. These are often potluck, unless John, the cooking enthusiast, and I are hosting. When we're all too busy or tired, they are takeout. The tradition takes instantly. John dubs them Funderfests, Phoebe concocts dances or plays to perform, I ask everyone to report on something that's happened since the last communal meal, and my mother, who endures our constant attention to Dad, gets us all to herself. Until Dad catches on.

I'm available, he says when one of us mentions a dinner in the offing. *I could come if somebody would pick me up and take me home.* My mother is gracious in her inclusion of Dad. She willingly hosts the events at her wheelchair-accessible apartment building; she tells us to invite Lois, who, in her increasing immobility, won't come.

My father doesn't participate easily in the cacophony. He doesn't seem to mind. Anything's got to be more interesting than sitting in his apartment, watching the Westerns channel for hours on end, but efforts to include him require backstories and fill-ins and self-censoring modifications. My sisters and I are well practiced at selectively revealing ourselves to him in order to avoid judgment. His presence alters every event: Whoever takes him home is tied to his exhaustion, and he always wants to leave early.

Whenever you're ready, he'll say to his escort, often just before the last fork has been put to rest on the table.

Shortly before his solo trip to Georgia, he comes to a family brunch at my mother's. We choreograph the arrivals, departures, and potluck assignments. Diane will bring Dad at noon after paying bills in the morning at his apartment. Margaret will work on his bills, too, but she'll come back earlier, stopping to pick up bagels at the good bakery on Dad's side of the river, the one we used to pass as we walked from school to the bus stop every day. John and I will come straight from home, stopping at the market to pick up cream cheese and tomatoes and red onion and fish—especially the smoked chubs Dad and John like, and a tub of whitefish salad. Greg will bring Phoebe later, and Phoebe, who has not inherited her maternal side's omnivorous gene, will eat a buttered bagel.

Brunch is filled with the typical land mines. When Dad asks Mom, again, if she'll come down to Georgia for the holiday weekend, she says she can't because she has to *work*. She lives fairly well off savings and a modest pension, but she supplements those with dog sitting and bed-and-breakfast guests. Greg and Margaret ask Dad's opinion about whether to keep or evict a habitually late-paying tenant, and as they lay out circumstances and context, Dad's mouth cements into a neutral line.

I've been out of the business a long time, he says.

Phoebe's birthday party was the day before. Mom was determined to get a cake for today and is disappointed when no one eats it, stuffed to the gills as we are after the meal, and, frankly, caked out. Even sweet-toothed Phoebe only picks at the icing.

I shouldn't have gotten it, Mom says.

But there are easy parts, too. Phoebe is chatty in her tales of her birthday party, its most successful games, the different kids' limbo styles. When she's talkative around Dad, even if not speaking directly to him, you can see he's mesmerized, lapping it up, basking in it. We engage in boisterous group speculation about the park informant, and I share my mixed feelings about Dad's offer to shoot anyone who shoots me.

Do you have any idea who Deep Throat could be? John asks.

No, Dad says. *In a small town like Monticello, you can't imagine the connections people have. It could be someone who remembers my father or was involved with him in some way. He helped a lot of people over the years.*

I remember one thing I really admired about my father. A man stole his cow and was caught red-handed. The police called my father in and identified the man. My father saw him cowering in the corner, looking so pitiful. He thought about what would become of him, and he turned around and walked out the door, even though the sheriff was agitating for him to press charges. But my father couldn't be a party to sending that man away.

So it could be a connection to him, or maybe it's someone with a relationship to the twins. Everyone knows the twins know me.

I TAKE DAD to the airport after checking the pockets of his vest to make sure he has the identification he needs and none of the pocketknives he likes to carry. He flies without incident. Jackie is waiting to meet him, and his maiden semisolo week at the farm speeds by. He is happy. He has Eddie at his beck and call, an all-day chauffeur. In a checkup call, I can't resist whining.

You don't need us anymore!

No, no, he rushes back. *I need you. Come quick. Come quick.* This is my dad at his loveliest. Playful, sweet, feigning need. Or real need: the good, natural kind that comes from an open heart.

All sorts of people fill in for the gap of daughterly attentions. Marshall Tinsley takes Dad for catfish and grits at his brother's restaurant the first morning, then drops Dad off at the courthouse so he can try for three hours, unsuccessfully, to ambush someone in the district attorney's office into giving him instructions on the protocol of meeting up with Deep Throat. Afterward, Dad walks himself a quarter of the way around the square (*I'm walking! I'm walking!*) over to Eddie Ray's, then hitches a ride home with Jerry Goldin. Dad drives himself down to the pond in the Explorer to check out the new dock and finds it satisfactory. Marshall comes back later to take Dad to the Lane Peach Packing Company down in Fort Valley, where Dad's on the hunt for tree-ripened peaches and a watermelon.

He finds peaches, but this early in the season only the messier cling-stone varieties are ready, the Flavorich and Sunbrite, Springcrest and Empress. Then he treats Jackie and Eddie to dinner in the town of Social Circle. That's just day one.

Over the next few days, he traipses hither and yon. He eats breakfast at Huddle House in Jackson with Troy, leaving nothing but a clean ring of ham bone on the plate, and is driven to a liquor store by Hard Time, whose moniker, I've found out, after asking directly, has nothing to do with incarceration or accosts. Instead, it comes from when Eddie tried out for varsity basketball as a high school freshman. The older members on the team said he'd have a "hard time" winning a spot. But he did.

Dad threatens repeatedly to go fishing; on Wednesday, he enlists Donna Coe to give him a riding lesson. He appends himself to the saddle with some pushing and pulling from Donna and Hard Time, and then he rides Dixie, the calmer of his two horses, across the length of the pasture. He's leaning to one side the entire time, listing, making Donna's heart race, but he stays up there, riding high.

I felt like John Wayne, he tells me, his voice as springy and fresh as a new rubber band. You can tell he was thrilled to have done it and come out okay on the other end. It's what he told everyone, including the cardiologist, he was going to do, and he didn't fall off and die or break a hip or paralyze himself.

Over the course of the week, he calls with questions, problems, status reports. *I can't get the computer to go on. . . . I can't make your recorder work . . . I'm gonna show Hard Time how to fish.* I call back and suggest checking to see if the computer's plugged into the wall, advise him to call the local Radio Shack to see if he can get a new tape recorder for his Deep Throat assignation, and wait for the fish tales to come my way.

Midweek, Dad talks to Deep Throat. *She didn't tell me anything I didn't already know,* he reports. No rosetta stones, no scoops, no details that push incompetence into illegality.

So you couldn't wait for me to come? I say, relieved.

I got it all on tape, he says, *so you can listen to it when you get here.*

I resent Jackie's success in making this possible. I think he's having a better time than ever and feel slighted. I used to be such a shining star. Everyone would comment on what good daughters Dad had, how lucky he was. Then I tell myself to shut up and be thankful. Thankful that I get a break, that the load has been lifted, even just a little. Thankful that he gets to be there, that this setup might get him there more often, at least for a while, until he turns on Jackie or she makes what is in his eyes some irremediable mistake, as pretty much everyone—except for maybe Holsey, who was about as close to a saint as I've seen walking the earth—eventually does.

ON FRIDAY NIGHT, Margaret and Phoebe and I get to the farm at 9 P.M. We find Dad at his kitchen table post. He's usually in bed hours before this, but he's stayed up to see us arrive safe and sound. Jackie is in the kitchen fixing dinner. She looks exhausted. She has allergies, she says, and it's been a bad week for pollen. The exhaustion or the pollen has exaggerated the bags under her eyes, the trait that so far is the single greatest indicator of our possible genetic connection. She's on the short side, too, which fits with Carolyn and several of the female cousins, but she has none of our hips or heft. She's a slim thing, unusually trim for her fifty-some years and given the lard-filled local cuisine she's eaten her whole life.

I wheel my suitcase into the smaller guest room, come back to the kitchen, help get dinner ready, then sit down next to my father. His two pillboxes lie at the edge of his place mat. Each holds a week's worth of medications. I don't like both boxes being out. That seems an invitation to mix-ups. When I've been in charge, I've kept

247

the boxes in my bedroom dresser and brought pills out to the table one dose at a time, depositing them in a ramekin at the center of Dad's place mat. The pills in the two boxes are in fact mixed up and half taken and in almost no discernable order.

Dad, have you been taking your medicine?

Yes, I have.

It looks like you missed some doses.

No, I didn't.

I look across the table at Jackie.

Has Dad been taking his pills?

I left that to him, she says. I want to ask what she was thinking, how she could do that, but I know. I can see her trying to help and Dad telling her, with all the confidence in the world and perhaps a smidge of harshness, that he didn't need her, that he'd keep it straight, that it was already laid out for him. I can see her perhaps even trying to reiterate her offer at some point, and his retort backing her into a silent corner. I can also see her feeling that she's taken on enough by coming to stay, fix dinners, and keep him company.

How about if I help you keep them straight? I ask.

Please don't, he says. *Whenever anyone tries to help, things only get messed up.*

Then I see his feet. They're swollen again, his ankles like tree trunks, fleshy cylinders of stopped-up, backed-up fluid.

Caught any fish yet? I ask.

I am the last one to bed. Before I leave the kitchen, I sit down with the pillboxes and try to figure out what's been going on. I discern the pattern of the pills, some of it coming back to me from the last time I was here and had to pop each prescription out of its blister pack and into the box. When I gain enough confidence to feel that I'm not actually making matters worse, I reorganize the boxes. I set up what looks to me like an obvious difference between the two containers, but I have a nagging feeling that obvious is in the eye of the non–stroke-addled beholder. So I get out a ramekin and

248

put the next morning's pills into it, and put that on top of the pill-boxes on his place mat. I'm hoping that if he gets up and to the table before I do, and I know he will, he'll follow the path I've set.

He could have had another stroke, I think as I turn out the lights.

MARGARET AND I STAND BY the horse barn on Saturday morning, a Howard-twin-built series of three stalls attached to an equipment shed, with a water line running to a spigot in the back. With every structure Elbert and Albert build, my husband's admiration for them increases.

They're masters of vernacular architecture, says John, himself a trained architect. I like the red they use to spray-paint everything.

Margaret and I are clustered in the bit of shade the building provides, and we are watching Donna give my niece a riding lesson. Donna rides Phoebe, the horse, as Phoebe, the girl, sits atop Dixie, usually the more cooperative and mild-mannered of the two mares. Today, though, Dixie is not going along with the plan, and no matter which way my niece tugs at the reins or clicks her tongue or squeezes her nine-year-old legs into the horse's barreled flanks, Dixie either stands stock-still or circles back to the barn. Finally, Donna attaches a lead to Dixie, and she pulls horse and child along behind her as she rides ahead, circling the pasture a few times so my niece won't feel shortchanged.

Donna has some worries, she told us while saddling up the mares. She commented on the care of the horses, which Eddie recently took on, in a way that bore no malice. At least that's how it seemed, so either she's a genuinely uncritical person or she's really, really good at faking it. She told us to watch out for the horses' ears, because she'd noticed the day before that the gnats had been at them so badly they were bleeding. She treated them with ointment and they look better already, but they are likely still sensitive. She also noticed some nicks on Phoebe's legs she can't figure out, and Dixie has a lump on her right rear leg that is of some concern. As she hoisted the saddle onto Dixie for the lesson, Donna noted that its cinch was shortened too many notches, and also that both horses' bits were too tight. She'd heard Eddie took a friend riding and the friend had fallen off. Presumably, this was on a separate day from when Eddie decided to go natural, riding one of the horses bareback and helmetless and using the horse's mane as a pommel. We're heard about this ride from Jackie already: Eddie fell and fell on his head.

Is Donna trying to tell us she's concerned about Eddie's care of the animals? I ask Margaret, assuming Donna's uncritical stance. The question could be phrased another way: *Is Donna trying to tell us Eddie's an idiot?*

CAROLYN DRIVES DOWN Saturday afternoon. At Margaret's request, Carolyn will stop at the airport along the way, picking up my brother-in-law, Greg, who's flying directly from his relatives' gathering in upstate New York. What I love about Carolyn is how family she is. It's not just that Funderburg is printed on our faces, gene-pool-wise, as if the dealer had only so many cards and kept reshuffling for each birth, or that she's willing to be enlisted in travel logistics, but that she walks in the door and is instantly among us, even when months and years have gone by. She helps and teases and loafs with the rest of us. I find her sitting on the couch with Phoebe one morning, both of them in their pajamas, having a lengthy, earnest discussion about their pet cats, including personalities, eating habits, and play styles. Margaret washes a blouse for her, and Carolyn takes the basket of freshly dried laundry and folds every last piece of clothing in it.

DAD LIES IN WAIT for me, stationed at the kitchen table with his new tape recorder in front of him. I pass by once or twice, then acquiesce, prepared to give the matter some attention, and then wash my hands of it.

You might find something of interest, Dad says, pushing the machine in my direction. Deep Throat turned out to be a local woman, a former City Hall employee. I press the "on" button. Every comment is clipped at its beginning and end, probably because Dad either fidgeted with the controls or left the machine on voice-activation mode. The result has the effect of coming in late to each person's thought.

From the portions I can make out, Deep Throat acts more as interrogator than as informant. *And what is your investment in the park?* she asks. *What was the value of the land you donated?*

The rest of the day, farm accounts are settled and general information is exchanged. I drive Dad and his checkbook over to Troy's to reconcile debts, and Troy tells us Bubba went into Jasper Memorial a few days earlier, was sedated for an MRI, and hasn't woken up since.

He's just "zz-zz-zz," Troy says, imitating a snoring Bubba. The hospital kept him overnight, but by the next afternoon, when he hadn't regained consciousness, they transferred him to Emory University's bigger, better-equipped hospital in Atlanta.

One twin, Elbert, comes by the farm to collect on an invoice. Compared to what Dad's been spending lately, it's a relatively small check I write out of his checkbook, less than two thousand dollars. It's a part of what's owed for the new dock and the installation of a swing set and the lowering of a barn wall and the putting up of a predator-proof henhouse and whatever other changes have been made in the month since I was last down.

This person I know wants to talk to you about the park, Elbert says, then gives me the last four digits of her phone number. I don't want to call her. I don't want to be sucked in. I don't want to filter information to my dad or have to represent him to others. But I can't figure a way out of it, so I call. She exudes urgency, and before

I'm clever enough to find a way out, we set up a meeting for three o'clock on Sunday.

I'll bring my boys out with me, she says, *because I like for them to see the open air.*

The next day, twenty minutes before the appointed Deep Throat meeting, I am down at the new fishing pavilion with Carolyn, Phoebe, and Dad. We're kind of fishing and generally messing about, and I feel like I'm on death row.

At five minutes of three, Dad says, sportingly, *Well, I guess I'll just run you up to the house and then come back down. If you girls want to wait*, he says to the carefree, unencumbered Carolyn and Phoebe, *I'll be back in five minutes.*

He heads for the driver's side, which I don't contest since Phoebe won't be with us. He rumbles the Explorer slowly up the path, over the cattle grate and onto the garage driveway, where we see a strange car parked around the other side of the house.

I guess she's here, I say. He pulls into the garage but leaves the car idling.

Dad, come in with me, I wheedle. I'm beyond reason at this point, desperate.

I can't, he says, and then laughs as I paw at his arm, careful to steer clear of his elbow. *I can't. But you'd better go. Bye-bye.*

No, I wail.

Bye-bye, he says. Har-har.

If you had an ejector button, you'd push it, wouldn't you?

Yes. Laugh laugh laugh. *I would.* Har-har. *Bye-bye.*

The meeting lasts fifteen minutes. I listen noncommittally as Deep Throat professes her desire to see justice done, her conviction that laws have been broken and monies misspent. I walk the line between letting her know how much I appreciate her concern about something so important to my father and saying anything that might be misconstrued as a willingness to join her crusade. She promises to be our eyes and ears, collects her boys from the picnic table outside, where they've been watching the open air, and leaves.

CAROLYN INTENDS TO STAY only one night but ends up staying two. She divulges some curious information along the way. First, my father recently sent her a check for four hundred dollars, the first time he's ever given her money, Golden Handshake notwithstanding. No one, including Carolyn, knows what prompted this unexpected gift. Carolyn also tells us he gave a check to Jackie, and that he asked Carolyn for her two brothers' addresses. We don't know for sure if he sent the boys money, since several checks have gone un-recorded in his register. The second item concerns a different type of currency. I pass by the living room and am surprised to see Margaret and Carolyn there, since I'd heard no voices. Margaret gestures for me to come over, beckoning with a hush-hush hand.

What? I whisper.

Tell her, Margaret whispers to Carolyn. Carolyn and Jackie had a DNA test almost two months ago. Carolyn paid the three-hundred-fifty-dollar tab, and two saliva swabs later, there is a profound indication—extremely high odds—that the two share no familial bonds.

I don't think Jackie's said anything to Uncle George, Carolyn says. *And I don't feel like it's my place to do that.*

At that, I turn and go into the kitchen, calling out to Dad before I reach the table. *Dad,* I say, as if I were bringing news of what was for lunch or that someone was coming up the driveway. *Did you know Carolyn and Jackie had a DNA test?*

No, he says, and waits for me to continue. But I don't. I just go about my business. Margaret and Carolyn come in the room. I let Dad wait another delicious ten or fifteen seconds.

Carolyn, I say, *tell Dad what you told us.* Carolyn sticks to the facts. She tells Dad her understanding of how the tests works, and that another, more expensive test is thought to be more conclusive. Dad says nothing for a while. Finally, he asks one question.

How much would that more accurate test cost?

SUNDAY MORNING I announce that I am going to fish, that I'm going to use up our red wigglers and catch some big cats. Dad says he'll come along. The day is sunny and the pond is pretty and Dad has me laughing in his running dialogue with his prey. *Okay, this is it. Now I'm getting ya. Here I come. I've got you cornered.*

He sits in a folding chair at a break in the dock railing; I circulate, aiming for the element of surprise. We are luckless and ready to call it quits when the twins pull up. I'm always better at understanding them at the end of my visits, when the filters of my northern ear come unclogged, when I can translate *skreet* or *skrimp* into *street* or *shrimp*. I follow along pretty well as Albert and Elbert talk to Dad about the crow killer, a man who will come onto your property with his gun and take out hundreds of crows at a time. The man doesn't ask to be paid; it's just something he likes to do, and I suppose the theory is that word gets passed along the crow grapevine that it's Armageddon over at George's Hill, best to stay away, and as a result fewer of Dad's trees will end up defruited and denutted. The twins came along during the crow killer's recent visit, and after the carnage, they strung up crow carcasses in the orchard as reminders. Once the conversation winds down, I tell the twins I've had bites but no catches.

Just put the worm on the hook and let it sit down at the bottom, says Albert. Or Elbert. *Then just wait. You'll see.*

My father has trouble walking over the uneven land between the dock and the truck. The cane he has brought is not enough. The twins go to either side of him and each takes an arm.

Take your time, one says. *No one's in a hurry.*

Just one step and rest, says the other. *That's what we tell our mother. One step and rest. That's all ya got to do. We got nowhere to go.*

When Dad can't raise himself into the seat of the truck, which is parked on an uphill slant, the twins just lift him in gentle and easy, as if he were a baby, a feather.

TROY COMES BY AFTER CHURCH to give us the report on Bubba, who's awake but not speaking. Just how conscious he is remains unclear. He's had a frontal-lobe stroke.

That's what they said I had, Dad says.

Yes, I confirm. *But yours was much milder, because you never stopped talking.*

Troy tells us that Bubba's son, Troy the doctor, is at his father's side, consulting on his care. No, Troy the younger has told the attending physician, they cannot split apart his father's skull the way they might normally do when someone has so much fluid on the brain. They are not to drill a hole to relieve the pressure. His father might not be able to take the trauma of the procedure.

He may get through this or he may not, Troy the elder says as he delivers the news to us around the kitchen table of 354. *You never know. He's been here a good long time, though.*

Meanwhile, Troy is minding Bubba's vast garden and eleven cows. Troy says Bubba loves those cows so much, and everyone knows it. *The Howard twins say that if Bubba does start talking again, the first thing he'll say is, "Where's my cows?" If he doesn't make it, those cows are gone.* Troy plays tough guy. *I ain't messin' with no cows.*

Five days after we leave, Bubba dies. He never recovered from the stroke, never talked again. Dad calls to tell me that Bubba is gone, only because I've asked him to call with any news, knowing that without the request, we might not find out for days or weeks.

I'd like to go to the funeral, I say. *Maybe you'll come with me.* His "yes" jumps across the telephone line, but then he leaves a message an hour later that after looking at the week's calendar, he doesn't think he can take the time to go, and he wants me to know so I won't work on making it happen. Maybe he just doesn't want to spend time amid all that church and emotion. But then I see on my  calendar that he has chemotherapy and the elbow surgeon on Friday, which is likely to be the day of services. I think of offering to switch around the appointments, or at least to try, but I don't. I don't call back. I don't go to the funeral.

14.

THE TRUTH IS TO LIVE

THE MORE MY FATHER'S HEALTH declines, the more his requests to be taken to the farm increase. Funerals aside, every meteorological shift, crop ripening, and animal birth is presented as a call to travel. The doctors who see my father regularly (Ellis, Schnall, and

Battaglia) back him on this. *It's the most effective treatment there is,* each one says. *If there were a way you girls could arrange for him to stay there longer or even permanently, I'd advise it.*

But my sisters and I can't quit our jobs, and even though he and Lois have more of a nagging than nurturing relationship, when we ask our father point-blank if he wants to go to the farm permanently, he says he can't leave Lois alone too long. When he's at the farm, he'll dial or instruct us to dial her twice a day. At the end of one long week, she tells him she misses him.

I miss you, too, Honeybaby, he says, then swivels around to face the back door. *But don't worry, I'm pointing my chair north.*

We know the end is coming. We don't know when, but it's beginning to feel like it can't be much longer, like no amount of will could prevail over such wear and tear. So my sisters and I ratchet up our efforts to get him to the farm as often as we can, aiming for once a month. We are aligned in goals, if not methods, which I am reminded of one Sunday when I accompany my sisters on their bill-paying trip to his apartment. We are trying to figure out the possibility of a late-June trip. Dad is no help. Ask him his availability and he's ready to go now, or later today, or, at worst, tomorrow. Diane's loyalty has displaced her own wound-licking, and she has said she is willing to go. She compares her schedule to his, which is complicated in that what he tells her doesn't jibe with what is in his pocket calendar, which doesn't jibe with the wall calendar, which doesn't jibe with Lois's master calendar. Dad repeatedly proposes one date, even though each time he says it, Diane tells him she's not available then. He says the date. Diane says she can't go. He says the date again. Again, she says she can't go.

I step into the impasse, taking hold of the pocket calendar. I see my father has written "OFF CHEMO" across one week, in capital letters and at a jaunty, upward angle. Oh, I think, he's got it under control. And then I turn the page, and "OFF CHEMO" is on the next week as well—an impossibility, since he has treatments three weeks out of every four. I turn the page and a third week has the same penciled-in banner of liberation. So does a fourth week. So does a fifth.

OFF CHEMO. OFF CHEMO. OFF CHEMO. OFF CHEMO. OFF CHEMO.

How my father insists on living. He talks up a storm about getting back up on Dixie and riding like John Wayne; he makes noise about how he's going to have Diane help him buy his new pickup truck; he buys thousands of dollars of stock in some company, based, he tells Diane upon interrogation, on something he read; he instructs the Howard twins to install oarlocks and oars on the aluminum boat that bears my name.

In the end, we decide on one long weekend in June, and when the time comes, I drive Diane and Dad to the airport. I urge Diane to take care of herself, to be as sybaritic as possible, to spend thirty-five dollars of Dad's money to upgrade her airplane seat to business class. Simply meeting Dad's basic needs will be exhausting, and on top of that, Dad's already told Diane that he's made an appointment with the local district attorney regarding allegations of park malfeasance, and that she has to go with him, and her job will be to make sure he doesn't say something "wrong." He also wants to get new satellite TV receivers and a telephone answering machine up and running after a May thunderstorm burned out the old ones.

I drop them at the curbside check-in. Diane hovers behind him as he leans on his walker to shuffle inside and to the bench of seats we know are to the right, the waiting place for wheelchair users. I'm fairly certain he'll run Diane into the ground and that she'll call from down there, telling stories on him that he'll relish and contest, and she'll return exhausted.

In fact, he makes good on his pickup truck threat immediately: When Diane won't take him to the Toyota dealership, he calls on

Hard Time to drive him, coming home in a cherry red four-door. She returns to Philadelphia swearing she'll never again take him by herself.

By July, I can tell my defenses are slipping and that I'll take my father to Georgia the next time circumstances dictate. But I won't rush the moment. We make a plan to send him down alone in the middle of the month, for Jackie to stay with him again, and for me to pick him up two weeks later. I'm not quite ready to go it alone, and when I find that neither my sisters nor John can join me, I lure my mother into going along by suggesting that she and I take Phoebe for the weekend, with neither doting parent present to interfere with our own doting. Then we'll bring Dad back.

Before Dad goes, though, he gets a call about the park. In response to our letter to the Attorney General, the Georgia FBI office wants to interview him. Hush-hush. He isn't to tell anyone.

He's going to blab it all over, says Diane, whom he's asked to call me and deliver the news of the interview.

No, I'm not! No, I'm not, I hear in the background. Despite the mysteries that surround my father, the endless questions I have about what motivates him, what he thinks, how he feels, he is, in a certain respect, miserable at keeping secrets.

On the morning Dad is to talk to the G-man at the farm, the week before Mom and Phoebe and I fly down, the G-man doesn't show. Dad calls, they reschedule. Dad promises me a full report. What I wouldn't give to be a fly on the wall. I call later to ask what the G-man talked about.

He talked like he had a mouthful of shit, Dad says. Nothing comes of the FBI's involvement. No one's indicted, although Dad does e-mail one of the people on his own suspect list to mention the FBI's investigation and how much easier things might be if the suspect were to come clean sooner rather than later. This makes me wonder, when I'm copied on that e-mail, about what legally constitutes harassment and false accusation. No funds are recovered. No playing fields are graded, no basketball courts are laid. Nothing happens at the park.

RIGHT BEFORE PHOEBE and my mother and I leave for the airport, it occurs to me to wonder the following about the imminent trip: what the hell am I thinking? There's Dad, whose needs come close to all-encompassing. There's Phoebe, who's not even in the double digits yet. She gets to have needs. Then there's my mother. Mom can be a worrier, and at eighty-one that trait only seems to be increasing. At the farm, that trait will probably be exacerbated by being in such ongoing proximity to her ex-husband. But she also knows how to have a good time wherever she is, and when we get there, she and Phoebe make great companions. They go on walks through the pasture together and play games and in the mornings, since they share the same room, Phoebe climbs up on Mom's bed and they lie on their backs and do Mom's physical therapy exercises together, even though Phoebe has not had her hip replaced. Through the wall that joins our two bedrooms, I can hear giggles alternating with counting off.

While Dad snores in front of a televised golf tournament, I slip away from the house for a short drive to the orchard, cutting off the driveway after the second cattle grate and circling around the rental house. Mom sits in the truck's passenger seat and Phoebe stands in its bed, holding onto the sides and giggling at every bump. We drive under the three old Stuarts, pecan trees so laden that their branches dip in surrender to the record-breaking crop they hold. It won't be harvested until late October, and at the moment, we are on the hunt for pears, the last of the small orchard's fruit to ripen. While I'm looking out my window, backing up under a tree so Phoebe can pick from the truck, I see the remnants of crows hanging from branches.

Whenever Phoebe's out of his sight, Dad asks her whereabouts. He is overly protective: if she sits on the edge of the fishing dock with her legs swinging over the side, he tells her to watch out, tells her this makes him nervous. Without complaint she gets up and moves. She doesn't flinch when Dad accuses her of taking his pen, a sparkly red roller ball that so clearly matches the set Phoebe always takes on trips.

I got that at the Farm and Garden this morning, he says. Phoebe says nothing.

But you can have it, he says. Phoebe takes it, says thanks, and walks away.

Later she calls me into her room.

Look, Leesee, she says, showing me a green version of the same pen. *This matches my set.*

Oh honeypie, I say. *I knew that was your pen. Granddad just gets a little confused. But you were very patient with him.*

I know, Phoebe says quickly, as if she doesn't want to make too big a deal of what happened. *I just wanted to show you.*

Dad calls out to me, *Leesee!* every two seconds. To fix him canned oyster stew; to write a check to Rami El-Jourbagy, the Egyptian émigré whose handsome high school age son is a fledgling tech support guy; to fetch Jerry Goldin a beer; to type up a fishing rights agreement for Marshall Tinsley; to look for his favorite and missing pair of Birkenstock sandals; and to go out and greet whoever has driven up to the house.

Jackie comes by several times. On one visit, she looks in the refrigerator and sees that the food has begun to pile up and that we'll be leaving much of it behind. *I'll be splitting those lamb chops with Mr. Troy,* she says.

Dad talks about getting a farm sign made for Mom, and while we debate whether it should go on the tractor, henhouse, or pasture, Jackie calls out from the next room. *While you're deciding,* she says, *you can make the sign for Jackie's Pavilion.*

Mom ponders and frets over what to have named. Finally, she decides on what she wants and takes me out to the patio to see it. We are looking south, across the fence line and over rolling hills and ponds and pastures, with the lumber company smokestacks in the distance.

What am I looking at? I ask.

Maggie's View, she says. Or, translated into my father's middle-name-obsessed lingo: Marjorie Jeane Lievense Funderburg's Panoramic View. This is my mom at her best. The rest of us come up with stuff. She names an experience.

Jerry Goldin names an experience, too. He stops by while the computer-fixing El-Jourbagys are trying to extract Dad's address book from the computer onto a disk, although I've tried to explain to Dad that the computer in Georgia and the one I've updated at Waverly don't hold the same information in their saved files. Jerry tells my mother some stories of his days as a state trooper, then shows her the Polaroids he happens to have in his pocket from his part-time position as the county's co-coroner. Jerry looks around at the motley assemblage of friends, family, consultants.

Who'd have thought, he says, *that in Jasper County, you'd have Muslims, Jews, blacks, whites, and mixed all under one roof?*

WHEN IT COMES to Dad's August trip, despite temperatures in the mid-90s with humidity to match, Margaret and I take him. Diane has warned each of us not to go down alone. *It's too hard,* she says. *It's way too hard.*

Margaret and I have figured that if we maximize the opportunity by picking him up at the end of one chemo cycle and bringing him home the night before the next, he can squeeze in about twelve days away. I fetch his suitcase from the apartment, then drive to the treatment clinic. He's still plugged in. He seems tired, groggy, and slow, but he's told all the nurses he's going to Big Foot Country. He's got his Stetson on, and his vest is packed with its usual detritus plus keys to assorted gates and doors and vehicles. He clowns around at the appointment desk on our way out, picking through the candy dish and answering, *Sweet,* when I ask what flavor he's chosen. He's been sitting in a soaked diaper for who knows how long. Two diapers, actually. This doubling up is something he's started to do, and it ensures that the fly of his pants truly cannot close. While I set up his next round of treatments, he canes to the bathroom to dry off and change, patting his vest on the way in search of spares.

I drive up to the door, and Dad canes to the car. I stand behind him, out of his way but within reach so I can catch him if needed. I put my hand between the top of his head and the car door frame and take the cane as it is handed off. Dad folds himself into the seat as slowly as gravity will allow, favoring tender spots and weaknesses he'll never talk about. But you can see they're there. Otherwise, he wouldn't have to parse the process into discrete and labored efforts: the lowering of his trunk onto the seat, the picking up of each leg to get it into the car, the shifting from an angled pose to a straight-forward one, the pulling, then buckling, of the seat belt, him still tilting onto one buttock, avoiding pressure on that overused, mal-functioning rear end.

Margaret meets us right before security so that she can skip the long lines reserved for the ambulatory. I have begun to recognize wheelchair drivers in the Philadelphia and Atlanta airports, to remember which are better at steering and gentling over bumps, which will take us not just to the parking garage but to the car, and which show irritation or patience when Dad has to make a long restroom stop. I know where the wheelchair lanes are at each checkpoint, and I know to allow time for Dad to be pulled aside and waved over with a handheld scanner as he always is. Once we're on the plane, I know that seat 1D is optimal for restroom access. I'll walk up the aisle to check on him during the flight, to bring him a sandwich or make sure he's breathing, and more often than not I'll find him either asleep or engaged with his seatmate, a college kid going back to Morehouse one trip, a Tennessee ham heir the next.

The weather is good, the plane takes off when it should, and we are in Georgia by early evening. We walk into the house to find boxes eclipsing all kitchen surfaces, the counters, the table. Dad has been spending time with the direct-mail catalogs that come in abundance to him and Lois, ordering with abandon and having everything sent to Troy's house, knowing Troy will bring all of it over in time for our arrival. It is Christmas in August: there is a handheld illuminated magnifier, a forged iron vertical paper-towel holder with a faux-rust finish, and a portable bug zapper. There are three vacuum thermoses, one-liter capacity each. Two are stainless-steel-sheathed, one is white plastic.

I had the idea, Dad says, *that we should take coffee with us when we go to breakfast at Dave's*. Dave's ribs are wedding-worthy; his coffee is not.

There are boot pullers, each with a curving metal hook attached to a wooden handle, and an illuminated chess training kit, endorsed by "Kasparov, World Champion."

So I can beat Diane, Dad explains.

My favorite, the Super SearchEye, is a safety-yellow handheld searchlight bigger but no heavier than a gallon of milk. It's blinding. It's huge, unwieldy, and for what? To see the Klan coming?

Margaret and I are not as worried about dangerous, cloaked strangers as we are about known variables, which is why we have squeezed in a forty-eight-hour trip to usher Dad into this next stint of time in Big Foot Country, with Jackie picking up after we leave. Things went awry recently with Hard Time, who, having entrenched himself at the fishing pavilion for hours at a time and day after day, presumably before or after taking care of the goats and chickens, was present when a nephew of Troy's came to fish. The most generous spin on what unfolded is that Hard Time too literally followed my father's instruction to call 911 upon encountering "intruders." So the police came, and when Troy's nephew tried to explain that he had a letter of permission sitting in his glove compartment, Eddie apparently told the law enforcement officers he was unaware of such a letter. The nephew left.

My father heard an account of this from Troy, and immediately sent Jackie and Eddie an e-mail, with copies to his daughters.

> Subject: Eddie Frank's Ungracious Behavior.
> dear Jackie and Eddie,
> it is distressing to have to write this e-mail about eddie's confrontational, ungracious behaviour toward one of my guest invited to fish on our lake.
> it may be that we can straighten this outwhen i return in about two weeks, I hope so, how ever to emphaxize my position, let me suggest that eddie not, fish on our pond until we do straighten this out. also, it might be a good idea for eddie not to take any of my liquor, vodka or wine,until that time I am not an indian giver and realize that there may be some wine that I had given Jackie that she should feel free to take home if she likes.
> by copy of this writing to franees smith [Dorothy's sister] i am requesting she pass it along to troy eugene johnson so that he may reassure his nephew that my permisssion for him to fish on our lak is still in tact and he is welcome to come back.the nephew should know that his grandmother was most gracious to me over sixty years ago when i spent a weekend at their house in the Glades.
> Keep well, continue your good work and enjoy life.love
> uncle george
> k
> Best Wishes

People always fall from grace with my father. Eddie didn't have as far to drop as some, considering how fervid Dad can be in his initial admiration, but still, descent was inevitable. I keep wondering about Jackie: Dad will mention that she's borrowed something from the house, maybe a DVD or ladder, without asking or returning it. Both actions are excommunication-worthy, yet he cuts off neither relations nor generosity. If she were a waitress or clerk, would he be more stringent? But she's not a waitress or clerk. She's on the city council, with connections, however tenuous, to the inner workings of local government. And she's willing to stay with him whenever he comes down.

Margaret and I felt uncertain as to how Dad's email would sit with Eddie. We had little evidence of how Eddie's mind worked, other than knowing that he had lost his memory for three years and wandered around in another state, Louisiana or Florida, spending his days walking and walking; that he preferred, he'd told me more than once, to treat a chronic toothache with alcohol rather than painkillers; that he was a Vietnam vet who apparently suffered from posttraumatic stress disorder; and, according to Jackie, that he saw our father as his commanding officer. We were sure, however, that delicate interpersonal situations are not our father's strong suit, and as we made our plane reservations, we traded worst-case scenarios that the email might inspire, which escalated from awkward Ingles encounters to patriarchicide. There were many ways for Dad to leave this life: on horseback or from cancer or on the motorcycle he's threatening to buy from Donna Coe's husband, but not, we hoped, from having provoked a fragile man into a murderous rage.

ON THE FIRST MORNING, as soon as Margaret and I are up and dressed, we find Dad waiting on us in his chair. We go to Dave's for catfish and grits, calling ahead to be sure the fish will hit the fryer before we hit the door, a door that acknowledges a changing world with its handwritten "Pescado Frito" sign. Dave's interior decor is singularly unchanging: cinder block and low ceilings, nature scene wallpaper covering one wall, a trailing plant making its way along the length of the wall opposite, wood-look veneer tables, rectangular and round.

Dad sits. Margaret and I walk down the center aisle to the cafeteria line at the far end of the room, with a hulking dispenser of sweet tea to the left. Trays and Styrofoam plates and cups and plastic utensils wrapped in napkins start the line. Everything is disposable except for dark green plastic coffee mugs, which once bore the name of a local bank but were bleached bare early on. Breakfast food is arranged from left to right as follows: toast and biscuits, bacon and sausages (fresh, country, smoked), scrambled eggs (plain and cheese), grits. You want butter on those grits, the ladies will put on a slab of margarine for you, and for your biscuit, foil-topped plastic tubs of jelly [jay-uh-lee]. To the right of the steamer table sits the cash register, and next to that a small table with a coffeemaker, sugars, and creamers. I have intentionally forgotten Dad's thermos, and so we drink from the urn.

Marshall Tinsley's nonagenarian father is often in for breakfast, usually in overalls, and one of Marshall's brothers, Willie, not Dave, is often ducking in or out of the kitchen. Aside from Poochie—a beautiful young woman with whom my dad flirts relentlessly but whose attempts to secure fishing rights on the pond he consistently ignores—I only know the name of one other employee, Miss Mary [May-ree], whose netted gray hair puts her closer to my father's age than my own.

Still chewing his last bite, Dad corrals Margaret into taking him home to pick up his orders for a blood-bolstering shot, which, sans insurance, would costs almost three thousand dollars per injection, and which has to be administered within twenty-four hours of the last chemotherapy treatment in each cycle. They'll drop the pre-scription at the hospital, he says, then come back to pick me up.

Wait here for Hard Time, he instructs as he tosses his wallet onto the table. In a vague reparations effort, he called and invited Eddie to breakfast, hanging up as soon as Eddie gave what Dad took as an affirmative response. So far, Eddie hasn't showed. A bell jangles as the door closes behind my father and sister, leaving me to effect the détente.

Marshall comes in and sits with me. We talk about this and that, and then there is a period of silence, broken finally by him.

What do you think of Jackie? he says to me.

I recall my graduate work at the Columbia University School of Journalism, my lessons in investigative reporting.

What do you think of Jackie? I say.

I would do anything for your family, he says. *You know that. But I don't really want to come around when she's there.*

DAD AND MARGARET DON'T RETURN. Eddie doesn't show. Finally, Marshall takes me in his truck and, in an effort that would be ri-diculous in a larger community, drives me around to find them. At the bank, Dad's red pickup is tucked into a handicapped spot. Mar-garet and Dad are walking out of the bank as we pull up. Margaret sees me.

He made me bring him here! she cries. *I told him we should go back to get you, but he said no.*

No, not at all, says Dad, who has increasingly been given to out-landish defenses. *Margaret insisted we stop here first.*

MY FATHER BELIEVES in the truth except for when he doesn't. We were talking about Grandfather one time, and the subject of his fabricated high school transcript came up. I admitted that the fabrication confused me.

I always got the sense that Granddaddy highly prized being truthful, I said, *but that wasn't truthful.*

You gotta know what the truth is, Dad answered.

So what is the truth?

The truth is to live so that you help other people and yourself. And you negotiate the inequities that confront you the best you can. He didn't pass Plessy v. Ferguson, *and you gotta be stupid to follow that as the truth.*

MARGARET, TROY, AND I sit around the kitchen table in the afternoon while Dad snores, his chair wheeled a few feet away to the middle of the sunroom floor, his head slumped forward, chin on chest. I tell Margaret and Troy what Marshall said about Jackie. Troy knows already. Perhaps Marshall has talked about his discomfort at church, where the two of them are permanently ensconced as ushers at the entry door. Troy says he's tried to counsel Marshall into letting any slights or discomforts roll off his back. Similar things have happened to him, he tells us. He tried to talk to Eddie about the incident at the pond with his nephew, no doubt in an attempt to smooth things over, and Eddie's feathers ruffled immediately.

Eddie said to me, "You act like you own the place," Troy says. *I stopped then. I could see there was no point.* Troy advises us against sharing this story with Dad. We all know it would get Eddie bounced permanently, which would raise issues of who would care for the menagerie and who would drive Dad around during the day. Just as I said to Marshall, Margaret and I say to Troy that we know our dad is difficult, we know that there's a price to be paid to get him help and support, and we're willing to pay that price as long as he's safe and his health needs are met.

Watch out for my dad, I say to Marshall.

Let us know if anything else happens, Margaret says to Troy.

SOON ENOUGH, the Taxol will fail, Dad's PSA level will return to its upward trajectory, and he'll shift to Taxotere, a different strain of chemo that never seems to do much good. Sores spontaneously erupt on his legs and, obsessive that he is, he won't stop bothering them, either picking at barely formed scabs or dosing them with iodine. His legs start to quit on him, he says, and he stops getting dressed. In September and October he sits around the Waverly apartment in his T-shirt, diaper, and bathrobe, legs up on a chair, watching westerns and waiting for daughters to visit or the phone to ring. Lois calls to tell me that he's admitted to having fallen in the bathroom.

We plan another Thanksgiving at the farm, despite his steady decline in energies, thinking that this, *this* might really be his last trip. Except for Lois, all of us will go, Diane and Mom included. Mom will stay at Troy and Dorothy's rather than on a couch, Carolyn will come from Atlanta and sleep anywhere, Hard Time is still banned from the property, and Marshall will be deep-frying another turkey.

Diane does double duty this trip, taking Dad down so that he can spend ten days before the holiday at the farm, Jackie staying nights. Instead of Hard Time's cousin coming in to do the housework, one of the Howard twins' sisters, Laverne, will clean and fix meals and watch out for Dad, who calls her Lavonne, which she doesn't correct.

Every time Laverne picks up my calls, I make sure to ask if Dad's treating her okay, if she's had any problems.

We're fine, she says each time. *He's just Mister George.*

After Diane leaves, I call and ask Dad what's he's been up to. *How's it going in Big Foot Country?*

Well, I got the idea that you should be able to see the pond from the sun porch, and so I'm waiting on the twins to come talk to me about clearing the underbrush. The twins will try to talk him out of it, but they will fail, and after equipment rentals and labor charges, the project will cost nineteen thousand dollars. *Yesterday I bought eight pounds of shelled pecans from Troy's brother Lorenzo. He sold them to me at six dollars a pound. At the shelling plant, they sell for seven-fifty. So I thought I might mail some out next week.*

Aren't your own trees yielding?

Yes! But the nuts fall on the ground, they don't fall in my pocket. Last year the twins picked up four hundred and fifty pounds, but then they just dropped them off at the plant. I'm waiting on those twins. Sonsabitches don't keep time. They're supposed to be here. Have you ever heard of CPT?

Yes, Dad. Dad rarely spoke about race with my sisters and me when we were growing up. I suspect he reserved such conversation for other adults, for the black men he'd met when he first came to Philadelphia, who were now judges and scholars and accomplished professionals, and whom he'd meet at the bar of the Inkosa Club, another place he didn't take my mother. Today, he'll speak freely about race and its manifestations: in economics, politics, religion, and, in this instance, colloquialisms such as Colored People Time, the self-deprecating claim that black people are constitutionally inclined to show up late.

Well, they run on CPT. Then George Davie Mohorne is supposed to come over later and we might go around and do a few chores.

Have you sent Diane on her way?

Yes. She left at quarter of seven. She should be home by now.

Did you two have a good time?

I think so, but you'll have to ask her. She should have a lot to report. Call her up. She should be home by now. We went to see the CPA and what else? We went to Wal-Mart and came back in an hour and a half.

How'd you do that? Did you just buy a pack of gum at the checkout counter and run back to the car?

Do you know what that crazy goddamn woman did?

What?

I told her to get me a pair of forty by thirty and she got me forty by thirty-twos.

Who, Diane?

Yes.

You mean, my "crazy goddamn woman" sister Diane?

Yes!

Whose idea was it to buy pants?

Hers! She said my fly was down. Doesn't bother me.

Yes, but it bothers everyone else on the planet.

Well. She should have gotten me forty by thirties. My fly's not down at my ankles.

Good point.

Call her and tell her that. Tell her she didn't do right by me.

Dad, are you drunk?

Drunk on coffee!

Sounds like you're having a good time.

Well, I have things to do down here.

Right. Not like at the apartment.

I don't have anything to do there.

Sometime during the next week, while Dad is still in Georgia, Diane and I meet at our gym. We compare recent conversations with him. We talk about how her last Dad Transport went, the only kerfuffle being when airport security found two large pocket-knives on his person, *Even though I asked him if he had any knives,* Diane says, adding that she discovered a third knife the next day, while putting his pants in the wash. We talk about how we might have to intercede aggressively in his finances if he comes up with more brush-clearing projects; his latest idea to sell the twins the farm; his idea to pay for Phoebe to switch to a private school if his

273

investments spike high enough; and his idea that the children at the Get Ahead House in the still-incomplete Funderburg Park should take up ballroom dancing.

We're stretching out on mats at the end, enjoying the smug righteousness of being on the done end of the workout. I say to Diane, *What will we do when Dad dies?*

What do you mean? she asks. *With all the extra time?*

I guess so. Without him there to harp at us. What will we talk about?

Mom, I guess.

15.

FREEDOM RIDER

*D*O YOU WANT MORE BEER? I ask my father in July of 2006. He nods and opens his mouth far enough for me to insert the straw I've put into a bottle of Heineken, his chosen brand. We are in his room in Muirfield, where he was remanded after a recent "pain crisis," and I have just proffered his death sentence of six months or less, a prognosis recently determined by his oncologist. I've informed him that we—Battaglia, Schnall, and my sisters and I—feel it's appropriate at this point for him to switch to hospice care. In the last three years, my father has had five surgeries, half a dozen trips to the emergency room, constant chemotherapy, and hundreds of doctors' appointments. He's been on a steady diet of blood thinners, diuretics, antibiotics, hormones, bone strengtheners, and supplements, many of them three times a day. Since June he's been dosed with various combinations of Percocet, Tylenol, and OxyContin, even though he has denied feeling pain until recently.

Hospice is just for additional supports, I say, and so that you don't have to take as many medications or go to the hospital anymore.

Can I go back up to the apartment?

We're working on that, I say. It's not looking good. We have to be sure you'd have enough care.

I wait many long seconds for his responses, parceling out bits of information as slowly as I can, keeping the silences until the cramp in my throat threatens to burst, to spill over into tears. At that point I add new information or repeat what I've just said.

When we went to the oncologist last week, she told you that chemotherapy isn't worth it for people who spend more than seventy-five percent of their time in bed. She said the side effects would outweigh the benefits.

He keeps his eyes closed, mostly, except to eat or drink or when he has a strong reaction to my words. Now they flash open.

Who told you six months?

The oncologist and your physician.

His eyes close. This is how it is with him now, everything slowed down, long delays between questions and answers, his head not even lifting up from his pillow.

With his permission, since I don't want to cause him pain by jostling the mattress, I am perched on the edge of his hospital bed. When he won't take any more bites of the brisket sandwich I've been holding up to his mouth—onions and horseradish topping on his, coleslaw on mine, dashes of Tabasco on each from the bottle we keep by his bed to doctor up the cups of V8 he drinks many times throughout the day, one of the last things he seems to have enthusiasm for—I talk with him about death. I put my hand in his, still so much bigger than mine, and he gives it a squeeze. I leave my hand there, curled inside.

EVER SINCE HIS EIGHTIETH birthday party at the end of May—he made good on his promise to stick around for it, and I made good on my promise to throw it: 102 people; invitation and RSVP lists; balloons and centerpieces and security-parking detail; a picture in the *Monticello News* that shows him with a paper towel hastily spread across his lap, covering the open barn door; and a pig that Troy declared John's best ever—the downward trajectory has been steep. John believes Dad was holding on for the party. Maybe so. He landed in Jasper Memorial less than a week later in acute pain, agreeing to go there only when Dorothy came out to the farm and told him he had to.

If Dorothy Mae says so.

Margaret and Diane brought him back to Waverly during a lull, but he continues to lose mobility and appetite and has increasing episodes of intractable pain throughout his body despite fentanyl patches and morphine bridges.

My sisters and I have been trying to get our footing since, to understand how hospice will apply to him, to merge what he needs with his dogged desire to be sprung from Muirfield and sent back up to the apartment or down to the farm.

Jackie will pick me up, he's said more than once. *You just need to put me on a plane.*

Then he'll say, *How much money's in my wallet?*

Why, Dad? What do you need money for?

I need to tip the wheelchair guy in Philadelphia, and then the one in Atlanta.

My father, once able to absorb disappointments with stunning equanimity, can no longer be counted on to remember or take in much of anything. *Who's John Howard?* he asked me yesterday, and he seems to have no overview of his own state. He knows that he's not hungry, but he doesn't know that he can't get out of a wheelchair by himself. If he has to switch from the chair to the bed, he insists on being left to his own devices even though twenty minutes will go by with no movement.

My sisters and I have tried to figure out what ground to stand on, how much to intervene, how much to take charge, how much to insist on informing him of his condition. Here's a man who's made it through life on smarts and hard work, yes, but mostly mettle, plunging forward despite logic, law, society, history, custom, emotion. If he chooses to ignore his own mortality, why should we make him face it other than to comfort ourselves, to ease our own burden?

CLARITY CAME with the opening of Funderburg Park a week ago, on July 15. Finally, this dream of a legacy had come true. Jackie, along with a volunteer park committee, followed through on her promise to get it done. The playing fields were leveled and sodded, the basketball courts poured, and a walking path around the park's perimeter set down. There would be speeches and ribbon cutting and barbecue.

The week beforehand, Margaret suggested we take Dad to the opening ceremony, and I signed on. We scrambled to consult his doctors and understand what we were risking. He might end up back in one of Jasper Memorial's eight beds. We might not be able to bring him home. We might break one of his fragile bones just by lifting him into a wheelchair or plane seat.

If anyone else suggested a trip like this, Battaglia said to me, *I would say you're crazy. But I know how much the park means to him, that it's his legacy, and if you girls could pull this off, it would be amazing.*

We didn't pull it off. We couldn't. We couldn't find a nurse to travel with us on such short notice, we couldn't scramble to figure out backup plans, what we'd do not if he died, which would be simple, but if he came close to dying, had another stroke, say, or broke his spine. In the end, I beseeched Battaglia to tell Dad he couldn't go, and when Battaglia said he didn't dictate to his patients in that way, I begged him to at least say it wasn't "medically advisable."

We can't pull it together, I said, speaking past the knot in my throat. *And we can't say no to him*.

BATTAGLIA DID INTERCEDE, but Dad conveniently and repeatedly forgot what he'd said, forgot all the way up to the day before the park opening. I had drafted in-absentia celebratory remarks for him that met with his approval. We had jointly picked a surrogate reader, and Jackie had promised to videotape the event. But at least once a day, Dad would ask if we were going to go.

We'll try to go back to Georgia, I said, *but not on such short notice. I know your spirit is willing, Dad, but your body is very fragile*.

One day, Margaret called me at home from Muirfield.

Lees, Dad says you're going to talk to the oncologist about going to Georgia.

I am.

Here's Dad.

The phone was passed.

Leesee.

Yes, Dad?

Are you going to talk to Sandy Schnall about me going to Georgia?

Yes, Dad.

Then tell Diane.

The phone was passed again.

Dad says you're going to ask Dr. Schnall if he can go to the park opening. Is that true?

No. *I'm going to ask her about taking him down sometime in the future*.

Diane repeated this to Dad.

Aw, shucks, he said.

BECAUSE THE HOSPICE decision hangs over us—not the whether of it, but the when—and because taking Dad to Georgia might kill him or come close to killing him, we are pushed to anticipate every eventuality as we determine if we can ever take him back to Big Foot Country again. Diane and I meet with Battaglia to ask final, clarifying questions about hospice, a significant principle of which, as we understand it, is to remove all therapeutic medications, retaining only those that alleviate pain.

Can he still get his blood thinner so he doesn't have a stroke . . . and then survive it? Diane asks.

Yes, the doctor says.

What happens if he has a pain crisis, if he goes into intractable pain? Can we handle the meds? We have learned the end-stage lingo.

You can handle it, he says. *And you can always get me by phone.*

WHILE MY FATHER'S HAND is still wrapped around mine, while patient call bells bleat in the hall outside his door, when I can't stand talking anymore about hospice, I tell him Diane's idea. Encouraged by our meeting with Battaglia, Diane has come up with a brilliant, wacky plan that is more proof of Dad's paternity than any DNA test could ever ascertain.

Here's the other thing we talked to your doctor about . . .

Diane has figured out that we can avoid the exhausting and possibly bone-breaking transfers involved in plane travel by renting an accessible van. We can strap his wheelchair into it and drive. With the help of Mapquest.com, she has calculated that it is thirteen hours and eleven minutes door to door, Waverly to 354.

If you need to rest, I say, *we can stop. If you're in pain, we can stop.*

If you need your diaper changed, we can stop. I don't mention that if he dies, we can stop, but that's part of the concept. *Does that sound good?*

Dad doesn't open his eyes, but he lifts his hand off mine and snaps his fingers.

I've got a name for it, I say. *I'm calling it Freedom Ride 2006.*

Freedom Ride, he whispers.

THE NURSES WHO SING to my father and kiss his forehead at the end of their shifts and cry in the supply closet when they can't get his pain to come back down tell us to go as soon as we can.

Don't let anyone say it's not his right, one says to me when we stop to chat in Muirfield's hallway. *It is his right to go and no one can stop you.*

At first her adamancy doesn't make sense. Of course it's his right. And then we start dealing with the administrators. The initial legwork falls to Diane and me, since Margaret won't be back from a family vacation until right before we plan to leave. Our idea is to take Dad to the farm for a week, and then come home.

You don't have a plan, Muirfield's chief administrator says.

We do, we say, and mention our reservation for a rental van.

Your plan is not adequate, she says. *It is not safe.*

But we've consulted all the doctors and nurses.

You'd be signing him out against medical advice.

How can that be? His doctors are encouraging us to take him, I say. *We specifically checked it out with his physician here at Waverly.*

I can overrule him, the administrator says.

WHEN DO WE GO to Georgia, Leesee?

Soon, Dad.

When is soon?

As soon as we can arrange everything.
Don't put it off.

WE'VE DECIDED TO GO ahead and start Dad on hospice care, even though we're hoping to leave within the week. We don't see any point in putting it off. Diane and Margaret have carried the weight of this task, meeting with the possible providers, selecting one, filling out the appropriate paperwork, and writing the checks. Then Diane calls me. The hospice company caseworker has been talking to the Waverly administrator and has told Diane that she needs to discuss this "idea" we have of traveling with our father. Diane found the caseworker oddly aggressive, not the gentle embrace we've all imagined the hospice experience to be. Diane has set up a meeting with her for the next afternoon.

I need you to come with me, Diane says. *I can't talk to her alone.*

Normally, an oldest-to-youngest directive would make me bristle, and the conversation would turn tense, maybe fall apart completely. Not this time.

When is it? I ask. *Who's going to drive?*

WHEN DO WE GO to Big Foot Country, Leesee?
We're hoping for the end of next week.
That far away?
It's not so far, Dad. See, here on the wall calendar? Here we are in July. I'm crossing off the days until we can go. See?
Well, I'm ready whenever.

THE CASEWORKER MEETS with us in Dad's cramped Muirfield room, which has the sterility of a hospital room except for its Colonial-style dresser and wardrobe. Dad lies in the metal-railed bed, his feet raised to aid circulation, a towel under his ankles to keep the heels from rubbing themselves into bedsores. We've taped photographs on the wall beside him: Dad and his cousin Eva Elsie at his birthday party; Phoebe at the farm, waiting to ride on the back of the 1972 Triumph motorcycle Dad bought from Donna Coe's husband and immediately gave to John; Lois's daughter, Gwen, who went to the birthday party in her mother's stead; John with Marshall Tinsley, standing in front of the porte cochere that Dad needled John into designing, then Marshall into building; and the fourteen cows Dad has insisted on buying in the last two weeks in some kind of arrangement with the Howard twins that involves his cash, their care, and alternating claims on the calves that will issue forth.

The caseworker arrives late, apologizing as she enters the room, clipboard in hand. She's a small, fit woman with curly brown hair, chewing a piece of gum in double time. She sits in Dad's wheelchair, the only available seat in the room.

I know you want to take your dad to Georgia, she says, *but the van is not going to work. It's not going to happen.* Diane and I look at each other. I ask the caseworker to explain what she means. We would be subjecting our father to intolerable pain, she says, using the same language as the Waverly administrator. We couldn't possibly handle the medication responsibilities, and she's talked to his doctors and they advise against it.

We know this isn't true.

Which doctors? we ask.

She looks through the papers on her clipboard and comes to the name of the Waverly physician.

But we just talked to him, we say.

When was that?

Last Friday. We went through all the details of how to manage the trip.

That was a week ago, she says. *A lot has happened since then. Your father's pain threshold has lowered. I'm a nurse, I specialize in palliative care pain meds, and I'm telling you, you'll torture him.*

I appreciate what you're saying, I say, *but this is what our father wants.*

How do you know this is what he wants? she asks, apparently assuming he's unconscious.

My father is awake, Diane says. *He can hear the conversation.*

Maybe he can hear it, but can he understand it?

Yes, both Diane and I say. *He can.*

Mr. Funderburg, she says, raising her voice and turning her attention to him.

Where are you? she asks. He answers correctly.

What year is it? Correct.

What month? Correct again.

What day of the week? He's off by two days. But who wouldn't lose track, stuck on his back, bored, isolated, not in his own home?

She turns back to us. We are obviously not bending. Nor is she. *I don't think you understand the possible consequences.*

I see where she's going, what she's hinting at. She's talking around the issue because she doesn't know who she's talking to. We're farmers. I look her in the eye. *You mean,* I say, *that he might die along the way?*

Yes, she says. *And if that happened, what would you do?*

We'd call 911, Diane says, telling her what the doctor told us when we asked the same question.

But does he understand? she asks, nodding in Dad's direction.

Dad, I say. He grunts. *Do you understand that if we go on this trip, you could die along the way?*

Yes, he says.

And how do you feel about that?

I would rather die in transit than not attempt it.

Let's step outside, the caseworker says. *We can talk more freely.* We walk out of the room, past the central nurses' station and out of the building, stopping under the long barreled awning that leads from Muirfield's automatic glass doors to its cut-curb pickup.

I don't want to be disrespectful, she says, *but it's like if a kid wanted ice cream and you knew it would give him a stomachache, would you give it to him?*

Yes, I said. *If he were dying.*

To do something like this has to be what the patient truly wants, she says, *not just what the family wants for him.*

This is *what he wants,* Diane says, exasperated, as I am.

I'm in a tight spot, she says. *I have to address everyone's concerns.*

I can't think of any concerns besides Dad's that matter . . . and then I remember the administrator, and I start to wonder what liability issues the facility might face, or fears it might face, or its lawyers fear it might face, if it were to endorse such a trip.

The caseworker, though, is working her way out of that spot in front of our eyes. Later she will tell us that Dad's response to my question was the turning point for her, the point at which she knew that indeed, this trip was his wish, not merely a misguided effort on the part of loved ones.

It's not that we can't make this happen, she says in the shade of the awning. *You should see some of the trips my patients have made.* She tells us about stretchers and ambulance planes, turning ferryboats around and getting to and from remote islands. *But you'd have to have someone with you. Someone who understood pain meds.*

Yes, Diane and I both clamor. There's a tiny ray of light peeking under the door. *We're happy to take someone. We'd love to take someone. We just don't know how to find them.*

Oh, the caseworker says, clearly having seized onto the challenge of the plan. *I think I've got the person.*

* * *

I GO HOME AND COMPLAIN to John about the mountainous resistance Diane and I have been facing, so much of it incomprehensible in its origins. He's silent as I rant.

I'm just going to say this once, he says when I pause to reload. *You and your sisters are some of the most practical people I know, but this time, I think you're off your game. I think this idea is crazy. That's how I feel. That said, if you still decide to go through with it, I will drive you.*

I have never loved him more.

IN AN EFFORT TO ADDRESS the vague critiques that assault us, we switch from renting a van to a thirty-foot-long RV that has a full-size bed in its rear. It also has a shower, toilet, and kitchen. I find an Internet cremation service (my father's preference) at the Web site FuneralDepot.com that will cover us in any state between Pennsylvania and Georgia. We order a week's worth of "comfort packs," which contain pain medications that go from mild to morphine.

The caseworker, who has done a 180-degree turn, is now completely in our corner. She arranges with a Monticello hospice for one of their nurses to meet us on arrival and check in during the week. She arranges equipment rentals for the farm, from a hospital bed to oxygen tanks. She gives me a checklist of items to pack, from gallon-size Ziplocs to potable water, wet wipes, and T-shirts slit up the back for easier access. And she calls me with the number of a coworker who could go with us. The coworker's name is Venus.

You need to set this up with Venus directly, the caseworker says. *Because you're going outside the state, she's going to be working directly for you. And don't be put off by how laid-back she sounds on the phone.*

LOOK, DAD, I'M CROSSING OFF today, which means just three more days.

Why can't we go tomorrow?

John's got to work, Dad, and he's going to drive us.

Oh, okay.

HELLO? VENUS CAMPBELL SAYS when I call. She sounds as if she's just woken up, although it's the middle of the day. I remember what the caseworker said and forge on. I ask if she's still willing to go to Georgia. She says yes, but then asks how hot it is there.

And are there mosquitoes? she asks.

The world depends on my answer.

Yes, I say, *but not more than up here.*

She doesn't ask about what she'll be paid, so I bring it up, using a figure the caseworker suggested. Venus says that's fine and asks when we need her to meet us at Muirfield.

At five on Friday, I tell her. *We'll be driving through the night.* Venus says nothing. *If, for some reason, Dad can't come back at the end of the week, we'll arrange for you to fly back.* She says nothing. I'm desperate to get a sense of her, to have some sign that she will truly be a help to us.

It's pretty generous of you to go on a fifteen-hour trip in a camper with complete strangers, then spend the week with them, I say.

I go where my patients need me, she says.

TWO DAYS BEFORE we are scheduled to leave, we have a final show-down with the Waverly administrator. Margaret, back from vacation, joins Diane and me, and we ask Lois to come down from her apartment so that we can present a united front.

We crowd into an office, Lois in her motorized chair, the hospice caseworker accompanied by her supervisor, the three daughters, and the administrator.

I'm sure we all want what's in my father's best interest, I say once everyone is seated, *which is why my sisters and I have made a plan that addresses every situation that has been suggested to us.*

We walk through the logistics of the trip. We've gotten to the part about stopping as needed, when the administrator interjects.

What if you need oxygen while you're on the road? she asks.

I don't have time to respond, to point out that if Dad stopped being able to breathe on his own we would not interfere, before the caseworker pulls out her cell phone and arranges a rental. The administrator says nothing more until I explain the cremation arrangements.

Funeral Depot, she says with a laugh. *I can't believe that exists! I was just being snotty the other day, talking to someone here, and I said, "What are they going to do? Call Funerals R Us?"*

I come to the final point, the one I think matters most to someone in the room. *We are willing, of course, to sign any liability waivers that Waverly would require.*

That's not our main concern, the administrator says, as she pulls out the waiver and hands it to Lois. *We just wanted to be sure you had a safe plan.*

WHEN ARE WE LEAVING, *Leesee?*

In about two hours, Dad.

Why can't we leave now?

We have to wait for Diane and Margaret to bring the RV, for Venus to come, and for John to get here from work.

Shit.

DIANE AND I MEET at the doors of Muirfield. She and Margaret have picked up the RV, watched the instructional video that focuses more on disposal of waste at the end of the trip than on road safety, and driven harrowingly curved suburban roads so slowly that people honked the whole way. Just to get out of the rental facility's drive-way, Diane had to stand in the road and stop traffic so that Margaret, whose prior big-rig experience was as a summer camp school bus driver in 1981, could turn the vehicle around.

Diane's eye position seems stuck at wide open.

We are insane, she says in lieu of a hey or an hola or a hello. *We are fucking insane.*

THE CASEWORKER INTRODUCES Venus to Dad.

I never lose an argument, he rasps.

Okay, Venus says. *I'm glad you told me that.*

This hat doesn't fit, Dad says when Venus puts the black Stetson on his head, a head so wasted his skull shows through. He's been on an appetite stimulant since June but can't gain weight, can't even main-tain it. *Something's wrong with the size.*

We drive through the night, John at the wheel except for the last three hours, which take us from the South Carolina border to the farm. The plan to put Dad in the back bed fails on two counts. One, he wants to sit up and look out the window, at least for the first half hour, so we put him in the bench seat just inside the entry door, surrounding and propping him up with the many pillows we've brought along. Two, we discover that the bed's position behind the rear axle turns it into something like a diving board every time we hit a bump. When Diane tries to nap on it, she is actually airborne.

Margaret rides shotgun most of the trip, up in the cab with John, listening to a mediocre book on tape and drinking from large cups of acrid coffee we get at the multiple gas stations we patronize, owing to the camper's average of seven to ten miles per gallon.

Dad shows no signs of pain, not once. He does get tired of sitting up, and so we convert his seat into a bed. We take turns sitting by him and holding his hand, something we've all started to do with him in the last month. We tell Venus to go ahead and nap when her shifts end, but she doesn't close her eyes or turn away from him.

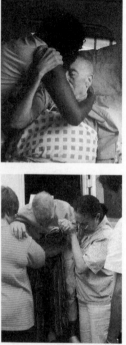

Venus, it is almost instantly clear to the rest of us, is extraordinarily gifted at her job.

When you're ready, she says to him before she moves any part of his body, *you tell me*.

We drive past Dave's Restaurant and Monticello's town square just before noon on Saturday, right on schedule. We ask Dad if he wants to see the park first or go to the farm.

Park, he says, although as we drive through, him propped up to look out the window, he cannot keep his eyes open. So we go to the farm, and Margaret points out that to the right of the driveway, underneath the ancient scuppernong vine that came with the property, Troy's watermelon patch is dotted with melons.

Pick one, Dad orders, eyes still closed.

Every day, the sun shines. Dad sits up for a few hours on Saturday afternoon, wheeled out to the sunroom and faced toward the horse pasture. Venus and I help him into the pickup truck, and the three of us go for a second look at the park. Dad is disappointed that no one is using the courts or trails, even after we observe that we are out in the heat of the day. Dad is in a T-shirt, striped pajama bottoms, deerskin work gloves, and his Birkenstocks, which now sit loose on his feet.

His feet. For the last year, since it became too hard for him to get into a tub by himself, they have been a crusty, calloused mess. In two days of unhurried sponge baths and lotion-filled massage, Venus transforms them, the paper-thin skin now soft and glowing.

John flies back to Philadelphia, to work the week and come back at its end for the return drive. Visitors come to the farm in a steady stream, bringing offerings ranging from tomatoes and figs to freshly laid eggs. We usher people into Dad's room whenever he's awake, setting up chairs by his bed, bringing in extra chairs as needed.

When he's not having visitors, Dad reads through the current issue of the *Monticello News*, looking for farmland to buy. He decides the willow oaks outside his window need trimming. He instructs me to find the phone number of a tree trimmer in his address book, then to call immediately.

But Dad, it's seven in the morning. On a Sunday.

Call him.

The Howard twins stop in at least once a day, checking in, bringing tomatoes, sitting with Dad. The first time they talk with Dad about the new cattle, he calls Diane into the room.

Write the twins a check, he says. *We've got to keep the money straight.*

On Monday, Troy and Dorothy come back from a family reunion, and they become part of the regular crowd, bringing along Dorothy's brother Howard or Dorothy's sister Hattie, who is visiting from Con-

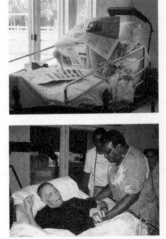

necticut and whom my father calls by her childhood nickname, Baby Sister.

While the Johnsons and Smiths visit, Dad's eyes are mostly closed. He occasionally makes a noise that shows he's paying attention, a small laugh at some joke. Finally, Baby Sister and her husband are ready to go back to Troy and Dorothy's for the night.

I'm leaving, George, she says from across the room. *But first I'm going to come over and give you a kiss.*

Dad's eyes stay closed, but he puckers his lips in readiness.

My sisters and I watch Venus, how gentle she is, what matters and what doesn't. She makes sure Dad has food and drink whenever he wants it, for example, but she does not insist that he eat more than he wants, which is almost nothing. She asks constantly if he's in pain. Venus is a talker. Among other things, we learn that her grandmother is the person who taught her how to care for people. She has two daughters and four grandchildren and she's raising her niece, Tatiana, who's close to Phoebe's age. Venus's favorite dinner is steak and baked potatoes. She briefly lived in another part of Georgia

but couldn't take the mosquitoes. She's a year older than I am and her birthday will come while we're at the farm. From other people, this would be chatter, soon intolerable. From Venus, it's soothing, tied to a funny comment or an incisive point. *I love my grandbabies but they drive me crazy. . . . Lise made me go fishing, and those catfish were taunting us. I'm gonna get one of those mugs. . . . Your dad is my patient, but I'm here to hold all of you together. I'm the crust around your pie.*

Venus soothes my father, too. I've never seen him so acquiescent. By day two, one of the daughters will ask him something like, *Dad, do you want to be turned?*

Yeah, he'll answer. *Go get Venus.*

Venus gets a guest room to herself. It's the least we can offer her, surrounded as she is. My sisters and I take turns sleeping in Dad's bed, and there's rarely a time when one of us isn't close by. But we decide to buy a baby monitor nonetheless, so that when he's sleeping the rest of us can hang out together in the kitchen or watch a movie and not worry that we won't hear his calls.

We balance the monitor on the windowsill by Dad's hosiptal bed and place its speaker on the kitchen counter. We ask Dad to give us a test run.

Yellow Fever, Yellow Fever, he says. *This is Sunshine, over.*

A few hours later, the three sisters and Venus are laughing and talking in the kitchen as we celebrate Venus's birthday. Dad was fine the last time anyone checked, but I suspect he hears the edge of our conversation and is lonely. We hear the monitor crackle.

Venus, I'm in pain, I'm in pain. Come quick. Come quick.

One morning, the dairy farmer Bryant Larmon comes by. He wears crisp denim overalls and a button-down shirt, the only outfit I've ever seen on him. His thinning white hair is slicked back against a ruddy scalp, and his hands and face are rough and spotted from years of sun. He brings us a box of tomatoes from his garden. He sits with Dad an hour or so, reminiscing about the various adventures they'd had over the years. How they went to a state fair and had their feet massaged. How Bryant couldn't figure out what kind of counter space to have in his new kitchen and Dad sketched out a work table for him, then went with him to the lumberyard to have the pieces cut. How they went to see Bryant's family place in the North Georgia mountains.

Sure was pretty up there, Dad says.

Finally, Bryant is ready to go. I walk him out to the kitchen where my sisters are sitting, we all chat for a while, and then as he's about to leave, he starts to cry.

It's just hard to say good-bye, he says.

Bryant must have gone straight from the farm to Tillman House, because the next thing you know, Ben Tillman drives up in a little GMC pickup, bright red with a Georgia Bulldogs sticker on the back. He's wearing a Maui T-shirt with the sleeves cut off, knee-length shorts under a grease-covered white apron, and white athletic socks peeking out of food-encrusted high-top lace-ups.

I heard your dad wasn't doin' so good, he says, as he pulls a cardboard box of food from the back of the truck and brings it into the kitchen. He's brought us chicken and dumplings, coleslaw, bread, and greens.

One of my sisters offers him a cold drink.

Nah, he says, *I got to get back to cooking.* Of course he does. It's the lunch rush, and he's the only cook. *All y'all take care now.*

293

We watch Ben climb right back into his truck and pull away. Ben Tillman, Mack Tillman's son.

DAD GROWS WEAKER EVERY DAY, and five days into the trip, he plummets. Diane and Venus have been monitoring his medications, trying to balance making him comfortable with keeping him connected to what's going on. Maybe they haven't given him enough. On Wednesday night, for the first time, Dad admits to pain. Nothing we do, no position we switch him to, is a relief. Diane calls the local hospice nurse, who encourages us to give Dad more morphine. He writhes in pain. Diane and I start talking, in another room, about what we'll do if he can't go back at the end of the week, about how long we both can stay and whether we need to start investigating hospital planes or interstate ambulance services. What would it mean if he had to go to Jasper Memorial? Could we let him die there?

But with Diane and Venus in close attendance, the increased meds do their work, and by the next day Dad has come out of his crisis. He is feeble, but stable, and we prepare to go. We pack the RV's storage compartments with miscellaneous items from the house, whatever we can find that has sentimental or practical value: books and kitchen tongs and a rug Lois wants.

The tree trimmer comes the day before we leave, giving the small grove of oaks an inverted buzz cut. Dad is pleased.

WE'RE IN THE RV, heading home. Dad is largely out of it, higher than a kite, swimming his hand through the air and following it, more or less, with his eyes. He talks about making wine in the fall, how we'll schedule that trip when the grapes are ready, how Troy will keep us posted as they ripen, how Margaret will walk barefoot on the grapes to squash them, and how John Reynolds is in charge of the whole process, but Dad will be glad to watch.

We take turns holding Dad's hand, sitting by him on the edge of the same banquette he used on the way down. He tells each one of us that he loves us.

My Dad, I whisper, touching my head to his chest. *My Dad*.

Margaret is behind the wheel when my father rasps, *I have a question for John Reynolds*. John sidles up and puts his hand into my father's. My father returns the grip. *John Reynolds*, he says, tears seeping from his eyes. *How are we going to keep this land in the family?*

SOONER THAN I CAN BEAR and at the worst moment or the perfect moment, my father will die. But right up until the very end, he will be racking off another layer or two of the Jim Crow sediment that lies at the bottom of every American's bottle. And I will have helped him along the way, gratified to discover my own devotion to him. I will have helped him toward a Good Death, squeezing out moments of joy and closeness where they come, bearing up under his habitual brutality, less susceptible to its insistent wounding than ever before. But I will be no less stunned when the day comes that there are no more to-do lists, no more commands to keep the money straight or blow my nose, no more pig candy on the driveway surreptitiously crossing the North-South, black-white, rural-urban, old-young, father-daughter divide.

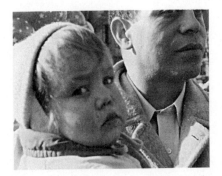

JOHN REYNOLDS'S MOJO MARINADE

*Makes enough mojo to marinate
a 100-pound pig.*

1 quart orange juice
1 pint lemon juice
1 pint lime juice
1 cup white wine
140 garlic cloves, minced
6 cups onion, minced
$\frac{1}{2}$ cup dried oregano
$\frac{1}{2}$ cup black pepper
$\frac{1}{2}$ cup kosher salt
$\frac{1}{4}$ cup ground cumin

Combine ingredients and let steep overnight.

Strain mojo through cheesecloth. Adjust salt.

Inject pig, being careful to distribute evenly throughout muscles.

Let injected pig rest 24 hours before cooking.

Follow directions stenciled on side of box, even though you don't really believe that a 100-pound pig can cook in 4 hours.

IN MEMORIAM

George Newton Funderburg

May 24, 1926–August 16, 2006

Lois Butcher Bye Funderburg
1926–2007

Lorenzo Lee Johnson
1923–2006

Sarah Burney Smith
1906–2006

Alfred Edwin Johnson
1921–2005

Vince "Cubo" Johnson, Jr.
1924–2005

Mack Henry Tillman
1937–2004

Holsey "Brother" Tinsley, Jr.
1917–2004

ACKNOWLEDGMENTS

This book is as much a testament to community as it is a tribute. For their encouragement to write what I saw, thanks go to John Feffer and the Spare Room Quartet; Karen Kurlander; Norman Vanamee; Alice Siempelkamp; Amy Gross; Donna Masini, Daniel Mendelsohn, and Stephen Simcock of I Cetona Cinque; and Alice Walker. And the MacDowell Colony.

Once the book was under way, many specialists came to my aid, generously giving of their resources and time, including Jasper County Library manager Nita Mix; University of Georgia horticulturalist Kathryn C. Taylor; Louisiana State University pomologist Charles E. Johnson; Fort Valley State University horticulturalist Anand K. Yadav; University of North Carolina public historian Karen L. Cox; and Columbia University Medical Center archivist Bob Vietrogoski. On growing peaches in Jasper County, I benefited from the insights of W. Phil Jordan, Holsey Tinsley, and Mary Ellen and Chick Wilson. Gregory A. Freeman's careful history of the Williams Peonage Farm murders in Lay This Body Down was immensely useful. Also useful was Francis Davis's first-person account of working on the Great Lakes' Night Boats, which brought dimension to that lost enterprise, as did materials and help from the Detroit Public Library, the Dossin Great Lakes Museum, Grand Hotel concierge and historian Robert M. Tagatz, and Hank and Mary Jo Healey.

Acknowledgments

For generous, discerning manuscript reads (sometimes more than once), I thank these brilliant editors and writers: Robert Gottlieb, Mamie Healey, Lisa Zeidner, Veronica Chambers, and Lisa Kogan. The clear vision of Robert Friedman and Jason Howard guided me out of tall weeds and into high cotton. Daniel Mendelsohn was my fellow traveler in the search for truth with a lower case *t*, history with a lower case *h*, and bacon with a capital *B*.

For careful shepherding of this project, thanks to my agent, Geri Thoma, who is a paradigm of constancy and level-headedness. Thanks also to my editors at the Free Press, Liz Stein and Wylie O'Sullivan, and the careful attentions of their colleagues, including Carol de Onís, Tom Pitoniak, Ann Kirschner, Suet Chong, Danielle Kaniper, and Elizabeth Perrella.

For all of the above, in addition to bearing up nobly under the pressures of being spousally attached to the project, I thank John Reynolds Howard. How lucky I am.

My sisters and mother own the same experiences I've written about, and I am grateful to them for their generosity in respecting my version. The greatest gift my parents ever gave me was my sisters.

Monticello deserves its own separate appreciation, as do all the people from there who have been so kind to me and my sisters, and who enjoyed, humored, respected, and put up with my father. A partial list includes Donna Coe, Bryant Larmon, Crawford Ezell, Jerry Goldin, Larry Lynch, Kathy Mudd, Mary Jim Ozburn and Mackie Jones, Floyd and Iris Moore, Frances Smith, Howard Smith, Eddie Ray Tyler, Judy Yielding, Albert and Elbert Howard and their family, the medical staff of Jasper County Memorial Hospital, Dave's Restaurant, Tillman House Restaurant, and Marshall Tinsley. Special thanks to Dorothy and Troy Johnson, who continue to welcome us when we come home.

My father's health issues were compounded and confounded by his pride, his will to live each day to the fullest, and his apparently superhuman tolerance for physical pain. In the midst of this,

Acknowledgments

many people provided succor and dignity, including the nursing and administrative support staff of Muirfield, and doctors Sandra Faye Schnall, David Battaglia, David Ellis, and Jack Abboudi. Thanks to the people of Odyssey Hospice and Abbey Hospice, who truly know what quality of life means, especially at its end, and to Venus Campbell, my fourth sister and number one bodhisattva.

To have finished this book shortly after my father's death was resoundingly bittersweet. I do believe he would have found a way to take pride in it, regardless of what words I'd put on its pages, for the simple reason that he was my dad and he loved me. I thank him, and will always thank him, for that.

ABOUT THE AUTHOR

Lise Funderburg was born in Philadelphia and educated at Reed College and at Columbia University. She has written for *The New York Times*, *The Nation*, and *Time*, and is a frequent contributor to O, *The Oprah Magazine*. She is an instructor in creative writing at The University of Pennsylvania and lives in Philadelphia.

www.lisefunderburg.com